The Antitrust Revolution in Europe

The Antitrust Revolution in Europe

Exploring the European Commission's Cartel Policy

Lee McGowan

Senior Lecturer in European Studies, Queen's University Belfast, UK

Edward Elgar

Cheltenham, UK • Northampton, MA, USA

Published by
Edward Elgar Publishing Limited
The Lypiatts
15 Lansdown Road
Cheltenham
Glos GL50 2JA
UK

Edward Elgar Publishing, Inc.
William Pratt House
9 Dewey Court
Northampton
Massachusetts 01060
USA

A catalogue record for this book
is available from the British Library

Library of Congress Control Number: 2009942053

Mixed Sources
Product group from well-managed
forests and other controlled sources
www.fsc.org Cert no. SA-COC-1565
© 1996 Forest Stewardship Council
FSC

ISBN 978 1 84720 146 1

Printed and bound by MPG Books Group, UK

Contents

Preface

Interest in European competition policy has never been higher and the literature has never been richer. In the last decade the European Commission has initiated a thorough review of all areas of its activities stretching from cartels and mergers to state aids and abusive monopolies. Competition policy can certainly be said to have 'come of age', and its recognition in the Lisbon Treaty as one of the few exclusive EU competences has enhanced its prestige and significance for students and researchers outside the two disciplines that have overwhelmingly dominated this policy area, namely economics and law. Yet beyond these disciplines, competition policy is little understood or often appreciated. Political scientists rarely study this area; even those working in the field of European Studies have also tended to underplay or overlook its importance as a European policy in the integration process. The absence of politics has long represented a major gap in the competition literature, and especially when the evolution of competition policy provides us with a great example of the European integration process. Over the last fifteen years, however, a small but growing band of historians and political scientists have finally begun to explore competition policy, stress its significance in the European integration process and shed new light onto the origins and actors as well as analysing the impact of competing economic philosophies and the appropriateness of rival theoretical approaches to understanding developments in this field.

This particular work comes at competition policy from a politics/public policy perspective and its focus on actors, ideas and policy developments aims both to complement and add to the existing economics and legal based literatures. This book explores the European Commission's cartel policy. Cartels have very rarely attracted the attention of political science, and yet cartel-busting has always been one of the foremost activities of the Commission and one that has consumed much of this regulator's time and resources. Cartel policy provides for a truly fascinating account of supranational governance in action as the Commission looks for ever more imaginative means to detect, unearth and penalise cartel offenders. The recent reform of the Commission's anti-trust provisions (through Regulation 1/2003) forms part of this modernisation agenda. It was a significant move and marked the first major overhaul of the Commission's cartel-busting activities since its inception nearly fifty years ago.

Some commentators claim the recent reform package constitutes a 'revolution' (Wilks, 2005), while others have opted to regard it instead as the latest development in a regime that has been continually marked by the neo-liberal turn of the 1980s (Wigger, 2008). Whichever reflects better the recent transformation of the policy, there is no doubt that for those of us interested in the area of competition policy (and cartel policy) we are living in interesting times and especially as we wait to see how the credit crunch and worst recession since the 1930s impacts on the competition arena.

Before commencing, however, there are a few stylistic points that need to be addressed at the outset. First, with regard to the numbering of treaty articles, this book uses the post-Amsterdam (post-1999) numbering only. Thus, Article 81 is referred to when cartel/restrictive practices policy is discussed (rather than its former incarnation as Article 85). This book avoids using both to prevent any unnecessary confusion although technically it should refer to Article 85 from 1958–1999. Another word of caution is needed on the numbering of treaty articles: at the time of writing the Treaty of Lisbon had still not been ratified by all 27 EU member states, with the Czech Republic, Germany and Poland still to approve the document. The treaty was ratified by Ireland at the second referendum attempt in October 2009 and approval came shortly thereafter from both Poland and the Czech Republic. The treaty finally came into force on 1 December 2009 and renumbered the treaty provisions. Under the Lisbon Treaty the competition articles now run from Articles 101–110.

The Lisbon Treaty will also adopt the term European Union throughout the entire treaty base. This book uses EU when referring to competition policy although it is currently technically correct to speak of European Community (EC) competition law. On a similar point it should be noted that in 1999, DGIV (Directorate-General Four) of the European Commission became DG Competition (or DG COMP). DGIV may be mentioned in Chapters 4 and 5 as the historical evolution of the policy is explored, but otherwise, DG Competition is used throughout.

Finally, I would like thank friends and colleagues for their support as this work was completed. I would like to express my gratitude to all the relevant staff at Edward Elgar for their patience and assistance, to all those people who kindly expressed their views on the draft chapters and the final text and those officials who provided insights into the workings and evolution of EU cartel policy. And finally, I wish to thank my immediate family for their support.

Lee McGowan, May 2009

Abbreviations

ABA	American Bar Association
AMCHAM-EU	American Chamber of Commerce – EU Division
BDI	Bundesverband deutscher Industrie (Confederation of German Industry)
BEUC	European Bureau of Consumers' Unions
BKartA	German Cartel Office
CBI	Confederation of British Industry
CDU	Christian Democratic Union (of Germany)
CEECs	Central and East European Countries
CET	Common External Tariff
CFI	Court of First Instance
CLP	Competition Law and Policy Committee
CMLR	Common Market Law Reports
CMLRev	Common Market Law Review
CSU	Christian Social Union (Germany)
DG	Directorate-General (of the Commission)
DG Competition	Directorate-General for Competition (European Commission)
DGIV	Directorate-General for Competition (prior to 1999)
DTI	Department of Trade and Industry
EC	European Community
ECJ	European Court of Justice
ECLR	European Competition Law Review
ECN	European Competition Network
ECR	European Court Reports
ECSC	European Coal and Steel Community
ECSC6	Original six founding members of the ECSC
EEA	European Economic Area
EEC	European Economic Community
EESC	European Economic and Social Committee
EFTA	European Free Trade Association
EP	European Parliament
ERT	European Roundtable of Industrialists
EU	European Union
EUMR	European Union Merger Regulation

EURATOM	European Atomic Energy Community
FDP	The Free Democratic Party (Germany)
FTC	Federal Trade Commission (US)
GATT	General Agreement on Tariffs and Trade
GNP	Gross National Product
GWB	Gesetz gegen Wettbewerbsbeschränkungen (German Law against Restraints on Competition)
G8	Group of Eight (industrialised countries)
ICI	Imperial Chemical Industries
ICN	International Competition Network
IT	Information Technology
ITO	International Trade Organization
MEP	Member of the European Parliament
MTF	Merger Task Force
NAFTA	North Atlantic Free Trade Association
NCAs	National Competition Authorities
NTBs	Non-Tariff Barriers
OECD	Organization for Economic Cooperation and Development
OEEC	Organization for European Economic Co-operation
OFT	Office of Fair Trading
OJ	Official Journal (of the European Union)
R&D	Research and Development
SEA	Single European Act 1986
SEM	Single European Market
SME	Small and Medium-sized Enterprises
SPD	Social Democratic Party of Germany
TEC	Treaty Establishing the European Community
TENs	Trans-European Networks
TEU	Treaty on European Union (Maastricht Treaty) 1992
TFEU	Treaty on the Functioning of the European Union 2009
ToA	Treaty of Amsterdam 1997
ToN	Treaty of Nice 2001
UNCTAD	United Nations Conference on Trade and Development
UNICE	European Employers' Association (now Business Europe)
WTO	World Trade Organisation

1. The origins and scope of European competition policy: themes and purpose

Some 53 years after the signing of the Treaty of Rome there is ample scope to debate the achievements, near misses and failures of the European Union (EU). One aspect of European governance, however, is undeniable, namely the priority and centrality of the competition principle throughout the history of the European integration process. As an issue of low politics, and one that is particularly complex, competition policy was arguably an ideal sector for initial functionalist co-operation towards the creation of a common (and later) single market. Even so it must be stressed that competition policy as an idea and logic was controversial in its own right among the states of Western Europe. It was a new departure and consequently, any plans to delegate powers to the supranational level not only were problematic but raised controversies about at which level power should be exerted, how it should be exercised and who should enforce it.

Nevertheless and with hindsight it is clear that these problems were overcome and that the development of competition policy within the EU represents one of the success stories of the entire European integration process and offers one of the first and best examples of supranational governance in action. Indeed, the EU competition policy regime gradually stamped its influence on the perceptions, structures and approaches of the national competition regimes within the EU as the latter have either opted to converge voluntarily with many aspects of the EU competition model or have been coerced into doing so as a necessary part of the accession criteria for the states of Central and Eastern Europe after 2004. This 'ever closer' interaction between the European and national competition authorities has been further boosted through the creation of the European Competition Network, which enables the agencies to share and swap information, and more importantly to develop their own set of norms and values. How did this all happen? Why did competition policy emerge as a suitable policy area for European integration and who are the drivers and actors within the EU regime? This book is very much concerned with unpacking the competition policy regime to provide answers to these questions and explores the actors, their powers and strategies at establishing European competition governance. Rather than providing a general overview of the full remit of EU competition policy this book focuses its attention primarily on the EU cartel regime and aims to illustrate how the European Commission has pursued cartels and to what extent its battles to uncover, dissolve and penalise cartellisation has been effective.

1. WRITING ABOUT COMPETITION POLICY

Although fewer areas of European public policy may seem to have been as widely researched, debated and analysed than European Union (EU) competition policy, a degree of caution is immediately required, for a closer inspection reveals that interest in this particular policy area has stemmed mainly from the disciplines of economics (including Bishop, 1993; Clarke and Morgan, 2006; Estrin and Holmes, 1998; Motta, 2004) and law (including Goyder, 2003; Jones and Sufrin, 2008; Whish, 2009). In stark contrast, few political scientists have opted to explore competition policy in terms of both research and teaching. Indeed, even most EU scholars (albeit with a handful of exceptions such as Cini and McGowan, 2009; Eyre and Lodge, 2000; McGowan and Wilks, 1995; Doern and Wilks, 1996; Wilks, 2007) have tended to overlook this field of enquiry, simply just acknowledge its significance on passing or dismiss its relevance altogether. This reality holds true for studies of the EU regime as well as studies of the individual national competition regimes. Few undergraduate modules on the EU include competition policy. The complexity and seemingly impenetrable labyrinth of the legal case law and the economic analyses of competition regulation may in part explain this seeming reticence to explore competition, and there can also be a tendency among economists, legal scholars and practitioners to reject a political dimension in the making of competition policy. Mario Monti, a former EU Competition Commissioner, provided an apt illustration when he declared that EC competition policy 'is a matter of law and economics, not politics' (Levy, 2005). Politics certainly plays a role in the regulation of competition and its exclusion (whether self-imposed or not) is simply no longer defensible.

EU competition policy has long represented one of the few areas where the Commission not only is responsible for direct policy implementation but also possesses wide discretionary powers as both a regulator and an enforcer of policy. Fortunately there are now strong signs that these knowledge barriers are finally being broken down as a new generation of political science/public policy researchers (Buch-Hansen, 2008; Büthe and Swank, 2007; Damro, 2006; Doleys, 2007; Lehmkuhl, 2008; Leucht, 2008;

Seidel, 2007; Warzoulet, 2007; Uydin, 2009; Wigger, 2008) shed greater and welcome light on the origins, institutions and workings of EU competition policy.

Politics matters in competition regulation and surfaces in relation to institutional design and powers, issues of transparency, degrees of politicisation, discretionary abilities and questions of legitimacy in the decision making process. Those regulators engaged in cartel enforcement may be surprised to find political scientists mulling over competition policy, but a closer examination of the intense debates surrounding the inclusion of competition in the ECSC Treaty and the shaping of the anti-cartel drive in the EEC Treaty clearly reveal examples of the political sensitivities at play. There can of course be little doubt that competition policy is a matter of economics, just as it is a matter of the law. As Cini and McGowan (2009) state:

> What is often forgotten, however, is that the reasons for having a competition policy, the form that policy takes – both substantively and procedurally – and how the policy is implemented and enforced are all at the core questions of politics. A political dimension demands that we stand back from the micro- and meso-analyses of the competition economists and lawyers to address broader questions of state, economy and indeed society.

Competition policy may not immediately catch the imagination of many political science students. At first glance it seems too arcane and complex, but its less than apt coverage is not so unremarkable. Indeed, let us go further and argue that the paucity of material from political science is part of a wider malaise in EU studies. There is an imbalance, and many of the main economic policy areas (with the exception of the euro) have been overshadowed by a huge interest in the 'high politics' arenas of security and immigration, the politics of enlargement and treaty reform. Although both topical and significant these areas should not be allowed to overlook the core areas where integration has proceeded the furthest. This imbalance has arisen owing to the unwillingness or degrees of uncomfortability for many about engaging with other disciplines, but in part it also occurs because such policy studies do not lend themselves easily to the leading debates within International Relations and Comparative Politics theories and approaches.

It is important for students of politics to engage with competition policy. It is one of only six exclusive core competences of the EU (Treaty of Lisbon), and students should recognise its significance in the creation of supranational governance, and need to question the politics behind its operationalisation and appreciate the growing relevance it will have for a new phase of government/industry relations in face of the current economic crisis.

This book has been written with the politics and public policy reader in mind, and aims to complement the numerous existing materials on this subject area from the disciplines of economics and law. As such it should be stressed from the outset that this work is primarily concerned neither with analysing the economic theories of competition behind cartel formation and practices (Bishop and Walker, 2002; Morgan, 2009) nor with the legal analysis of collusive agreements and a substantial case law that already exists (Korah, 2007; Sufrin and Jones, 2008; Whish, 2003). Its attention concentrates rather on the institutional structures and decision-making processes of the EU supranational cartel regime, and specifically the role and activities of the European Commission and the evolution of cartel policy. In adopting this approach it recognises the contributions from both economics and law. Indeed, this book should prove invaluable and informative for students of both law and economics as each discipline brings its own distinct slant and focus.

Still, from a political science perspective, if there has been little work done on EU competition policy as a whole there has been substantially nothing that has been done on the two core aspects of anti-trust, namely cartels and monopolies. This book begins to redress this omission by examining cartel policy. It focuses on the one aspect of its competition brief which has occupied much of the European Commission's limited resources from the very outset, namely restrictive practices (under Article 81), which includes the pursuit, identification and termination of cartel arrangements. The European Commission takes the lead in shaping and setting the policy, and in establishing the parameters within which it is applied in practice. Even though certain aspects of policy enforcement have been decentralised since regulation changes in 2004, and despite the fact that the Commission now works within a network of competition actors and institutions to which it has delegated some of its earlier responsibilities, it remains the dominant player in the European competition policy game.

This book addresses a paradox. Although the anti-cartel drive represents the oldest aspect of the EU competition regime and has been the one which has consumed most of the European Commission's Competition Directorate General's (DG Competition) human resources and time, the area of cartels has been under-researched in favour of the other aspects such as merger control and more politically sensitive areas such as the liberalisation of the public utilities (especially in the energy sector) and state aid (Doleys, 2007; Thomas and Wishlade, 2009). The paucity of political science literature in this area is unfortunate, for the pursuit of cartels opens up a truly fascinating world of 'dawn raids' and intrigue where secretive agreements are concocted in smoke filled rooms, in luxury holiday resorts and have even been subject to covert taping (see Connor, 2001) by the FBI in the USA.[1]

In the first half of 2008 alone the European Commission raided the offices of a very prestigious list of companies (such as Unilever, Procter and Gamble, Lufthansa, and Lloyd's Register, to name but a few) in their search for cartels (*Financial Times*, 30 June 2008; *Irish Times*, 21 June 2008). The study of cartels has, according to two competition law specialists (Harding and Joshua, 2003), received little distinct exploration even in the legal literature, and the highly probable explanation for this situation rests with competition law's focus on market structures rather than investigating the moral and ethical issues of anti-competitive activities. Cartels are a reality of modern business life, but just how problematic are they and what exactly is competition policy?

2. UNDERSTANDING THE COMPETITION PRINCIPLE AND THE ENFORCEMENT OF COMPETITION POLICY

It is an undisputed fact among neo-classical economists that competition is a necessary prerequisite for a free market economy, although there may indeed be a variety of different approaches to defining what competition actually entails and means (Scherer and Ross, 1990). Being anchored in the principles of free-market capitalism the origins and development of competition policy across Europe after 1945 have always retained a degree of controversy and policy evolution must be set against trends in wider economic models and varieties of capitalism (Buch-Hansen, 2008; Wigger, 2008). A competition policy strives to secure the creation and maintenance of genuinely competitive markets. As one commentator has described it, 'central to the classical definition is the notion of perfect competition which provided a benchmark against which all other forms of competition should be judged' (Gavin, 2001: 108). Thus, the commitment to competitive markets is rarely questioned. Cini and McGowan (2009) note that 'Competition' has been defined as the 'struggle or contention for superiority, [which] in the commercial world . . . means a striving for the custom and business of people in the market place' (see also Bishop and Walker, 2002; van den Bergh and Camasasca, 2006). Wilks identifies the reality that 'there are both economic and political rationales for competition policy' (Wilks, 2005: 115). The political aspect centres on the readiness of individual governments to allow business actors the freedom to compete in the market in order to protect the consumer from any potential exploitation from the power of big business. Although the economic rationale raises more points of controversy it is very much steeped in 'neo-classical' economic approaches which highlight the advantages and desirability of both productive and allocative efficiencies. Ultimately, efficiencies will be greater where the health of the economy is subject to strong competition rules and they are very much linked to the competitiveness agenda which arose in the mid-1990s and continued as a central aspect of the Lisbon Agreement. A sizeable literature on the economic theory of competition policy has developed from Smith and Mill to the Chicago and Austrian Schools. It is not the intention to deal with this here and readers are strongly encouraged to consult the above-referenced works.

The pursuit of perfect competition has long been a cherished concept of neo-classical economics and the market has been regarded as the most effective instrument to allocate resources and determine prices. Accordingly, competition between firms is to be welcomed as it unleashes dynamic effects which can be transformed into greater efficiencies, innovation and, ultimately, lower prices for the consumer. Economic theory illustrates the argument through two ideal types. The first type refers to a world of perfect competition where the existence of numerous suppliers prevented any likelihood or possibility of collusive agreements to control price. This ideal model remains largely utopian in nature as the realities of many actual markets are typified more by models of imperfect competition (type 2), where considerably fewer players exist and can (determine price) and do deliberately set out to thwart competition through the pursuit of anti-competitive agreements. Even Adam Smith, with his talk of the 'invisible hand' of the market, recognised that competition was an abstract notion which could not exist in its purest form in the real world.

Instead of pursuing some abstract notion of perfect competition, competition authorities have preferred to opt for the looser concept of 'workable competition' (Clark, 1940; Sosnick, 1958). On the one hand such an approach is, in terms of theory, a much vaguer concept, but on the other hand it reflects developments on the ground. Either way a state of actual competition cannot simply be taken for granted even if there are be ethical and social objections to the absence of competition. Markets can be manipulated by firms deliberately to distort the benefits and efficiencies of competition. Some firms strongly resist any such calls for competition and seek to undermine such objectives by engaging in a number of anti-competitive practices which include dividing up markets and fixing prices in order to increase or maintain their profit margins.

A state of firm to firm competition is often resisted and fought because it generates uncertainty. In contrast engagement in anti-competitive practices is deemed to provide greater predictability. By acting collusively or by abusing a dominant market position, cartel members may be able to charge higher prices and reap substantial gains. Given this context competition policies are designed and drafted to prevent, deter or threaten firms from acting in such a fashion. In the lack of strict competition application and enforcement such incentives are easily lost, and without it, as the former command-led economies of the former communist states in Eastern Europe readily illustrated, prosperity and growth suffer.

Competition requires regulation because, as Doern and Wilks (1996: 1) have affirmed, '[n]either competition nor the market is inevitable or natural. Markets have to be created through processes of social change and public regulation . . .', and while there is indeed some consensus that competition is a good thing, there is little agreement about what 'workable competition' implies in concrete policy terms. In other words, and in order to safeguard and ensure the benefits arising from the competitive process, the market has to be 'policed', and this in turn requires the establishment of a regulatory framework which requires strict enforcement. In practice, competition policy needs to strike a balance between the imposition, by legislation, of necessary restrictions upon unbridled economic competition and the elimination of harmful restrictive practices which prevent a coherent integration of markets. Competition policies are constructed around what practices are not allowed, and in this sense are negative policies as they seek to prevent rather than to promote certain activities. However, caution should be applied because competition policy may not always be driven by the desire to promote competition and thus enhance consumer welfare (in terms of both prices and protection). There can be other factors at play which can centre on the distribution of wealth and concerns about economic power residing in the hands of the few. There has always been a concern about the extent of economic power and the degree to which cartels and monopolies are undemocratic. Competition policy can also be advanced to defend the position of small and medium-sized enterprises, which provide both potential competitors to their larger neighbours and supply most jobs in the economy. Competitiveness is another objective of competition policy. In the EU context competition policy has been advanced as a means of furthering economic and political integration by breaking down privately constructed barriers to trade between the EU member states, thus realising a fully functioning Single European Market (SEM).

EU competition policy constitutes one of the largest, if often unheralded, success stories of European integration and has two main objectives: firstly, to create and sustain a single market that fosters intra-EU trade and competitiveness; secondly, to promote economic and political integration. It has achieved both. The most distinguishing feature of EU competition policy is that it represents a clear example of European governance in action, but what issues does it deal with, who are the principal actors behind competition policy and to what extent has the policy become Europeanised?

3. INTRODUCING THE EUROPEAN UNION COMPETITION REGIME

From a European perspective the development of a competition policy framework has been a gradual process which commenced after 1945. The first steps towards the first coherent regimes occurred in the United Kingdom (from 1948) and West Germany (from 1957).[2] From the outset the adoption of these domestic policies reflected new thoughts on industrial structures and competitiveness and were influenced indirectly and directly by the well-established US competition model (initiated under the Sherman and Clayton Acts in 1890 and 1914 respectively which sought to ensure that economic power (in the shape of banks, oil, and railroad companies) was not concentrated in the hands of a few powerful trusts). At its core competition law essentially was seeking to balance the perceived benefits of economic collaboration against the potential economic and political problems that could ensue. Although the UK, West German and the later domestic competition regimes in Europe all differed slightly in terms of structure, institutional design and decision-making processes, they all shared the same objective of promoting competitive market structures and breaking up anti-competitive behaviour such as market-rigging, price-fixing cartels and abusive monopolies, which had been an endemic feature of the European business environment for the first half of the twentieth century.[3] These anti-competitive pursuits still remain very much a threat in the early twenty-first century. The realities that many of these acts occurred on a cross-border scale effectively left the national authorities ill-equipped to tackle and investigate them, and consequently led to greater pressure for both greater inter-regime co-operation and new modes of international competition governance. Competition policy, for example, therefore assumed central importance in the European regional integration process, and found reflection in the objectives of both the European Coal and Steel Community of 1951 and the European Economic Community Treaty of 1957 (Cini and McGowan, 2009; Leucht, 2008), and both are discussed in greater detail in subsequent chapters. Article 3(g) TEC explicitly declared that competition should not be distorted in the common market while the substantive law is spelt out in Articles 81–90 (TEU).[4]

However, the treaty articles simply outlined the objectives and did not spell out how such objectives were to be realised. A state of competition between companies could not be taken for granted or assumed to occur without some form of regulation, and thus it necessitated the creation of a government agency effectively to police the market place. Set within the context and ambitions of a customs union it would have been simply counter-productive to dismantle trade barriers between the member states if private industry had been allowed to remain free to engage in cartel-like restrictions on competition and undermine the advantages of opening up the markets in the first place (Von der Groeben, 1961). In short, the realisation of a truly integrated market and flourishing intra-EU trade could be ensured only if the market place were actually policed. In the West German case, for example, the Christian Democratic-led government under Konrad Adenauer had established the Bundeskartellamt (BKartA) or Federal Cartel Office in Berlin in 1957 (McGowan, 1993; Sturm, 1996) to protect competition. The same logic of regulation and the need for some form of institutionalised control at the supranational level to secure and maintain competition discipline within the common market was also recognised.

Consequently, the six original member state governments established the European Commission's legal competence through Regulation 17/62 (and simultaneously sidelined both the Council of Ministers and the European Parliament) to operate as an autonomous and quasi-judicial competition policy-making institution. The regulation equipped DG Competition with exclusive powers of investigation (including the infamous 'dawn raids') into suspected violations of the EU's competition rules and enabled DG Competition to codify, exempt and impose fines on offending firms.[5]

In effect, and in terms of governance, Regulation 17 identified the Commission as the principal actor in the administration and implementation of competition policy decision making and assigned it the roles of judge, jury and executioner. Only the European Court of Justice (and after 1989 the Court of First Instance) was granted the power to overturn Commission decisions. In short, the Commission's role in competition policy places it in an altogether different position from its work in most other EU policy areas, because in the competition policy arena the Commission is the decision maker. Further elaboration is required. Responsibility for the day to day investigations lies with DG Competition which is obliged to consult one of the two Advisory Committees (one for restrictive practices and the other for mergers) before its reaches a decision which has to be endorsed by the College of Commissioners.

In hindsight the member states had created a powerful supranational agent (Seidel, 2007) which has continually advanced its power through the adoption of guidelines and notices, and in so doing has altered the terms of the principle/agent relationship (Lehmkuhl, 2008). The decision to initiate an EU competition regime heralded the advance of a Community legal order which would in time ensure strong degrees of convergence on the realisation of a European cartel policy.[6] This nascent European regime laid the basis for the development of a competition policy which was constructed on increasingly shared norms and gradually helped to disseminate a competition culture throughout the Community and beyond.

The fledgling EU regime developed slowly. We should not underestimate the challenges that faced the new supranational European Commission and not least in terms of recognising its powers. As such the historical narrative of EU competition policy is one of incremental growth but also one that simply failed for the most part to show up on the radar screen of political science for most of the 1960s and 1970s, albeit with some exceptions (Allen, 1977).

A sudden metamorphosis in the mid to late 1980s brought competition to the fore, and this transformation finds explanation in a number of factors. Firstly, timing was certainly crucial and changing economic philosophies (boosted by a neo-liberal agenda) pushed competition as a means to encourage innovation and efforts to restore European competitiveness, especially in the United Kingdom and West Germany. Secondly, the Commission had matured sufficiently by this stage to assert its own analyses and powers and, thirdly, was assisted by the rulings of the Court of Justice (and after 1989 also the Court of First Instance) in Luxembourg and the accumulation of a considerable amount of competition case law. Personalities, as a fourth explanatory factor, also played a substantial part at the European level as a series of dynamic and forceful Competition Commissioners (including Peter Sutherland, Leon Brittan, Karel van Miert, Mario Monti and Neelie Kroes) all propelled competition forward as the only credible solution to European economic dynamism as vociferously as they challenged state intervention in the economy. Finally, it should be emphasised that although competition policy was not identified as a specific non-tariff barrier to be eradicated under the 1992 single market programme, it rapidly became a central pillar to its very success. In short, national government mindsets and strategies on competitiveness (notably even in countries which had traditionally displayed a rather lukewarm interest in competition policy like France) had changed significantly enough during the 1980s to enable the competition principle to take hold and have had an irrevocable impact on the domestic competition arena.

4. THE FIVE ASPECTS OF EU COMPETITION POLICY

Today the EU rules themselves extend over five substantial areas (see Table 1.1): these target firstly the endemic existence of cartels and restrictive practices (such as price-fixing and market-sharing agreements) under Article 81 (formerly Article 85 EEC). This article prohibits all agreements 'which may affect trade between member states and which have as their object the prevention, restriction or distortion of competition within the common market'. Cartel policy rapidly emerged as the core activity in terms of staff, time and resources, is one of the most developed aspects of policy and will be returned to in greater detail from chapter 2 onwards.

The second aspect of EU competition policy centres on merger control. Merger policy (which had originally been deliberately omitted from the Treaty of Rome, although it had appeared in the Treaty of Paris establishing the ECSC) was added as a belated weapon to the Commission's arsenal in 1990 (through Regulation 4064/89) after the member states bowed to the wishes of the Commission and growing demands from the business community (most notably the European Round Table of Industrialists (ERT) and the European Employers Association (UNICE)) for a level playing field and a one stop shop for assessing EU mergers which exceeded specified thresholds.[7] Mergers and joint ventures may have anti-competitive implications because they could lead to a situation where a monopoly or oligopoly is formed (i.e. a process of concentration). EU merger policy has been well received by the business community, and the Commission has generally won praise for its efficient handling of mergers even if some of the member states (such as Germany) have now and again expressed their concern over the possibility of politicised decision making within the College of Commissioners.

The third and fourth key aspects of EU competition policy focus on monopolies which are abusing their dominant position in the market place under Article 82 (formerly Article 86 EEC) and efforts to inject greater competition and liberalisation into the public utility sectors which had traditionally been exempted from the competition provisions such as telecommunications and energy under Article 86 (formerly Article 90 EEC). In the case of the latter the Commission can point to developments in the airline, energy and telecommunications sectors to highlight the significant advances of creating a single and competitive market over the last twenty years although progress has been more limited in the services sector. EU monopoly policy (i.e. where one firm holds a monopoly position) is designed to catch and penalise those companies which deliberately set out to abuse their dominant position within the market and as such these actions can have a detrimental effect on competition. The Commission has been involved with a long drawn out tussle with Microsoft, and in 2004 imposed a fine of €497 million on the company for refusing to provide rival suppliers with the necessary interoperability information to challenge it. This ongoing case illustrates the Commission's resolve to stoke

*Table 1.1 Tracing the expansive development of EU competition policy**

	1957	1960s	1970s	1980s	1990s	2000+
Restrictive practices/ cartels	0	1	2	3	4	4
Abusive monopolies	0	1	1	2	2	3
Mergers	0	0	0	0	4	4
Liberalised utilities (telecoms, energy, postal services)	0	0	1	2	4	4
State aids	0	1	2	2	3	3

Notes: *This table excludes the coal and steel industries which fell under the ECSC Treaty. The table has been developed from Schmitter, 1996.

Scale Coding
0 = No EU Competence
1 = EU Competence but largely dormant
2 = EU Competence and slowly developing
3 = EU Competence and active
4 = EU Competence and very active

controversy. Abusive dominance assumes the form of using market power to cut prices and drive out competitors (predatory pricing) or to charge high prices where consumers have little alternative but to pay up. Assessing dominance has proven problematic for DG Competition officials, as it has required specific definitions of relevant, product and temporal markets. Such economic analyses are often queried and to date monopoly policy has constituted the least active of the Commission's competition policy activities (Cini and McGowan, 2009).

All the above four areas bring the Commission into dealings with the business world, but uniquely the fifth area, which centres on the granting of state subsidies under Articles 88–90 (formerly, Articles 92–94) involves direct contact with member state governments and has proven arguably the most contentious and politically sensitive aspect of the EU competition brief. State aid policy is of a different order and deals with the potentially anti-competitive effects of national grants of subsidy to industry within the context of the EU's single market. State aid has featured as an aspect of government/industry relations to varying degrees across Western Europe since 1945. The use of such subsidies have often been justified as an essential aspect of government driven industrial policy and are designed as ways to secure employment particularly in peripheral and economically depressed regions, as issues of national prestige such as Air France and Olympic Airways (Featherstone and Papadimitriou, 2006), or attempts to create European champions (for example, Bull, to compete directly with US and other international companies). Trying to control levels of state aid has been a particularly difficult task for the Commission. Although DG Competition adopted an increasingly aggressive stance towards state aids from the mid-1980s onwards many member states appeared reluctant to abandon the granting of subsidies. In many ways national reaction to state aid reflected different models of capitalism in play. To assist its efforts the Commission even launched its own scoreboard in 2001 to embarrass and cajole member states into granting less aid. In the period from 2000 to 2006 most state aid cases were recorded (see Commission, 2007) in Germany (some 148), closely followed by Italy (105), Spain (70) and France (63).

This short overview of EU competition policy has highlighted several factors to note: firstly, the willingness of the member state governments to delegate powers in the competition arena to the supranational level (see McGowan and Wilks, 1995); secondly, the expansion over time of the policy base as the Commission has gained in confidence and expertise; thirdly, a gradual policy convergence of rules across the entire EU; and, lastly, the exporting of the same EU rules to third (for example, potential accession) states as part of the *acquis communautaire*. In the course of the last two decades the EU competition policy regime has changed out of all recognition. This metamorphosis from a sleepy backwater to the forefront of Commission activity owed as much to changed economic thinking with the ascendancy of neo-liberalism and the accumulation of an ever expanding case law as well as growing confidence within DG Competition (formerly pre-1999 DG IV) and its ability to attract very high calibre recruits. These developments facilitated the pro-competition drive of a succession of very capable competition commissioners who have all driven competition policy forward.

By the end of the 1990s a puissant and prestigious supranational competition regime had exerted its force and power on both business undertakings and companies and member state governments. The supranational competition order was not however problem free by any means. It has always had its detractors who have pointed to the so-called faults or weaknesses within this system, such as, for example, the length of time taken to settle cases, a lack of transparency, weak analyses of the facts that have settled cases, too much room for politicisation, and at times Commission officials have been charged with being too dogmatic in promoting the competition principle over other factors. The Commission has noted the criticisms and has endeavoured to respond to its critics, and to this end has on regular occasions moved to overhaul the competition machinery and its own practices. How well it has done so remains open for debate.

The Commission has regularly sought to modernise its practices and update its procedures across all five areas of activity, and usually as a means to facilitate speedier and more consistent decision making. It initiated, for example, the most far reaching changes in its handling of cartels (McGowan, 2005) for over forty years in 2004 when it replaced Regulation 17 with a new regulation (Regulation 1/2003) which also coincided with internal restructuring within DG Competition and the creation of a new cartel unit. This latter regulation simply reinforced the realities of supranational governance and effectively created something akin to a 'federal' regime, with the Commission located like a ringmaster at the very centre determining which cases it will investigate and which it will pass to the national authorities (Wilks, 2005).

On reflection various trends have been recognisable in competition regulation within the European Commission since the late 1980s. These can be labelled 'modernisation', and 'Europeanisation' (Cini and McGowan, 2009), and both have made their presence felt in terms of both competition policy and specifically cartel regulation. Modernisation was the label given to the Commission's competition policy reform programme which commenced in the late 1990s. The pressures for updating the EU cartel rulebook in 2004 were driven by calls for changes in the substantive analysis which constituted competition decision making and to reduce the administrative burden placed on the Commission before the two most recent waves of EU enlargement in 2004 and 2007 respectively occurred.

Notions of Europeanisation emerged as a highly fashionable concept in the field of European Studies in the late 1990s. Its definition may be contested (Harmsen and Wilson, 2000; Featherstone and Radaelli, 2003; Risse et al., 2001) but essentially it refers to the impact of the European Union governance structures on the politics, polities and policies of its member states. In the context of this book the process of Europeanisation was most aptly displayed through the convergence of all national anti-cartel legislation in line with the rules under Article 81 TEC (McGowan, 2005). In trying to assess how far these changes have bought benefits to the wars against the cartels it is necessary to turn towards the theme of this book and to highlight the dangers of cartellisation.

5. THE SECRET LIFE OF CARTELS

Cartels have long represented an established aspect of commercial activity. They were particularly pronounced as an essential, accepted and even government-orchestrated feature of business activity in German-speaking Europe throughout the first half of the twentieth century

(Gerber, 1998). The existence of such activities and practices can be traced as far back as Ancient Egypt (Herlitzka, 1963: 121). When and wherever cartels emerge they impact on the operation of markets and the positions of other actors and traders. Whether such impact may be termed negative or positive is open for debate. Any comparative and historical examination reveals that perceptions (ranging from toleration, agnosticism to outright hostility) have differed from state to state over time. The propensity towards cartels today may often be driven as much by cultural norms and historical tradition as by economic benefits. Yet, perceptions changed dramatically after 1945 when cartels were generally perceived as undesirable.

The origins of EU cartel policy have to be understood in the context of three factors: the imperative of the drive for the realisation of a single market, the historical context which shaped policy after 1945 and the influence and leading role of the US experience on the European regimes (Leucht, 2008; Schulze and Hoeren, 2000). Cartels were identified as an immediate target from the outset when Article 85 of the European Economic Community (EEC) Treaty specifically prohibited all agreements 'which may affect trade between member states and which have as their object the prevention, restriction or distortion of competition within the common market'.[8] In retrospect, the decision by the six founding EEC member states to commit themselves to competition discipline and simultaneously recognise the logic of a supranational dimension is significant, given the unfamiliarity of the majority with anti-trust. It is also worth recalling that member state positions on the competition policy rules certainly varied, and there was a tussle between France, the Netherlands and West Germany over both the meaning of competition policy and differing approaches on policy management.

Although cartels were identified over fifty years ago by the EEC Treaty as the first and primary target of the EU's competition policy order, the EU cartel regime took time to form, and its enforcement until the 1980s has been described as hesitant, patchy and largely ineffectual. It is never a straightforward task to pinpoint specific chronological turning points or periods in any policy's development, but this book suggests four periods of development (see chapter 6) for EU cartel policy. In each the position of DG Competition and cartel policy developments can be examined with reference to both the substantive and the procedural regimes. Accounting for internal changes is one aspect of competition policy which is generally well covered (Wilks and McGowan, 1996), whereas there has been considerably less attention paid to the external variables. Any examination into the evolution of EU cartel policy cannot be completely separated from developments at member state level. This allows recognition of the varieties of capitalism literature (Albert, 1993) which emphasises the spectrum of capitalist models across Europe and the variable impact of competition policy (see Wigger, 2008) on liberal, co-ordinated, state and transitional economies. Policy development must be considered against changes and events in the wider economic and societal spheres. Wigger does this in an innovative manner by adopting a critical economy perspective to the development of EU competition policy in which she traces the impact of Ordo-liberalism, embedded liberalism and neo-liberalism on the evolution of the competition regime, and especially on Commission thinking (Wigger and Nölke, 2007). It is not the intention here to retrace this particular wider narrative, but readers are strongly urged to consult such emerging literature. How far can the Commission really operate a single cartel policy when so many different cartel traditions have prevailed and continue to exist at member state level?

Cartels are generally held today to represent the most pernicious form of anti-competitive behaviour, and condemnation of cartel agreements has become the norm. Cartels are an endemic aspect of global business activity and recourse to them has been labelled as akin to cancers in the market place, and even theft.[9] They arise when companies participate in 'deliberate, highly organised and covert collaborative' (Harding and Joshua, 2003: 1) practices which have been agreed by a number of independent firms from the same or similar sphere of economic activity. Cartels are effectively safe havens to escape and prevent competition. For the most part hard core cartel policy can be described as a combative struggle between those large corporate interests which seek to create anti-competitive agreements and the antitrust regulators who are determined to catch and penalise such activity.

Cartels are now universally 'recognised as the most aggressive violation of competition law' (OECD, 1998). Cartels have been prioritised as the key element of the Commission's entire competition policy brief over the course of the last two decades, and particularly under the last three competition Commissioners, Karel van Miert 1993–9), Mario Monti, 1999–2004) and Neelie Kroes, 2004–10).[10] All three have stressed the importance of battling cartels as a means of defending consumers (Kroes, 2008). This book explores the Commission's role and strategies in its pursuit, identification and termination of cartel arrangements.

Secret horizontal agreements which divide markets, fix prices and prevent newcomers from entering the market embody the classic shape of a collusive agreement. Cartels in the contemporary world are generally recognised as problematic because they have been primarily designed to serve and work in the interests of their members and not the consumer or the overall health of the economy. Kroes (2006a) summed this up neatly:

'cartels strike a killer blow at the heart of economic activity. This makes it harder for us to deliver the Lisbon goals of high growth, job creation and innovation'. They work to the detriment of the consumer through the imposition of higher prices.[11]

In the short term recourse to cartellisation may indeed prove beneficial, but in the longer term and in today's environment such hard-core cartel arrangements are certain to have detrimental repercussions. As a means to extract higher rents from their customers such covert operations prevent competition and innovation. Secret agreements which divide markets, fix prices and prevent newcomers from entering the market represent the classic shape of collusive agreement and the most harmful for the competitive process. It is interesting to note that certain economic sectors (such as the pharmaceutical, paper, cement and glass markets) seem more prone to cartellisation than others. The world of cartels is inherently unstable. The formation of cartels proves immensely intricate, incites many jealousies among the parties and ultimately the strain leads many to collapse. Still, cartels thrive in the modern world and cartellisation continues to remain a strategic option for many companies on a short term, and for some on a much longer term, basis.

In the medium to longer term cartels will always enjoy higher (illegal) profits than otherwise would be the case in the face of open competition.[12] The profit maximisation incentive ensures that cartels remain very much an endemic reality in the modern world. Concerns have also been raised about the connections between economic power and political power.[13] Condemnation of cartel agreements has become the norm. In the last decade competition regulators in both the EU and the US have intensified their determination to hunt and break up as many cartel agreements as possible that can be unearthed. The difficulties of such a task should not be underestimated and the regulators are constantly engaged in battling a seeming propensity on the part of the business world for cartellisation. Indeed, viewed from a longer term perspective this book depicts the Commission's struggle as a series of battles that can be interpreted as an ongoing cartel war.

Attitudes globally towards cartels are changing fast and pressure is growing against the growing number of international cartel arrangements. We are now living in the 'Age' of the international cartel. Indeed, cartels are not just more prevalent today but have become much more sophisticated in their design and ways of concealment. In the past often the classic type of cartels occurred in sectors of the economy where market shares were relatively stable and where brands could not successfully differentiate between products. Importantly, there tended to be fewer players in such cartels and each member was easily able to check for anyone breaking ranks. Recent events in the UK reflect the reinvigorated determination of the Office of Fair Trading (OFT) to crack down on cartels. As an example, in its investigations into the country's four largest supermarkets it alleges (and in theory this seems difficult to co-ordinate and the charge is clearly rejected by the supermarkets) that the supermarkets have used the largest consumer companies, 'as a switchboard to swap information that enables the supermarkets to co-ordinate the prices of thousands of products from soap to cola' (*Economist*, 3 May 2008: 18). This particular case illustrates the real difficulties in proving actual deliberate collusion but it also suggests that the current probe is much more than just a sweep by the competition regulator, and indicates that the authorities perhaps know what they are looking for, and this raises the issue of whistleblowers.

Arguments in favour of permitting cartels to operate legally are usually predicated on notions that such agreements can protect employment and can assist sectors of the economy which are under threat and especially 'if they can lead to technical improvements and enable firms to adjust to a harsher economic climate and growing international competition'. There has to be exceptional justification because, as cartels are designed to work in the interests of their members, their wider impact on the economy and consumers has to be considered. The degree of conflict can be observed on two fronts, which can be identified as institutional and procedural. Organisational changes within DG Competition, and a more aggressive determination to tackle cartellisation within DG Competition, typify the former, while amendments to the EC restrictive practices regime under Regulation 1/2003, the reform of the leniency programme (in 1996) and even tougher notices on fining infringements reflect developments in the latter.

The stakes and costs in this war have been raised. For example, the sixteen highest fines in EU cartel history occur after 2001. The goal of eradicating cartels may be a laudable aim, but the task is an onerous one which continually challenges the energies and resources of all anti-trust regulators. How the regulators respond and pursue cartellisation ultimately determines the scale, intensity and number of such anti-competitive practices. It is too naïve to expect a sudden increase in the number of competition policy researchers, and this book is not advocating such an objective. There should be, however, greater recognition and realisation of this core policy arena among those studying the EU. How can this be achieved? There are two paths to traverse. The first sets out to make the theme more exciting to non-specialists, and the second seeks to reach out and place discussions of competition policy more in the mainstream by engaging in theoretical discussions.

EU cartel policy has developed in an incremental fashion and has become over time increasingly proactive and combative. The Commission's current resolve is displayed in a number of strategies and reforms since 2000 which include internal organisational changes within DG Competition, the adoption of new administrative rules under Regulation 1/2003, refinements to the leniency programme, a new and tougher notice (June 2006) on fining infringements and efforts to foster greater international co-operation, as well as a number of more innovative mechanisms and tools such as its 2008 White Paper on Private Actions. The stakes and costs in these cartel wars have been raised. It is not just coincidence that the highest fines in EU cartel history have all occurred in the last decade, though whether high is high enough remains an issue. The Commission possesses considerable discretion in setting the fines and has opted to shed more transparency on how and why it calculates the actual fine. Fines form a part of a deliberate strategy to deter cartel formation. Yet, no matter how laudable the goal of eradicating cartels may be it remains an onerous task which continually challenges the energies and resources of all anti-trust regulators.

How the regulators respond and pursue cartellisation ultimately determines the scale, intensity and number of such anti-competitive practices, at least in theory. Can they in practice create sufficient deterrents ever to overcome the attraction of cartellisation?[14] Judging just how successful an enforcement agency the Commission is depends on a number of factors which include how many cartels it unearths, how many fines it imposes and how many potential arrangements it deters. Although statistics are available for the first two we will never be in a position to provide an answer on the EU rules as a deterrent. It is practically impossible to speak with the firms concerned, and thus all reference points relate to cartels which have been unearthed. As onlookers we will simply never be in a position to know enough information about the scale and scope of cartellisation or the strategies of the firms involved, but we can make general assumptions about the nature and degree of such anti-competitive activities from cartels which have already been detected. That said researchers should also avoid the danger of relying on the Commission's own assessment of its strategies.

6. ORGANISATION OF THE BOOK

The chapters which follow provide an analysis of the origins, evolution and workings of European Union cartel policy. Chapter 2 provides an introduction for the political scientist reader to the world of cartels. It offers a definition of the term cartel, explains the rationale and characteristics of cartel practices, before moving on to highlight some of the dangers that cartels pose and exploring the fragile nature of these collusive agreements. Chapter 3 provides a historical narrative of the acceptance and encouragement of cartels, especially in Germany in the period from the later 1890s until the end of the Second World War and identifies the absence of any substantive regulations at all.

The following five chapters centre on the European supranational regime. EU cartel policy provides a number of avenues for exploration and chapters 4 to 7 explore the Commission's role and response to cartellisation over the last five decades. They demonstrate how the Commission has constantly expanded its competences, adapted its approaches and continually sought to refine its strategies to combat cartel proliferation. In short, these chapters provide a historical overview of the four phases of EU cartel policy and illustrate how the Commission has steadily become more active in its pursuit of cartels through new Notices and Guidelines. Chapter 4 outlines the major shift in governments' attitudes towards cartels in Western Europe which developed immediately after 1945. Special attention is given to the ECSC Treaty. This chapter shows how this fledgling European policy came to be influenced by the antitrust tradition in the United States.

Chapter 5 centres on the provisions of the EEC Treaty until the signing of the Treaty of Rome in 1957. Both chapters 4 and 5 focus on the positions of the West European states in the negotiations of both treaties with reference to competition issues. They explore the institutional framework which governs the EU competition regime and touch on key elements in competition decision-making. They also account for the administrative framework which was agreed and put in place under Regulation 17 to deal with restrictive practices. Chapter 6 examines the development of EU cartel policy from 1962 until the end of the 1990s, which it divides into four key chronological phases of activity. Chapter 7 deals with the European Commission's plans to modernise its anti-cartel strategies in the twenty-first century. It explores how far the latest reforms, administrative developments and internal restructuring have placed the Commission in a position effectively to combat or at least control cartellisation. In each of these last two chapters policy substance will be explored by means of using specific case examples to illustrate developments. The final chapter casts an eye to the future of policy development and raises questions about the likelihood of growing international co-operation and the search for international rules. It also ponders how far the recession and economic difficulties facing the Western industrialised nations will impact on and alter the Commission's anti-cartel drive in an era when certain leaders such as Nicholas Sarkozy, the French president, have openly questioned the neo-liberal competition mantra and pondered what competition has ever done for Europe (*Financial Times*, 22 June 2007). Before embarking on the history of European cartel policy it may be helpful to turn our attention towards defining what constitutes cartellisation and to explain why cartels are deemed to be problematic.

NOTES

1. The lysine cartel is a US antitrust case and is one that provides a fascinating example of cartel organisation and activity. This particular cartel comprised the world's five leading lysine producers and was constructed round price-fixing agreements. Lysine itself is an amino acid and is essential for human nutrition and development, but as it cannot be manufactured by the body, it is normally obtained from food. The meetings of the cartel were carefully staged to avoid rousing any suspicion especially as one of the cartel's main customers (the poultry industry) was holding its own conference simultaneously in the same town as the cartel met. To this end cartel members started in separate hotels and arrived at the meeting at different times. This meant there were a few empty seats at the start of the meeting, and some of the participants joked that these seats had been reserved especially for their customers, and one even said they were for the US Federal Bureau of Investigation (FBI). Little did the cartel participants know that as the meeting took place, FBI agents posed as hotel employees and recorded everything that occurred. The material collected by the FBI provided ample evidence of the cartel's ambitions and objectives.
2. The framework for both these evolving competition regimes was laid down in the 1948 Monopolies Act and the 1956 Restrictive Trade Practices Act in the United Kingdom and the *Gesetz gegen Wettbewerbsbeschränkungen* (Law against restraints on competition) in West Germany. For overview of the historical evolution of both see S. Wilks, 1996, 'The Prolonged Reform of United Kingdom Competition Policy' and R. Sturm 'The German Cartel Office in a Hostile Environment' in G.B. Doern and S. Wilks (eds) *Comparative Competition Policy: National Institutions in a Global Market*, Clarendon Press, Oxford, pp. 139–184, pp.185–224.
3. The main characteristic of the UK system (see Wilks, 1999) is its institutional and statutory complexity. Considerable room was built into the process for substantial ministerial discretion. In contrast, the German system, which was centred on the Federal Cartel Office, was largely a bureaucratic and judicial model with some possibility for ministerial control.
4. In the EEC Treaty (TEC) this general objective was originally to be found under Art. 3(f) and the articles pertaining to competition ran from 85 to 94. Under the Treaty on European Union it became Art. 3(g). The numbering of the competition articles was amended under the 1997 Treaty of Amsterdam and is to be altered again when the Treaty of Lisbon comes into force.
5. The amounts of the fines have been steadily increasing over the last two decades. For example, in 2001 the European Commission imposed fines of €462m on Hoffmann-La Roche (vitamins cartel); €296m on BASF (vitamins cartel); and €184m on Arjo Wiggins (paper cartel). In 2002 €250m was levied on Lafarge (plasterboard cartel) and €149m on Nintendo (for price-fixing), while in 2003 Hoechst was fined €99m (food preservative cartel). The 'hitlist' will continue to grow, but so too do the determination and resolve of many companies to conceal their anti-competitive activities by all means possible.
6. See recital 1, Council Regulation (EC) No 1/2003 on the Implementation of the Rules laid down in Articles 81 and 82 of the Treaty, *Official Journal of the European Communities*, OJ 2003 LI/1.
7. The Commission automatically became the one stop shop for processing merger

applications where the firms involved had an aggregate worldwide turnover of more than ECU 5 million; where at least two of the firms involved had an aggregate EU-wide turnover of more than ECU 250 million or where at least two of the companies involved held more than two-thirds of their aggregate EU-wide turnover within one and the same member state.

8. It should be noted that some types of agreement (and this to some extent reflects earlier more sympathetic perceptions) were entitled to exemptions from the EU competition rules where agreements contributed to improving the production or distribution of goods, promoted technical and economic progress or ensured that consumers reaped considerable benefits. Prior to 1 May 2004 such exemptions under Art. 81(3) were solely at the Commission's discretion to bestow if an agreement's beneficial effects were judged to outweigh any detrimental impact on competition.
9. US antitrust has always displayed an aversion towards the concentration of economic power and questioned its actual impact on notions and concepts of democracy if economic power is in the hands of a few powerful players.
10. Monti described cartels as a 'cancer' on the European economy in the XXXI Report on Competition Policy 2001, European Commission, 2002, p.4.
11. In its 2005 report on hard-core cartels the OECD noted that collusion resulted in significant percentage increases in prices. In Japan it was estimated that cartels raised prices by on average 16.5 per cent, in Sweden and Finland by around 20 per cent and in the United States there were examples of price increases of the magnitude of some 60–70 per cent.
12. The economic gains are difficult to quantify and vary from case to case.
13. US antitrust has always displayed an aversion towards the concentration of economic power and questioned its actual impact on notions and concepts of democracy if economic power is in the hands of a few powerful players.
14. In exploring EU cartel policy the academic researcher relies very much for primary material on a number of official publications (such as the Commission's annual competition policy report, DG Competition's Competition Policy Newsletter and information rich web-site as well as Court rulings) and on interviews with officials from DG Competition. Commission information provides statistics on the formal decisions, the number of firms involved in each case, the level of the fines and information on where and to whom leniency notices have been issued. The researcher also needs to be able to digest the existing range of secondary sources which extend across the disciplines of economics, history, law and politics.

2. Uncovering cartels: understanding the approaches and complexities of collusive agreements

Agreements between private companies have long constituted a regular aspect of business life. Such agreements have been designed to provide benefits for the undertakings concerned and to offer them new opportunities. There are occasions, however, when certain forms of agreements, although they may indeed be advantageous for the parties concerned, have adverse and negative effects on rival competitors, work to the detriment of consumers and undermine the competiveness of the economy in general. The issue centres on how far such arrangements impinge on the competitive process and the creation of competitive markets. Attitudes and views have differed over time, but in today's economic and political climate one particular form of agreement, namely the cartel, is now considered to be the most particularly damaging form of all anti-competitive behaviour. Cartels provide an excellent illustration of covert agreements which have usually been constructed to secure profit maximisation, and by their nature deliberately set out to thwart the competitive process.[1] Two essential facts about cartellisation and collusive activities should always be borne in mind. Firstly, recourse to cartellisation is not a new development, and for some commentators cartel formation stretched as far back as Ancient Egypt (Herlitzka, 1963: 121). Cartels have impacted ever since on the operation of markets and the positions of other actors and traders. Whether such impact may be termed negative or positive is open for debate. Any comparative and historical examination reveals that perceptions (ranging from toleration, agnosticism to outright hostility) have differed from state to state over time.

Secondly, cartels are not rare episodic creations but constant endemic realities of business life, past, present and future. The propensity towards cartels may not be as prevalent as during the interwar period, when it has been estimated that some 40 per cent of world trade was co-ordinated by international cartels (Nussbaum, 1986: 134), but they continue to thrive and today can often be driven as much by cultural norms and historical tradition as much as by economic benefits. Since the early 1990s hard-core cartellisation agreements have emerged again as a global phenomenon which proliferate in a wide range of economic sectors from vitamins and escalators to glass making and bitumen. The growing number of international cartels being uncovered from the mid 1990s onwards reflects a hardening of attitudes from the competition authorities (Whish, 2009). This priority response has led to more resources being dedicated to cartelbusting, more cartels being unearthed and the imposition of higher fines on cartel members. All in all cartels have also begun to attract more sustained and substantial media coverage in recent years. But what is a cartel, what sort of a threat does it pose, how do we measure the success or failure of a cartel arrangement, why has their presence suddenly become so problematic and who is charged with detecting and penalising such agreements and how well can this be done? These questions have informed academic research and publications on cartel policy from scholars from economic, legal and business backgrounds.

Indeed, the history of specific cartels, the degrees to which economic sectors have been prone to cartellisation and a substantial literature (Levenstein and Salant, 2007; Harding and Joshua, 2003) on why cartels are formed and how they operate already exists.[2] It is not the intention of this chapter to replicate these debates and issues owing to space constraints, but also because they justify lengthy debate and could form several books in their own right, especially as so much disagreement and dissent exists between many of the leading cartel researchers, both past and present. There are differing views over the stability of cartels, the actual duration of the anti-competitive activity and degree of profitability of cartel arrangements (Evenett, Levenstein and Suzlow, 2001; Levenstein and Suslow, 2006). Much of this stems directly from the difficulty of conducting research on cartels, which by their very nature are clandestine and covert agreements, and there is considerable room for 'measurement error, unobservable variables and sample bias' (Levenstein and Suslow, 2001: 2). It becomes difficult to make generalisations, but not impossible, as this chapter aims to show.

From a politics perspective this work is concerned with reviewing neither the economic theory nor the considerable legal case law, but instead keeps the focus on the development of the EU regime and its pursuit of cartels. It cannot, however, ignore the economic and legal contributions and does not intend to. Indeed before accounting for the powers and practices of this supranational regime it is necessary to provide an overview of the complexities of cartel studies and to introduce the cartel. This chapter is divided into five sections which cover a series of key themes that permeate all discussions about cartels. It begins with a short overview of humankind's propensity towards secret agreements in business and to alert readers that the practice has an established history and reflects a cultural disposition which remains as strong as ever. The second and third sections both provide a definition of the term cartel and isolate the characteristics of such collusive agreements. The following section considers what variables lead to cartels. It begins to address some of the assumptions about the nature and purpose of a cartel agreement and the issue of cartel stability.

1. RESTRICTIVE AGREEMENTS AS HISTORICAL TRADITION

The cartel represents one of the oldest forms of anti-competitive practice and has featured in commercial life in the Western business environment for well over a century. Its origins are much older. Writing at the end of the eighteenth century in 1776 Adam Smith correctly identified how 'people of the same trade seldom meet together, even for merriment and diversion, but the conversation ends in a conspiracy against the public, or in some contrivance to raise prices' (Smith, 1976). Smith's infamous supposition really marks a turning point and gives recognition to the dangers posed by cartels and other anti-competitive creations which work against the interests of consumers. Different terms and concepts have been deployed ever since to explain the emergence of anti-competitive practices. Restrictive practices, the law of monopolies, and restraints of trade are just some. The proliferation of notions and changing perceptions about the degrees of severity of such activities have rendered some degree of confusion among non-economists and non-lawyers. One of the central aims of this work is to shed greater light and clarity onto the world of the cartel for the non-specialist.

Agreements between companies represent one of the five main areas of modern European competition policy as identified in chapter 1, and by their nature and scope consume much of the time and energies of the modern competition authorities. Not all agreements between companies, however, are illegal. There is ongoing debate about where the borders lie between an agreement and a concerted practice but these discussions are mostly linguistic in nature and have little bearing on legal definitions. For the antitrust regulator the real distinction centres on collusive and non-collusive activity. Agreements are unlawful when they have been designed to fix prices, share markets and restrict output (the so-called horizontal agreements) and are punishable by fines, and in some jurisdictions (UK and USA) also come with the threat of imprisonment for the chief executives concerned. Vertical agreements involving firms at different levels of the market (i.e. manufacturer and distributor) are also covered by restrictive agreements legislation in most states and certainly in the EU context. Vertical agreements prove to be far less problematic to the competition regulators than the horizontal variety of cartels.

To appreciate the cultural dynamics of business cartels fully it is necessary to recognise the reality that what we now regard as the classic form of anti-competitive practices have a long history and tradition which do not begin at the end of the eighteenth century but are considerably older and originates much further back in time. It is possible to identify laws governing what in effect amounts in our modern day understanding to types of competition law that have been promulgated over the course of the last two thousand years of human history. It is not the intention here to provide a chronological survey of such practices and legislation but simply to underscore the reality and age-old pedigree of restrictive agreements. Whether Egyptian Pharaohs, Roman Emperors or whether medieval monarchs and feudal Lords, evidence can be unearthed of numerous anti-competitive agreements. One of the earliest recorded examples of competition law is generally held to have been enacted (Lex Julia de Annona) under the rule of Julius Caesar by the Roman Republic around 50 BC (Palatzke, 2008) to protect the corn trade. In this case heavy fines were imposed against anyone directly, deliberately and insidiously stopping supply ships to maintain high prices. The Constitution of Zeno was passed in the early Byzantine Empire (AD 483) to punish any trader involved in the fixing of prices for clothes, fishes and urchins (Whish, 2009: 497). In the Middle Ages evidence of cartel activity was recognised with the passing of legislation (*constitutiones juris metallici*) in late thirteenth century Bohemia under Wenceslas II. Early Modern Europe also demonstrated an increasing interest in the power of monopolies and cartels (Braithwaite and Drahos, 2000: 185–186), and one of the examples of an anti-cartel statute can be found in legislation enacted under Charles V, Holy Roman Emperor, in the early sixteenth century to prevent losses resulting from monopolies and improper contracts which many merchants had established in the Spanish controlled Netherlands.[3]

By the start of the seventeenth century the notion of a restraint of trade was slowly being developed in English law. It centred on agreements between independent companies and their impact. England's approach was based on prohibiting agreements which ran counter to public policy, and this concept became the early forerunner of modern competition law that commenced with the passing of the Sherman and Clayton Acts in the United States of America in 1890 and 1914 respectively. These laws were directed primarily against the huge American trusts which had become identified as synonymous with monopolies and had led to questions and public debate about the compatibility of economic power in the hands of a few and concerns over a perceived threat to democracy and the free market (chapter 4). The giant oil and railroad companies were the first major monopolies broken up under United States antitrust laws.

US antitrust law simply codified past American and English common law notions of restraints of trade. Indeed, the very first section of the Sherman Act states that 'every contract, combination in the form of trust or otherwise, or conspiracy, in restraint of trade or commerce among the several States, or with foreign nations, is declared to be illegal. Every person who shall make any contract or engage in any combination or conspiracy hereby declared to be illegal shall be deemed guilty of a misdemeanor, and, on conviction thereof, shall be punished by fine . . . or by imprisonment not exceeding one year, or by both said punishments, at the discretion of the Court' (US Department of Justice, 2009).[4]

By the start of the twentieth century some European states had opted to introduce moral codes on competition and laws to regulate monopolies and cartels as in Germany in 1909 (see chapter 3), before deciding on more stringent and enforceable antitrust codes. Other states rejected such course of action. The US codification of the common law position (Peritz, 1996) on restraint of trade was to have a widespread effect, in both coercive and voluntary forms, on subsequent competition law development beyond its own borders. In post-1945 Japan, for example (Sanekata and Wilks, 1996), the US practically imposed the competition statutes, whereas in the European context US experience and US trained European lawyers came to shape debates (see chapter 4) as cartels became a central tenet of both the founding ECSC and EEC Treaties.

Its inclusion in these treaties reflected a gradual acceptance of the desirability of competitive markets which came to be associated with lower prices, better quality goods, more innovation and greater efficiencies (see Asch, 1983; Bishop and Walker, 2002; Motta, 2004), at least in terms of perfect competition. This belief was further reinforced by both moves towards demonopolisation, liberalisation and privatisation and the growing globalisation of trade, markets and companies in the final decades of the twentieth century.

However, some caution should be applied because there is not always any correlation between having a rigorous regime on paper and the enforcement of its rule. This reality became too evident in the Japanese case where the strict rules were more or less overlooked. In contrast, the fledging EU regime strove hard to develop a coherent competition policy. The majority of the European Commission's competition brief from the very outset from the signing of the 1957 Treaty of Rome was to focus on restrictive practices which include the pursuit, identification and termination of cartel arrangements. Article 81 was to spell out the objectives, and the regulatory procedure was agreed by the six member states and laid out in Regulation 17 from 1962 (and discussed in chapter 5). The study of European Union (EU) cartel policy makes for a fascinating case study in terms of the European integration project. Competition policy represents one of the few areas where the Commission not only is responsible for direct policy implementation but also possesses wide discretionary powers as both a regulator and an enforcer of policy. For the most part cartel policy amounts to a combative struggle between large corporate interests to maximise profits and to conceal their price fixing and market sharing activities and the regulator, but the overall picture is larger. The exploration of cartel policy (be it national, regional or supranational) necessitates both the recognition of the motives of and the interplay between a set of four key interlocked actors (Harding and Joshua, 2003). This includes – see figure 2.1 – the cartel members (who constitute the offenders

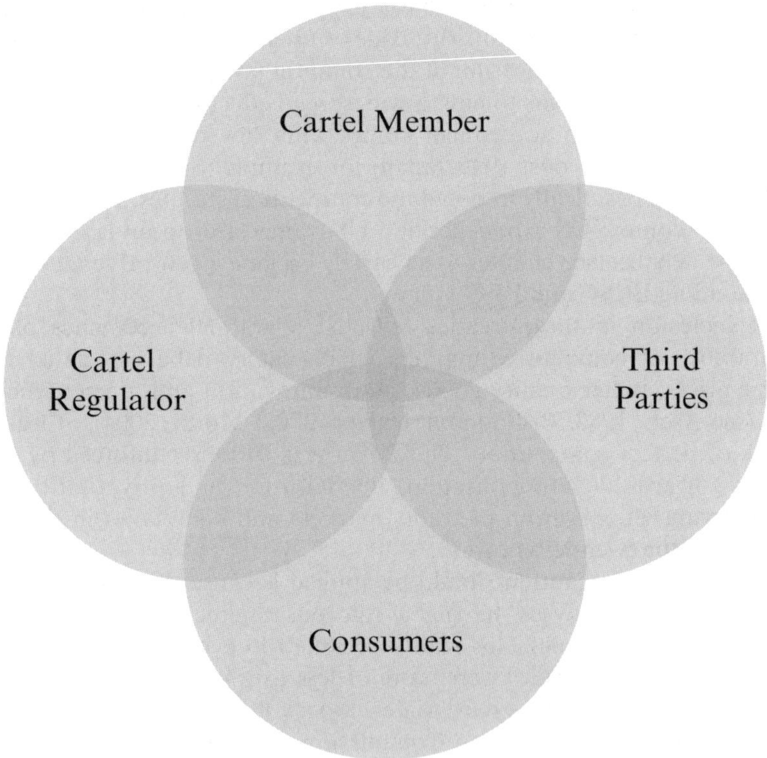

Figure 2.1 Mapping cartels: a complex relationship between actors, victims and regulators

or aggressors), the cartel regulators (in their guise as referees or police service), third parties (rival competitors who are not part of the cartel arrangement) and other victims of the cartel (consumers and the wider public). All four constituencies (see Figure 2.1) feature as integral players of any cartel regime though their roles and impact vary enormously. This work focuses primarily on the first two groups. Before proceeding to consider EU cartel policy and the institutions of cartel governance attention needs to turn to providing a definition of what a cartel is before we can consider whether it is both disruptive and damaging.

2. THE DEFINITION OF A CARTEL

The word cartel has a very complex etymology (Harding and Joshua, 2003: 12), and the origins of the word derive from the Medieval Latin word *cartellus* (little card) and has translated very easily into English and most other main languages to become *Kartell* in German, *cartel* in French and *cartello* (letter of defiance) in Italian. Within the existing literature on cartels it is possible to identify at least three different contexts in which the term cartel is utilised. The first and oldest references to the cartel possess military connotations, as the term cartel was applied to an official agreement between governments at war to cease conflict temporarily in order, for example, to allow the exchange of prisoners. In this context cartels are equated very much with the notion of a truce. This book deliberately recognises this military tradition in its adoption of the concept of the European Commission's cartel wars.

This idea of 'ending hostilities' through an agreement also found reflection in the world of politics with specific reference to a group of political parties, factions, or nations which united in an agreement for a common cause. In this instance a cartel becomes synonymous with a political alliance between a block or a group of parties. This took the form, for example, of references to the Cartel Parties in the German government which essentially comprised a temporary coalition of the competing parties under Otto von Bismarck, the German Chancellor in the 1880s (von Strandmann, 1969) which was deliberately designed to resist the rise of Social Democracy. Ideas of a truce and an agreement tie in with the third and most familiar usage which identifies a cartel as a group of companies, countries or other entities which agree to work together. In the business context a cartel is a group of legally independent producers (usually in the same industry) who formally agree to co-operate together to influence and fix market prices, to limit supply, to restrict competition and even to divide profits.

Over time the word cartel in the English language has developed more negative overtones and today suggests a degree of undesirability, though this was not always the case, particularly in the period between the two World Wars. The existence of cartels runs counter to classic theories of open competition and the free market and the inherent dangers posed by cartellisation (see Kronstein, 1973) have ensured that the formation of cartels is illegal in many Western countries including Australia, Canada, the United States and throughout the European Union. Three of the most infamous contemporary examples to illustrate the current and more negative connotations of the term cartel are to be found with reference to the De Beers Diamond Cartel, the Organisation of Petroleum Exporting Countries (OPEC, and see Mason and Polasky, 2005) and the Colombian drugs cartels in Latin America.[5]

3. ISOLATING CARTEL CHARACTERISTICS

A business cartel is a formal agreement between independent firms which are active in the same or very similar areas of economic activity and which deliberately concoct an arrangement among themselves to stifle direct competition. Rather than engaging in open competition with one another, cartel members instead opt to reach agreement (see Box 2.1) on issues such as the fixing of prices, the determination of total industry output, the allocation of customers and market shares, bid rigging and the division of profits (see Jephcott and Lübbig, 2003). Understanding why certain firms opt to create such agreements necessitates an awareness of specific market conditions. Cartels usually emerge in a market or economic sector where there are a small number of manufacturers (i.e. oligopolistic markets) who are producing similar products. In such markets rival firms usually rely on heavy product differentiation through advertising (as in the brewing and glass sectors) and other marketing ploys to distinguish themselves from rival brands. This costs in terms of both advertising and, ultimately, lower profits as the goods have to be competitively priced.

Entry into collusive agreements is regarded as an avenue to escape the degree of uncertainty of oligopolistic markets and to profit maximisation as if the market was itself a pure monopoly. In short, the undertakings concerned engage in collusive activity as a means of exerting market power which they would not otherwise have and by doing so restrict competition (Motta, 2007). However, the central aim of maximising profits works very much against the interests of the consumer. Caution is needed here because economic insights into the conditions for successful conclusion are irrelevant for the most part in the mindsets of competition authorities (Monti,

BOX 2.1 ESTABLISHING BASIC CARTEL CHARACTERISTICS

i) Cartels are a combination to divide up markets and fix prices (generally higher to maximise profit) amongst themselves;
ii) Cartels can restrict cartel members – when fixing production and sales targets, the more efficient members are not often allowed to increase output. Indeed, price fixing arrangements are often designed to suit the least efficient member – quotas must therefore be depicted as a hindrance;
iii) Cartels seek to prevent new firms entering the market; in practice goods retailing at high prices always attract companies. Cartel arrangements will aim to frustrate such new competition. Cartels frequently operate to the detriment of consumers in terms of both product quality and price.

2007: 324), which are more keen to distinguish between express and tacit collusion, and the focus is very much fixed on the former. It is these hard-core cartels which should always be the focus (Motta, 2007) of any competition authority, because if unchecked and successful, they can cause considerable damage to the competitive environment and the consumer.

When investigating cartel activity it is important to differentiate between horizontal co-operation and vertical co-operation. The former represents the most prolific form of cartel and ranges from hard-core cartel activity to joint ventures and efforts to promote research and development and takes place between firms operating on exactly the same level of production. Horizontally (those manufacturing similar products) based cartels nearly always fall foul of the competition rules. Concerted practices on the other hand represent a much more subtle form of collusion than the hard-core cartel, and the onus rests firmly on the competition regulator to prove the existence of any such anti-competitive agreement. Evidence, and usually in the form of an economic analysis, is needed. This gives rise to one of the most difficult problems for any competition authority when it commences its investigations and especially in oligopolistic markets. What might look initially as if it is collusive activity (e.g. similar price rises) may in fact be nothing more than straightforward parallel behaviour and a response to a rival competitor's move. Prices that are set under this scenario are normally determined by 'dominant firm price leadership' than any collusive agreements. Indeed, firms in such markets are highly interdependent, and each is very much concerned with and monitors the actions and reactions of its rival competitors.

The European Commission's 1984 Woodpulp decision provides an excellent illustration of the difficulties that confronted the regulator. In the Commission's decision it had uncovered a cartel comprising Scandinavian and North American exporters of Woodpulp, and its decision was explained through its analysis of parallel pricing within the specific market which the Commission traced back to the mid 1970s. On appeal, however, the Court of Justice (ECJ) rejected the Commission's interpretation in 1993 largely on the grounds of insufficient evidence. This case outcome shocked DG Competition staff, as the ECJ had supported a similar line of argument in the Dyestuffs case in 1973 where strong co-operation and seeming evidence of parallel pricing were deemed sufficient by the Commission to declare the existence of a concerted practice. The oligopoly problem confronts all competition regulators. It is in issue where experience and the development of case law have facilitated the roles of the competition regulators and compelled staff in DG Competition to identify more foolproof and concrete evidence of illegal activity. But while cartelbusters search for harder evidence, the cartel members are working to ensure that such evidence is either limited or non-existent. In other words, firms have taken to not leaving any paper trails, any electronic records and have even held meetings outside the EU to determine the nature of their cartel (see chapter 7). A financial levy may prove high enough to prevent collusion, but there is a second issue which has been highlighted by some commentators (Martin, 2004), where firms operating in oligopolistic markets do not really need to worry about too much competition as they can reach a stage of 'equilibrium market performance' without collusion. Under such a scenario firms can edge much closer to the position of a monopoly than is often realised (Chamberlain, 1947). There is nothing a competition authority can do about it.

Cartels can also centre on firms involved in vertical co-operation, which occurs between firms operating at different levels of the production chain (see, for example, Grundig–Consten).[6] Such agreements may be in the form of exclusive markets (where only one distributor is allowed to sell a particular product) or in the form of exclusive purchasing agreements where a distributor will agree to source all of its supplies from one particular supplier. The Nintendo case represents a more recent example.[7] Vertical agreements have never quite attracted the same attention from the regulator as have horizontal agreements and are generally not deemed to possess the same degree of danger. Consequently, they are not considered in this work.

4. UNDERSTANDING CARTEL ARRANGEMENTS AS PRIVATE AND COLLUSIVE TREATIES

The reality that a firm will opt for a cartel agreement rather than openly compete with its rival competitors should not be so surprising. The crucial aspect in any oligopolistic market revolves around the behaviour of an individual firm towards its rivals and the assumptions that it makes about its competitors and their reactions to any of its own price moves. Gauging responses is always going to prove problematic. Much depends on the nature of the specific market in question, and firms involved in the sector will always be alert to the risks of potential retaliation. Both considerations present business concerns with strategic choices and have duly given rise to a series of competing economic approaches and theories. A substantial economics based literature on this issue has emerged over the last thirty years and has postulated a variety of suggestions as to why and how firms opt to set prices.[8]

The crucial core of all such collusive agreements for the regulator is whether the agreement is a covert arrangement which deliberately aims to lessen competition. In economics collusion is a situation where firms' prices are higher than some competitive benchmark (Levenstein, 1995; Motta, 2007: 2). Economic theory is not so concerned about how these prices were secured, it does not offer any explanation of how to differentiate between collusive and non-collusive behaviour but does provide some suggestions (Gavin, 2001: 114). Exclusive collision is said to emerge through the form of an organised cartel which is constructed around shared information and constant communication between its members.

The analysis of collusion in modern industrial economics is based on the so-called concept of incentive constraint (Motta, 2007: 5) where firms weigh up their commercial and strategic situation to determine whether profit can be maximised furthest through engaging in collusive agreements or not. The calculation has been labelled by economists as deviation. Basically, if a firm makes more from collusive activity, and firms always calculate the possible impact of any fines if a cartel arrangement is unearthed, then this is the course of action a firm will stand to take. Much of the existing literature explores this theme. It is important to know what reasons facilitate collusion and important for anti-trust regulators to know. But what constitutes explicit collusion, what forms does it take and how is it detected and punished? There are different types and degrees of collusion and to do them all justice and 'to describe them all would require an entire book' (De Jong, 1973: 99). Hard-core cartels can be sub-divided into two basic types that can broadly be identified as either a price fixing cartel and/or a market sharing cartel.

4.1 The Price-fixing Cartel

Price-fixing agreements typify the best illustration and most undesirable aspect of cartel activity. Price-fixing arrangements are always caught under the EU anti-trust rules, but so are other agreements which directly or indirectly suppress price competition (Whish, 2009: 507).[9] At its simplest, if rival competitors display rather similar list-prices and have a range of uniform discounts, or prices that change in tandem, cartel activity may be expected. Cartel members go to great lengths to avoid detection and to conceal the evidence. A price-fixing cartel, however, may become more visible and more vulnerable to detection when it raises prices. The more frequently or regularly prices change, the greater the chance that purchasers will realise that prices are moving together or changing by the same amount or percentage. The regulators are also continually monitoring markets. Buyers are well placed to notice when prices rise by identical amounts at similar times. Caution should always be applied here because even where prices are identical or even where they have seemingly aligned simultaneously there still may be no definite evidence of cartel activity. Moreover, actual apparent price differences can equally conceal collusion. Analysing price movements over a certain period of time may prove fruitful in uncovering price-fixing cartels and the possibility of an agreement to restrict competition. Still, further documentary proof is needed and usually in the form of emails, letters and, in the US case, phone tapping to confirm the existence of an agreement.[10]

The formation of a price-fixing arrangement is never that straightforward. Questions such as how long the offence should last, who should be allowed to join the arrangement, let alone determining the actual prices, often make it difficult to secure. It will be easier the fewer the differences between the firms in terms of both their products and their production costs. The firms will find it harder to agree on a common price if the differences in their products are substantial, for example in terms of quality. This explains why economists tend to think that cartels are generally formed in markets with similar type products rather than those which differ. If firms operate at different levels of cost, then they will have different prices at which they maximise profits, making it harder to agree on the common price. For any cartel to work effectively the firms involved must be in a position to control supply to maintain an artificially high price. Collusion is easier to achieve when there are a relatively small number of firms in the market and a large number of customers, but the problems of engaging in cartellisation should not be underestimated. There are downsides for any prospective cartel member, as some are always going to be more efficient than others and some are going to be more susceptible to price changes than others. Cartels affect their participating companies in different ways and this helps explain why some cartels are short-lived. The incentives for firms to cheat can be considerable and it has been customary for cartels to monitor their members. In efforts to deter any cheating, cartels have been known to threaten penalties for cartel members who break free from the arrangement and to exclude these same companies from any future activities, both legal and illegal. In an effort to avoid the break-up of an existing agreement, members often seek to strengthen the benefits of sustained co-operation and create other incentives and inducements.

4.2 The Market-sharing Cartel

In addition to the price-fixing route firms can also opt for a second classic means to maximise profits and maintain their proportion of the market through specific territorial sharing arrangements. Such agreements are often designed to discourage members from cheating (Slade, 1990) and tend to divide up a country (such as the USA) or a regional grouping of countries such as the EU between the members of the cartel. Such exclusive market creation has its advantages, as it ensures that a cartel member is safe in the knowledge that another member will not encroach on its customers. In such market-sharing agreements firms will determine and agree their share of the market in advance. The cartel members will normally also meet at regular intervals to determine how well the cartel is operating, whether its terms should be renewed and how to share the most lucrative contracts (bid-rigging). Such meetings increasingly occur in other jurisdictions and as far from the gaze of the national competition regulator as possible and aim to make it appear that actual competition is occurring in the market. Collusive tendering (which takes the form of bid suppression, complementary tendering and bid rotation) is one of the most difficult forms of anti-competitive activities to uncover and the regulators often hope to collect their information and evidence from whistleblowers.[11] If cartels are difficult creations to monitor and detect from the outside they are also difficult to maintain even from within. This reality is positive news for the cartel regulators, who can focus their energies and attention on those markets where such collusion is potentially most profitable (Posner, 2002).

5. STABILITY AND FRAGILITY

Doubts have always existed about the actual stability of cartel agreements. Often such doubts have been linked directly to a cartel's duration, as most break up (Suslow, 1991). This may seems a plausible conclusion, but any such analysis is much more problematic than it may first appear because the secret world of cartels is one of ever changing cartel patterns (Ellison, 1994). The fact that cartels come and go, that members temporarily withdraw, that actual membership can change and that cartels often merge, demerge and remerge on a regular basis suggests instability, but the picture is actually much more complex than it initially appears. It certainly provides the regulators with something of a severe headache and a real challenge as they try to establish if a cartel exists and to find sufficient evidence to prove it. The European Commission has to tread cautiously (Whish, 2009: 104) and always ensure that it has identified collusive activity, as opposed to some form of parallel behaviour where firms are simply responding to market conditions and not party to any agreement. It can also be difficult to pinpoint the exact creation and cessation of a cartel agreement because they can alter in shape, membership and objectives over the duration of the arrangement. What may look like three or four cartels over a thirty-year period, for example, could in fact be just one cartel. For example, Eckbo (1976) and Griffin (1989) may have both studied the sugar cartel but both disagree in their respective analyses over the timing of its actual duration.

Most cartels do not last for anything more than the immediate short term, and empirical studies of cartel activities during the course of the twentieth century reveal that the mean existence of a cartel lasts generally from somewhere in the region of between just over three to nearly eight years (Levenstein and Suslow, 2001: 5). Some cartels, of course, last for a considerably shorter period and some for as little as one year, while others have endured for a much longer time. Some economists believe that nearly all price-fixing cartels are inherently unstable (Stigler, 1964). Indeed, the pressures and internal rivalries often lead to the collapse of many cartel arrangements. The European Commission's experience of cartelbusting to date seems to suggest this may be the correct assumption. However, caution is required because not every collusive agreement is so fragile. Some are much stronger and endure for much longer (Whish, 2009: 99). The sustainability of any cartel agreement depends heavily on the ability of its members to coordinate their activities successfully and maintain a strong allegiance to the benefits of the cartel. It has generally been assumed that the more firms that exist within any given market, the more difficult it actually may be to establish and coordinate a cartel. In contrast, the fewer the number of firms in the industry the easier it becomes for other members of the cartel to set up and to monitor each other's behaviour. However, the evidence is decidedly mixed (Levenstein and Suslow, 2001: 8) on whether a larger number of members actually creates greater cartel instability or stability. Some authors have presented contrary evidence. In his study of 989 cases which came before the US Department of Justice Posner (1970) found that 52 per cent of collusive agreements which possessed ten or fewer members managed to last on average for six years or more, but that 64 per cent of cartels with ten plus members lasted for the same period or more. Even where there are only a handful of companies within a cartel the existence of just one cheating firm is sufficient to undermine the collusive behaviour of the entire cartel.

Again it is assumed that cartels tend not to last for very long in industries with low barriers to entry, because the threat of potential rivals entering the market generally reduces the gains to be had from collusive behaviour. Although new producers may join a cartel, when membership levels increase this often makes communication, negotiation, and enforcement more difficult. Cartels are also deemed to be most effective when the demand for their product is not very price sensitive. Circumstances sometimes dictate that firms will seek to break their deal or not meet the full terms of the collusive agreement. The incentive for cartel members to cheat on their agreements is relatively high and undermines the stability of the cartel. If they all cheat the cartel collapses fairly quickly. Interestingly, evidence strongly indicates that demand stability is often a core factor in the duration of cartel agreements. The weaker the demand for a given product, so the weaker the cartel turns out to be and the more likely to dissolve.

Whether cartel members opt to cheat depends on whether the short-term returns for cheating outweigh the medium and long-term losses which result from the possible breakdown of the cartel. For example, a cartel member may cheat on any previously agreed prices or production quotas and thereby sell more of a particular product at higher prices (than operated by the cartel) or opt to lower prices. Indeed, an undetected price cut will help a company to attract customers who are buying from the other members, as well as customers who are not buying the product at all. Some of these price adjustments may be subtle, including better credit terms, faster delivery, or related free services. For this reason cartel members closely monitor each other's moves and often appoint one member to act as policeman to an agreement.

The longer the time firms in the cartel can cheat without detection, the greater the gains from doing so. Therefore, if monitoring is difficult then there is a higher probability that some parties to the agreement will cheat and make the agreement increasingly unsustainable. There are a number of factors which potentially make a firm's ability to monitor a cartel problematic. These include the number of firms in the industry; the characteristics of the products sold by the firms; the production costs of each member, the behaviour of demand and, finally, the frequency of sales and their characteristics. Homogeneous (similar) product markets lend themselves to facilitating an agreement on prices and/or quantities, but they are also easier to monitor and detect. Indeed, firms are all too aware that a change in their market share is probably due to a price cut (or quantity increase) by another member. In contrast, where products are differentiated, changes in quantity sold by a member may simply be due to changes in consumer preferences. The first case provides a clear example of collusive activity, whereas the second may just be explained by a switch in consumer demand and does not entail any form of anti-competitive activity.

Cartel arrangements are not static creations, but are constantly adapting and changing to both reflect and meet altered economic circumstances. This makes them difficult for the regulators to detect. The potential instability of price-fixing cartel arrangements is usually heightened by one or more of the following factors; an economic downturn; the arrival of non-cartel members into the industry and the subsequent pressure on the cartel's agreed price regime; over-production by the cartel members which breaks the price fixing agreement. The prisoner's dilemma has been often used (Whish, 2009) to explain why cartels have not lasted, and argues that all collusive agreements tend to fall eventually because, although price fixing is in the joint interests of all members of a cartel, it is not a profit maximising equilibrium for each individual firm and, thus, the correct incentives will entice whistleblowers willingly to break ranks (see chapter 7).[12] In short, to what extent members of a cartel will choose to cheat on the agreement depends on whether the short-term returns on cheating outweigh the medium and long term losses which result from the possible breakdown of the cartel.

The world of collusive agreements is amazingly complex and is a difficult one for researchers to traverse, given that we are dealing with formally closed cases only. Nevertheless, some general observations can be made about the nature, duration and stability of cartels. Firstly, anti-competitive agreements between private undertakings in specialised and highly concentrated sectors seem more able to endure and over a longer time frame than in those sectors where firms have a much reduced share of the market. Secondly, homogeneous markets seem to possess a greater propensity towards price fixing and thus, may also be easier to establish and manage. Thirdly, it is interesting to observe how certain sectors (e.g. steel, paper and cement) are more attracted to being involved in cartel arrangements than others, but fourthly, how many firms have a history of cartel activity and are in effect repeat offenders. Finally, cheating appears to represent another key characteristic of many cartel agreements and one that provides greater instability and encourages other members to cheat. Once armed with such knowledge the cartel regulator is placed in a much better position to confront and tackle cartels and can adapt its procedures and modernise its weapons accordingly, but how successful have the regulators been in anti-trust enforcement? This has been exactly the trajectory pursued by the European Commission and especially since the 1990s (chapter 7).

Most national jurisdictions in Western Europe started to develop their own domestic anti-cartel legislation in the latter half of the twentieth century. It aimed to halt and deter any agreements that seek to fix prices, engage in bid rigging, place restrictions on output and share markets. The adoption of anti-cartel rules has thrown up three core questions: firstly, are all cartels to be viewed in such negative terms or are there times when collusive agreements can be defended; secondly, whose interests should take priority (the consumer's or the producer's) and, thirdly, who are the regulators and what criteria do they use to identify cartel activity? Such pertinent questions have dogged researchers and commentators for the last fifty years. For Friedman the main problem for all regulators centred on the definition of the public policy criteria and getting the balance between the values of co-operation against the benefits of competition (Friedman, 1972: 308). Attitudes towards cartellisation have depended, of course, on changing circumstances and shifts in economic philosophies and approaches between different cultures and among different economic and political regimes.

There are, it should be stressed, occasions when co-operation between firms actually finds justification (Harding and Joshua, 2003). These mostly relate to special markets or sectors of the economy that require a degree of protection. For example, arguments can be and are made supporting greater advances in defence related industries or cases can be made for certain sectors to be excluded from the reach of the competition regulator altogether, as occurred with the development of the EU's Common Agricultural Policy. A distinction in cartel activity needs to be drawn between public and private cartels. In the case of public cartels, the government may establish and enforce the rules relating to prices, output and other such matters. Export cartels and shipping conferences are examples of public cartels. In many countries, crisis cartels (as in Europe in the 1970s) have been permitted by national governments in industries deemed to be requiring price and production stability and/or to permit rationalisation of industry structure in order to fix prices and ration production and distribution in periods of acute shortages. Examples of such activity have occurred in Japan in the steel, aluminium, shipbuilding industries. Such cartels were also allowed in the USA during the 1930s in the coal mining and oil industries. Cartels came to feature as part of German government policy between 1933 and 1945 (see chapter 3). Such examples might be considered now of historical interest only, but this would be an error. Cartel agreements covering products such as coffee, sugar, tin and, more controversially, crude oil are examples of international cartels which have publicly entailed agreements between different national governments. Western European governments allowed the formation of 'crisis cartels' (in the steel industry) in the 1970s (chapter 5).

In contrast, private cartels entail an agreement on terms and conditions from which the members derive mutual advantage but which are not known or likely to be detected by outside parties. Private cartels in most jurisdictions are viewed as being illegal and in violation of antitrust laws. A factor facilitating the formation of cartels and influencing their duration certainly centres on the actual risk of being detected by the authorities. Is it strong or weak? The second key question which arises from any prospective cartel member's perspective is how potentially damaging are the sanctions which could be imposed, if any collusive comes to light. Sanctions are a crucial aspect of any successful cartel enforcement regime. The available sanctions vary from regime to regime. Whereas the EU antitrust system allows for the imposition of substantial fines for serious infringements (and these are set ever higher for habitual cartel offenders) the US regime also makes use of criminal sanctions (i.e. prison sentences) alongside its fining arrangements.

6. CONCLUSIONS

Cartels are generally held today to represent the most pernicious form of anti-competitive behaviour and arise when companies participate in an agreement as a means of deliberately escaping from the costly realities of competition. In other words cartels can be visualised as a safe haven, and as such are effectively the outcome of 'deliberate, highly organised and covert collaborative' (Harding and Joshua, 2003: 1) practices which have been agreed by a number of independent firms from the same or similar sphere of economic activity. Experience seems to suggest that collusive activity often occurs in those sectors with few players, easy access markets and/or in those operating on small profit margins and facing lower rates of growth. Much, however, still remains unknown about why and where cartellisation occurs and the available evidence can often be contradictory.

In the short term recourse to cartellisation may indeed prove beneficial, but in the longer term and in today's environment what are being deemed hard-core cartel arrangements are certain to have serious and detrimental repercussions because, starved of the dynamic and innovative effects of competition, they often become uncompetitive in the real market. Such secret agreements which divide markets, fix prices and prevent newcomers from entering the market represent the classic shape of collusive agreement and the most harmful for the competitive process. Indeed, it is interesting to note that certain economic sectors (such as the pharmaceutical, paper, cement and glass markets) seem more prone to cartellisation than others. Condemnation of cartel agreements has become the norm and recourse to them has been labelled as akin to cancers in the market place and even theft.[13] The world of cartels is inherently unstable. The formation of cartels proves immensely intricate, incites many jealousies among the parties, and ultimately the strain leads many to collapse.

The war against cartels is an enduring and timeless conflict which pits the regulator against the interests of the firms involved. We should recognise cartel formation and its pursuit as a form of economic based warfare. Cartels have no respect for national borders, and as international trade has become more global in nature so cartels have moved their activities onto the international stage. In providing the reader with a general introduction into the world of the cartels this chapter has attempted to identify some of the commonly held perceptions and assumptions about the nature of cartels and collusive market behaviour or what has been described by two authors as cartel delinquency (Harding and Joshua, 2003). This book now turns to explore the evolution of the European Union's cartel regime.

NOTES

1. Experience and existing case studies (see Eichner, 1969; Genesove and Mullin, 1998; 2001) illustrate how this goal is not always achieved, as in a number of short-lived sugar cartels.
2. Levenstein and Salant have pulled together an excellent collection of 61 essays and seminal articles (from an economics perspective) from the 1890s to the present century on various aspects of cartels and cartellisation. This edited two volume collection covers a variety of themes which include, amongst others, the historical overview of cartels; identifies the problems that cartels create within markets; explores the issues of enforcement; investigates the particular challenges brought by natural resource cartels; considers the issues of collusion; and also explores the internationalisation of cartel activities.
3. An example of one of the leading entrepreneurs from one of the richest family businesses (Fugger) in Europe and one that was heavily involved in cartel activity is provided by Strieder *et al.*, although the original work dates from 1931. Jakob Fugger II (or Jacob the Rich who lived from 1459 to 1525) built up an extensive empire and practically held a monopoly in the mining and trading of copper, silver and mercury throughout Europe. He is alleged to have secured the election of Charles V as Holy Roman Emperor in 1519 by bribing the electors and was rewarded with money, land and monopoly rights.

4. A full copy of the amended Sherman Act can be found on the US Department of Justice's web page at www.usdoj.gov/atr/public/divisionmanual/index.htm.
5. The De Beers Diamond Cartel is one of the most written about cartels and centres on one of the most desirable items. The cartel was in operation for over 100 years (Farrelly, 2001). De Beers was originally founded in the late 1880s by Cecil Rhodes, though his actual involvement in the diamond 'rush' dates back to the late 1860s. De Beers rapidly emerged as the main owner of all the diamond mining operations in Southern Africa, and the company grew and developed throughout the twentieth century. Concerns had often been expressed that De Beers was operating a cartel the origins of which can be traced back to 1889 when Rhodes had skilfully negotiated an agreement with a diamond syndicate based in London. This arrangement centred on the export of a fixed quantity of diamonds and an agreed price for those diamonds (see Epstein, 1982). Several court actions were filed against De Beers in the US in 2001 for infringing the antitrust rules and fixing prices. In 2004 the De Beers group admitted to some price fixing agreements before a US court and agreed to pay $10 million and in so doing has allowed De Beers' executives to enter the US, which is one of the world's largest diamond markets. More recently De Beers has reached a settlement of a number of civil actions that were within the US. (See also Spar, 1994.)
6. This case centred on the relationship between two companies, Grundig and Consten. The West German company, Grundig, had appointed the French company Consten, as its sole distributor of its (Grundig's) electrical appliances throughout France. The details of this arrangement, however, were upset when a third party (UNEF) opted to buy Grundig's products in West Germany before exporting them onto the French market. Grundig objected to UNEF's actions in France but the ECJ ruled against Grundig's attempt to provide Consten with exclusive rights which deliberately infringed Article 81 (restrictive practices) under the EEC Treaty and was illegal (see Whish, 2009: 115–116).
7. This case centred on an anti-competitive agreement between Nintendo and seven of its official distributors in Europe which deliberately sought to maintain high prices for video and computer games across the EU. The arrangement lasted from 1991 until 1998 and it compelled each distributor to prevent exports from one territory (EU member state) to any other territory (EU member state) through any unofficial distribution channels. Any of the distributors party to this agreement who ignored the provisions risked being boycotted by Nintendo or being supplied with smaller consignments. Consequently prices varied enormously across the EU and were highest in Germany and the Netherlands. The Commission imposed a fine of €168 million on Nintendo and its distributors.
8. Readers are directed to the following authors as excellent examples: Abreu, D., Pearce, D., and Stachetti, E. (1986) 'Optimal Cartel Equilibria with Imperfect Monitoring', *Journal of Economic Theory*, 39(1), 251–69; Ellison, G. (1994) 'Theories of Cartel Stability and the Joint Executive Committee', *Rand Journal of Economics*, 25(1), 37–57; Jacquemin, A., and Slade, M.E. (1989) 'Cartels, Collusion and Horizontal Merger' in Schmalensee and Willig (eds), *Handbook of Industrial Organisation*, Vol. 2, New York, Elsevier Science Publishers, 415–73; Lanning, S.G. (1987) 'Costs of Maintaining a Cartel', *The Journal of Industrial Economics*, 36(2), 157–74; Porter, R.H. (1983) 'Optimal Cartel Trigger Price Strategies', *Journal of Economic Theory*, 29(2), 387–400; Ross, T.W. (1992) 'Cartel Stability and Producer Differentiation', *International Journal of Industrial Organisation*, 10(1), 1–13 and Sluewaegen, L. (1986) 'On the Nature and Significance of Collusive Price Leadership', *International Journal of Industrial Organisation*, 4(2), 177–88.
9. The formation and operation of cartel agreements are usually constructed around higher prices (and often some 20 to 40 per cent higher than what they would have been), lower output, reduced product quality and less innovation.
10. Companies have become more adept at concealing such relevant information and usually dispose of faxes, e-mails and all other correspondence between the members. In

response, the regulator is left to consider whether it is dealing with a concerted practice. Concerted practices can also contravene the EU competition rules if such loose agreements are designed to limit competition, but the onus rests with the competition authority to prove that co-ordination has taken place.

11. In 'bid suppression' schemes, one or several competitors (who would otherwise be expected to tender) opt not to submit a tender or withdraw a previously submitted tender so that a competitor's tender will be accepted. In 'complementary bidding' (also known as 'protective' or 'shadow' bidding) some supposed rival competitors submit tenders which are specifically intended to be too high to be accepted (or, if competitive in price, then on special terms that will not be acceptable). Such tenders are deliberately designed to give the *appearance* of a genuine tendering process. Finally, in 'bid rotation', all cartel firms participating in the scheme submit tenders, but by agreement each firm has secretly agreed a turn at being the lowest bidder. A strict bid rotation, of course, defies the laws of chance and suggests collusive activity. Rotation schemes tend to be fairly sophisticated to avoid detection.
12. Cartel members are normally better-off being party to the agreement than engaging in actual competition. However, even a cartel member may seek to outwit its own 'associates'. For example, a slight deviation (for example, in a reduction in prices) may capture a larger share of the market demand and lead to greater profit margins. In other words, the members of a cartel always have an incentive to 'cheat' on their agreement, which explains why cartels are generally difficult to sustain in the long run.
13. US antitrust has displayed an aversion towards the concentration of economic power in the hands of a few leading corporations or individuals, and also questioned the compatibility of such economic power with notions of democracy.

3. The rise of the cartel: toleration, encouragement and the control of cartels in Europe, 1871–1945

Although it is certainly tempting – and it would have been a much more straightforward exercise – to keep any study of EU cartel policy completely focused on post-1945 developments, it would have been short-sighted. European cartel policy may essentially be a post-1945 phenomenon, but in order to appreciate its developments and the decisive break in continuity from practices in the first half of the twentieth century that it represents it is necessary to push further back, and at least to the last quarter of the nineteenth century. Only then can we understand the wider context, stages and drivers shaping the history and development of anti-trust policy. This longer time frame also allows for a brief discussion of the adoption of the modern world's first substantive cartel legislation in the United States of America in 1890 which not only pre-dated the European integration process by some sixty years, but initially challenged European assumptions of the desirability of cartels. Opting for this longer time-frame has its challenges and necessitates knowledge of a considerable business and economics based literature on the period prior to 1945. This chapter provides a brief overview and aims to draw out how, where and why the number of cartels expanded and, more importantly, how states responded to the process of intensifying cartellisation, both domestically and internationally.

The period after 1870 to the end of the Second World War is generally held to epitomise the era and triumph of the cartel as an accepted form of business activity, and one which was completely unregulated as cartels became facts of daily life across many branches of industry. The actual picture is somewhat more complicated. Business historians (Fear, 2006) have charted the rise and fall and repackaging of cartels over this period. Closer inspection reveals a somewhat mixed history in so far as cartellisation has displayed a stronger resonance in some states more than others and for different reasons. Different regimes over the course of the last one hundred and forty years have at times tolerated, even encouraged and combated cartels. The changing variable in the equation has centred on each individual state's response towards the desirability or urgency of cartel regulation as the European states were at different stages of economic and industrial development. Indeed, the picture becomes even more complex because on occasions some aspects of collusive activity may be deemed a legitimate course of action in different states and in different time frames.

Still, within this era it is possible to identify a number of critical junctures in the history of cartellisation which encapsulates the rise of the cartel. Three general and introductory observations can be made in relation to, firstly, pinpointing time lines (i.e. the origins and development of cartels); secondly, identifying those countries which were more susceptible to cartels than others; and, thirdly, locating those economic sectors which have proven most prone to cartellisation. Cartels began to emerge across Europe as an omnipresent form of business activity and, above all, in the German speaking countries of Central Europe, and especially the newly unified German state after 1871. They reached their apex during the interwar period when they came to underpin the economic structures of both Nazi Germany and Fascist Italy and other economies which either accepted and/or sought protectionist measures to thwart unwanted competition from foreign rival companies. Recorded evidence reveals that such forms of cartels were more prone to emerge in those large scale and heavy industries that proved costly to run and maintain in the face of open competition (Mirow and Maurer, 1982: 11–35). Some of the first and most established examples of cartellisation in the period running up to 1914 occurred in the production of aluminium, chemicals, cement, fertiliser, paper/cartonboard, salt and steel. It is interesting to observe how these same sectors have continued to engage in cartels even up to the present day.

Trying to explain why cartellisation impacted on some European states more than others and why certain industries displayed a readiness to engage in collusive activity in the period after 1870 is a complex task which extends far beyond the confines of this particular book. Nevertheless, this chapter highlights some of the explanations and issues that help explain the cartellisation process and why it occurred where, how and when it did. It is now divided into five sections. The first provides the background to the rise of the cartels in Europe; the second traces the origins and spread of cartellisation in Imperial Germany and questions why this state showed most propensity towards this course of action, and the third introduces the anti-cartel experience in the United States as a means of comparison. The following section outlines the developments and trajectories of cartellisation in the inter-war period and signals the emergence of the first anti-cartel policies in Europe. The fifth and final section focuses attention on the appearance of the international based cartel.

1. THE RISE OF THE CARTEL IN EUROPE

Nineteenth century Europe was relatively peaceful. A state of more or less peaceful co-existence prevailed in Europe and lasted from 1815 until 1914 (with a few exceptions such as the Crimean War, sporadic internal revolutions and the unification drives in Germany and Italy).[1] This period gave rise to a growing population, scientific inventions and discoveries, a rapidly emerging rail network and growing international competition as many businesses expanded. The significant appearance of cartels towards the end of the nineteenth century cannot be properly understood without recognising the economic and political context from which they emerged. The three main European powers (France, Germany and the United Kingdom) had rapidly industrialised, witnessed phenomenal economic growth and found themselves locked in a competitive struggle for markets with each other.[2] The period after 1870 was marked by the shift towards economic protectionism and steered away from earlier mercantilist and freer trade position. Tensions between these powers for markets, resources and labour fuelled the move for larger companies and cartellisation. It was an age of 'competitive imperialism' (Beaud, 2000).

Many of these early cartels may have been created to meet expectations in domestic markets, but as they matured they reinvented themselves and adapted their strategies and alliances to build collective and collusive international arrangements as they sought to escape the dangers of so-called ruinous competition. Germany has most often been recognised as the archetypal economy in Europe which was truly underpinned by a higher degree of cartellisation. Although evidence of cartel-like activity can be traced back to the second quarter of the nineteenth century in several German states in the form, for example, of the steel-wire cartel (Kastl and Metzner, 1963: 461), the Neckar Salt Union (established in Wurttemberg in 1928), the *Oberlahnstein* Association to regulate the price of pig iron in the late 1840s, and later tin plate cartels, cartels only really begin to multiply and become an endemic aspect of the German business environment in the five decades after the unification of Germany in 1871.[3] There was scant governmental interest in cartellisation during this period. This reality was mirrored in other European states. Rather than feeling any necessity of regulating business activity, successive governments of Imperial Germany resisted state intervention and supported free markets where businesses, as private associations, were left to make their own agreements. The new German polity required a strong and powerful economy, and cartels had become a means of securing this objective. 'Without them, the state could not expand its own sphere of economic power . . . cartels played the role of industrial organisations to combat foreign competition and particularly the Americans trusts' (Nörr, 1994: 29).

Cartels emerged first in the heavy industry sectors as a response both to the economic uncertainties unleashed by overproduction and an ensuing fall in prices and then spread almost contagion-like to most sectors of the German economy by 1900. There was (Harding and Joshua, 2003: 71) certainly a 'formidable community of pro-cartel interests and actors in Wilhelmine Germany (1888–1918)' (heavy industry, big agriculture, the government and many economists). Cartels simply emerged to represent the accepted face of German business practices and statistics illustrate how the number of cartels had gradually climbed slightly from a modest 4 in 1865 to 8 a decade later before jumping significantly to 90 by 1885 and further to 210 in 1890. Estimates (Vito as quoted in Pace, 2007: 5) place the number of cartels past the 300 mark by the end of the 1890s. The upward trend had been set, and by 1905 there were some 400 cartels in operation (Henderson, 1967: 54) involving some 10,000 companies. The figures continued to augment and had climbed to 700 by 1910 before surpassing the 1,000 mark by the end of the First World War (Schröter, 1996: 132). It is necessary to distinguish the varying nature of cartel agreements which can be assessed in terms of duration, power and effect. The majority of cartels were clearly short-lived; some of the most potent, the best known and most established were to be found in the basic industries of coal, steel, iron, coke and potash. It could even be argued that, as many cartels have a short life span, the need for any anti-trust policy was obviated. This position has to be rejected, given the propensity of cartels frequently to re-invent themselves and a small number did have lengthier life spans. Whenever and wherever cartellisation is allowed to flourish unhindered it does impact negatively on consumers. In short, German business and moral traditions prior to 1914 were much more directed by planning and issues of stability than any notions of competition and competitive markets.

Cartels rapidly spread to many sectors of the German industrial economy, so much so that there were even separate cartels in place in the manufacture of both soft and hard toilet paper (Liefmann, 1930). This upward trajectory in Germany was replicated, albeit in a less pronounced fashion, in its bordering territories and most notably in Austro-Hungary, where some 200 cartels were in existence in 1914. Again cartel activity was most pronounced in the heavy industrial sectors such as coal and iron (Resch, 2002). Other leading European states such as France, Italy, Spain and the United Kingdom did not remain immune from the cartel drive, but their individual experiences never reached the numbers or solidity of their German counterparts.[4]

2. THE LAND OF THE CARTELS – GERMANY

How do we explain such developments and a propensity towards cartellisation in the German speaking countries? A range of general assumptions have been made in the past which have sought to explain cartels, for example as a response to economic difficulties, as a reaction to protectionist tariffs and as the vehicles for the banks to make greater profits, but are these correct? They have also been deemed to reflect Germany's form of 'organised capitalism' which centred on self regulation and a close relationship between business and the state. They have been presented as an attempt to bolster German economic development in a world which was increasingly being carved up by various powers into largely protectionist zones. In order to understand the cartellisation process it is first of all necessary to appreciate the economic and political context of recent German history. Germany had undergone a truly massive and fairly rapid transformation from a largely agricultural based economy to an industrialised economy (Pierenkemper and Tilly, 2004) during the course of the nineteenth century. During this period Germany's population rose from 22 million in 1800 to some 40 million by 1870 and 56 million by 1900 and Germany became an increasingly urbanised society. Harding and Joshua (2003: 64) put forward four very convincing variables for researchers to consider when trying to explore and explain the rise of the cartel in Germany. The four variables relate to broad economic trends (including industrialisation, the economic downturn in the 1870s and overproduction), the type of market in question, the political context (nation building and protectionism) and business and regulatory culture.

In part the economic changes were facilitated by the creation of the German *Zollverein* (customs union with no internal barriers to trade between its members), which came into existence in 1818 and greatly accelerated cross-border intra-German trade among the states in Germany. The *Zollverein* was a Prussian creation to invigorate growth and had its own parliament, currency. The economic benefits resulting were almost immediately apparent as the Prussian state underwent a period of nearly thirty years of economic growth from the late 1840s. The economic expansion scaled new heights in the immediate period following the unification of Germany in 1871.

Industry was flourishing and really beginning to challenge the dominance of British manufacturers for the first time. Expectations were high, and the economic boom period of the *Gründerjahre* (founding years of the early 1870s) heralded the emergence of leading banks such as the Deutsche Bank, which provided the capital for the expansion of German business interests. Some forty-seven banks were established in 1872 alone.

However, the boom was short lived and the German economy unexpectedly descended into a rather lengthy period of depression from 1873 until 1896. Of course, there were some glimmers of prosperity within this time frame (as occurred between 1879 and 1882), but for much of this period the economy seemed to be in a state of crisis which impacted on government aspirations, business confidence and the public. The *Reich* government responded to these turbulent times through a variety of mechanisms. It moved Germany away from being a free enterprise market economy (based on Manchester liberalism) towards protectionism. The re-appearance of tariffs was specifically designed for the agricultural sector and to protect the interest of the large land owning aristocracy east of the Elbe from cheaper foreign grain imports. Tariffs also came to feature in industrial goods and especially in relation to iron, but how far did these impinge on business and produce cartels?

On the one hand the recession led to the collapse of many smaller family run firms, but it also gave rise through mergers and acquisitions to the creation of larger business interests. This concentration process of economic power was another hallmark of the age. The revival of protectionist duties and technical barriers to trade in the 1880s was conducive towards greater monopolistic tendencies. Business certainly found itself compelled to respond to the deteriorating situation and challenging times. Above all it wanted to limit competition where possible. Initially, the first wave of cartels to emerge in the immediate years after German unification can effectively be labelled as a 'product of necessity' in difficult times, but as members came to realise the advantages of such private economic agreements so cartels came to flourish, even in times of prosperity. Instead of pursuing the competitive process, many German businesses adopted the somewhat safer and more secure environs offered by cartel membership. The creeping process of cartellisation was tolerated by the new fledgling German state in an effort to enable German industry to rival its British competitors. These aspirations culminated in the desire for territorial expansion (which became typified in the *Reich*'s drive for colonial possessions in the 1880s and the huge shipbuilding programme (which required iron) after 1900.[5] Against such a background any notion of competition and competitive markets became a secondary concern. Most cartels of the period were not the outcome of an alliance of small firms seeking some form of a defence arrangement against a more dominant market player (though that is how some of the first originated), but rather were designed as part of an offensive strategy and usually included the largest market players.

Consequently collective agreements were quickly recognised as a viable and even desirable form of business activity. The coal mining industry provides a good illustration of this deepening process of concentration. In Rhine-Westphalia, for example, some 40 per cent of the mining companies ceased to exist between 1873 and 1890 although production trebled and the number of people working in the mines effectively doubled. This industry also represented one of the most well known cartels at the time in the form of the Rhenisch-Westphalian Coal Cartel (Gebhardt, 1957: 206). This cartel was established in 1893 and quickly limited production and helped to bring greater stability through, among other things, higher prices which finally reached their 1873 levels in 1913. This particular cartel employed over 5000 people, consisted of 67 firms in 1912, had its own headquarters, and managed about 1400 different prices for varying coal qualities (Peters, 1989). The recession thesis seems entirely plausible and fits well with certain collusive agreements. In this sense cartels came to be classified as *Kinder der Not* (necessity's children) and a form of protective collectivism that arise in times of economic depression and falling prices, failing firms and falling wages. But are these assumptions always correct? Three examples provide useful illustration.

The rail/steel sector offers another prime example of collusion as a defence strategy. The railways had expanded rapidly from the first line between Nuremberg and Fürth in 1835 across the German states and facilitated both trade and communications. Their expansion plays a significant role in Germany's industrialisation and greatly increased the demand for steel. Initially most of this product had been imported from Great Britain, but as the Germans developed, copied and honed the techniques of their British rivals so they quickly became self-reliant. Germany went from being a net importer to producing by 1863 some 85 per cent of its needs. However, following the sharp fall in steel prices in the 1850s the main producers sought refuge in a steel/rail cartel which was formed in 1859 and survived practically intact until the First World War (despite a small cessation in the boom years of the early 1870s). It not only proved to be one of the most enduring examples of cartellisation but was one which remained highly profitable. There was a desire on behalf of the cartel members to keep the activities of cartel arrangements hidden from the public gaze. Interestingly, the rail/steel arrangement was one of the first cartels to come to the wider attention of the general public when Eugen Richter questioned its motives and practices in a speech in the Reichstag on 5 May 1879 (Liefmann, 1930: 23), and in particular the cartel's decision to charge higher prices for steel on the domestic German market than it did in international markets.

Another industrial sector which opted for the cartellisation route was potash. This sector displayed some unique features. Low entrance set-up costs meant that many companies were able to enter the market and sink wells. However, this reality proved immensely problematic because it led to too many players in the market place in the 1860s and 1870s. In a normal competitive market the abundant supply of potash should have pushed prices down for the consumers at the cost of the producer. To avoid any such scenario the potash producers established a cartel which simply maintained artificial prices and simply expanded to bring in new members. In short, in the absence of competition over-inflated prices prevailed within a highly inefficient sector. Often higher cartel membership equates with greater instability, and this cartel ultimately collapsed in 1909 only to be reinstated by the *Reich* government several years later. Interestingly, this sector was further protected from competition when the German government ruled out any possibility that foreign (non-German) companies could buy into the German potash industry. The potash cartel survived due to the absence of any competition, and the situation was rectified only after the First World War when the number of cartel producers fell from 228 to forty (Liefmann, 1930: 87).

The chemicals sector housed two main cartels. The first (the so-called Dreibund or Union of Three) comprised BASF, Agfa and Bayer, while the second (the so-called Dreiverband or Association of Three) included Hoechst, Cassella and Kalle. Attempts at merging the two however encountered resistance from suppliers and came to nothing. It is striking that cartels increased and flourished from the mid-1890s onwards in times of economic growth and prosperity (Kleeberg, 2004) and began to get more notice in some of the daily papers. Cartels can be depicted as a response to Germany's rapid industrialisation and in effect be deemed defensive agreements for firms facing both economic downturn and increasingly inefficient industrial sectors, but this angle is just one explanation of the cartellisation process in Germany. The examples above cast doubt on such arguments.

Another crucial dynamic which has been used to explain the rapid industrialisation process throughout Germany centres on the growth and role of the banks. The banks had certainly developed almost out of all recognition in the fifty years after 1840, but how strong a connection exists to cartellisation? Gerschenkron (1962: 15) has argued that the rush towards cartellisation in Germany reflected the wishes of the banks to protect their investments, and undoubtedly there is sufficient evidence to connect the banks with a spate of industrial and technological developments. Banks clearly facilitated the development of such specific capital intensive industries as the electro-technical sector which often bred cartels, but trying to correlate the two facts has often risked overstating the economic power of the banks. The banks form just part of a story that must also recognise other features of Germany's form of so-called 'organised capitalism' which included the interlocking directorates, supervisory boards, collusive agreements. It is still important not to over-exaggerate the power of the banks (Feldenkirchen, 1991). Certainly the banks were represented on the supervisory boards and possessed voting rights but they did not dominate proceedings and developments. Their focus and presence in heavy industry reflects the need of such sectors for substantial capital investment.

Cartels were simply as much a feature of business practices as were the banks. It was generally assumed that the cartels themselves provided the mechanisms to control any instability in the market place and to prevent dangers of competition. In this time-frame anti-cartel measures were extremely rare. The first tentative steps in the direction towards some form of regulatory system and rules on collective market behaviour actually encouraged cartel activity, as the *Reichsgericht's* (the supreme court until 1945) judgment in the infamous Wood Pulp cartel demonstrated. This case from 1897 centred on the existence of a wood producers' cartel in Saxony the avowed aim of which had been to prevent 'ruinous competition with one another and to obtain an agreed price for the producers' (Nörr, 1994). In order to do this they established a joint sales agency for all parties to the arrangement whereby all members had agreed to pay a fine if any opted to break the 'contract'. One such company did, and by challenging the nature of the agreement gave rise to the case. The anti-competitive agreement was approved by the court which (in the absence of any competition legislation) based its decision on the existing Civil and Commercial Codes. This outcome paved the way for the rapid expansion of the cartel industry in Germany. At closer inspection the judgment on this cartel is significant for two main reasons. Firstly, it determined that the freedom of contract took precedence over the freedom of competition. Secondly, it maintained that cartels were not necessarily against overall public policy. Indeed, it is important to stress in this context that most observers did not favour an outright ban on cartels (and this may help to explain the court's decision). Rather this decision should be interpreted as the Court's determination to have cartel contracts brought before the judges where they could be struck down.

It is also interesting to note that the original complaint arose from one of the members of the cartel and not from the consumer. In this time period the notion and realities of consumer interests were practically non-existent (Gerber, 1998: 105), and this meant that demands for greater cartel regulation were rather limited. Consumers were largely identified as workers whose interests were represented by the growing trade union movement and the SPD, but cartels were far removed from the main issues of the party's programme. In retrospect, the court had neither truly appreciated the potential negative effects cartels had on economic growth nor sufficiently grasped that the development of a free economy is based on genuine competition in the market place.

The 1897 ruling marks a decisive stage in the history and evolution of German competition policy, as it constitutes one of the first building blocks of a regulatory framework and it also marks the realities of an emerging competition community of lawyers and state officials. There is evidence of a growing interest in the dangers presented by the absence of fair competition from the late 1890s and public concerns led to some debate in the *Reichstag*, for example, over a rise in coal prices in 1900, several draft bills to combat cartels and even a government enquiry from 1902 to 1905 (Voigt, 1946: 174) on the extent of the cartel problem. The survey uncovered 395 cartels (and identified 132 in the brick sector, sixty-two in iron, forty-six in chemicals and some nineteen in coal). In retrospect, there was a creeping recognition of the desirability of competitive markets and the danger posed to their attainment through cartellisation. This growing awareness found reflection among social scientists (essentially legal scholars and economists) and also in the passing of the *Gesetz gegen unlautern Wettbewerb* (law against unfair competition or the UWB) in 1896. This law was not an attempt to secure genuine competition between companies, but is best described as a moral code and was basically concerned with ensuring that people in business operated according to 'fair rules' when competing with one another and in their relationship to the consumer. In other words this law aimed to ensure that people did not conduct their business activities in a manner which might offend good morals such as entrapping customers through misinformation; obstructing customers through price wars and selling below costs; and making unauthorised uses of another name or trademark. Although the UWB was revised in 1909 there was scant interest among successive pre-war *Reich* governments for some form of regulatory control of cartellisation, even given the growing number and transformation of the cartels themselves. Indeed, calls for the creation of a cartel office in 1908 had fallen on deaf ears within government.

Towards the end of the nineteenth century it had become clear that many of the original domestic cartel arrangements in Germany now dominated many industrial markets. For example, by 1907 it has been estimated that 100 per cent of the potash industry, 90 per cent of the paper industry, 48 per cent of the cement industry, 36 per cent of glass production and 50 per cent of raw steel production were subject to cartel agreements (Nipperdey, 1994: 248). Cartellisation did not always equate with stability, and some agreements were highly unstable and dissolved quickly. These cartels underwent a further metamorphosis and evolved into transnational agreements. By 1914 there were some 110 such international cartels and nineteen were located in the chemical sector, eighteen focused on transportation (including liner shipping), and some twenty-six centred on coal and other metals. Each had its own peculiarities and had been designed for either national markets or international markets, and increasingly all strove to restrict competition. Virtually all such collusive international agreements at this point in time contained German companies, although partners from Austria, Belgium, France and the UK were also strongly represented. One of the issues arising from the outbreak of the First World War was that it actually compelled states to industrialise further and thus anchored the status of cartels in the war geared economies.

3. THE APPROACH TO CARTELS IN THE UNITED STATES OF AMERICA

When accounting for the development of cartels and cartel policy in Europe it is impossible not to contrast and compare with the response to the same phenomenon in the United States. Indeed, the US model of anti-cartel policy certainly differed in style, substance and approach and challenged European perceptions until 1945. It is certainly tempting to assume that US antitrust is the model upon which all later policies are based. While there is some truth in this assumption, it is important to remember that competition policy is shaped as much by domestic considerations, as some (see Cini and McGowan, 1998) argue, such as historical traditions which have a bearing on the role of the state, and cultural attitudes towards industry, as they are by external policy borrowing. Contrasting the American model very briefly against the emergence of the main European models (i.e. the larger and most significant) demonstrates this point.

The US possesses one of the first and strongest legal bases in terms of antitrust and it is built on the 1890 Sherman Act and both the Clayton and the Federal Trade Commission Acts from 1914.[6] Together these acts represent the bible of US antitrust policy. The American antitrust (or competition) tradition embodied in these laws grew from a populist movement in the late nineteenth century (McChesney and Shughart, 1995) which centred on a suspicion of unchecked economic power, and the development and expansion of large trusts brought increasing concerns about notions of democracy and accountability. The United States had also undergone a rapid wave of industrialisation which mirrored the country's rapid expansion westwards to the Pacific Ocean from the 1830s onwards. The drive west was followed by the railroads and enhanced trade and economic growth. In the second half of the nineteenth century the first cartels emerged in such sectors as tobacco, oil, steel, and the railways (Beaud, 2000: 176).

By the late 1880s huge enterprises, especially the railroad companies, were swallowing up small firms at a frightening rate. These large businesses raised concerns about potentially abusive monopolies. Pressure for antitrust legislation was driven initially by the social, moral and political effects of big business rather than being driven by economic theory. In short, US antitrust began as an attempt to defend the individual entrepreneur against large companies (or trusts). There were numerous protests about the dangers posed by cartellisation from both other business undertakings which were affected by such illicit agreements and also the wider public. Fears were expressed about the power of many capitalists and the number of large companies and the near monopolies in such economic sectors such as sugar, petroleum and steel.[7] This discontent fuelled the emergence of the first anti-cartel legislation at state level in 1887 (Hovenkamp, 1994) and preceded US Congress's passing of the Sherman Act in 1890. The US antitrust Acts are therefore not simply legislative texts but also embodied the values on which America was built: individualism, fairness and free enterprise (Whish, 1988: 16). As free and fair competition was viewed as the economic embodiment of political freedom and democracy, surrender to the unaccountable economic power of the monopolist would have undermined the ideological foundations of the American state (Neale and Goyder, 1980: 16). This does not mean that the American approach to concentration was unquestioningly hostile. Rather, it tended to focus on the need for balance, and on the fostering of a positive pro-competition ethos.

The Sherman Act omitted the word competition completely and placed its emphasis with concepts and positions of economic power rather than market structures. The Act contained a definite prohibition against 'monopolization of trade and commerce', but also declared 'every contract, combination in form of trust or otherwise, or conspiracy, in restraint of trade and commerce . . . to be illegal'. There were no provisions for exceptions and those found guilty of such practices were to be subject to financial and penal penalties. The seemingly clear objective and powers to prosecute every trust disguise the reality that this was not a particularly 'effective piece of legislation' (Peters, 1996: 43) and was beset by a vagueness in terms of both style and the use of language, and consequently the job of the courts was made more difficult when it came to assessing what actually constituted clear abuses of power. Little distinction, for example, was made between those restraints of trade which could be deemed beneficial and those which were problematic. This particular Act was also powerless to prevent the growing trend towards greater economic concentration.

Accordingly, the later Clayton Act of 1914 should be recognised as an attempt to tighten up the law, given the growing concerns about the power of monopolies. It attempted to specify the different types of activity that could be deemed illegal restraints on trade. This Act, for example, included price discrimination and also sought to tackle trade practices (including tying and exclusive dealing arrangements as well as mergers) which threatened to undermine competition. It went one step further and cleverly forbade 'all unfair methods of competition' and identified the newly created Federal Trade Commission as the primary institution to undertake investigations of industry and to initiate proceedings against companies which were engaged in unfair practices. These American antitrust laws had set the scene and direction of the US tradition, but would it find reflection in Europe?

4. THE TRIUMPH OF THE CARTEL, 1919–45

The realities of prevalent cartellisation were to reach their ascendancy in continental Europe during the interwar period from 1919 to 1939 and assumed two general phases. The first phase, which covered the period following the First World War until the Wall Street Crash in 1929, was marked by a continuation of the cartel trend but also by a growing number of embryonic rules on competition as governments slowly came to appreciate and recognise the potential dangers from cartellisation. After a brief lull in both cartel formulation and government intervention between 1929 and 1933 the history of the European cartel underwent a decisive change in direction post depression, especially in both Germany and Italy, and entered a second and more intense phase when the state authorities altered direction and both encouraged and compelled cartellisation. It has been estimated that cartels controlled approximately 40 per cent of world trade between 1929 and 1937 (Nussbaum, 1986: 134).

Although agreements often involved German partners it is important to stress that cartels were not just a German phenomenon. They had become a reality in most industrialised nations and had existed prior to 1918 in all four leading West European states (i.e. France, Germany, Great Britain and Italy) and beyond. They covered a range of sectors such as chemicals, electricity, glass production, iron and steel, metal and minerals, textiles and cardboard (Pace, 2007: 8–10). Many cartels had become international entities. In an excellent study of cartellisation Schröter (1994) divided European states into four different groups. In the first and largest group he identified those states that were strongly in favour of cartels, and included within this category Austria, Belgium, Czechoslovakia, Finland, France, Germany, the Netherlands, Norway, Sweden and Switzerland. In a second group he listed those states that not only tolerated cartels but were also laying the first foundations for some form of regulatory bodies, such as Hungary, Italy, Poland and Spain. In a third cluster he placed those states which were rather ambivalent towards cartels (Bulgaria, Denmark and the UK), and in the final group those countries which were steadfastly opposed to cartels such as Yugoslavia, Australia and New Zealand. It is neither possible in this chapter to assess the correct classification of these states nor is it the intention. Instead the remainder of this chapter focuses particularly on events in Germany, which became the first state to introduce a system of cartel control, although comparison with other states and especially France and the United Kingdom will be made where appropriate. These three states represented the main building blocks of the interwar period despite their very different historical, cultural and legal traditions. All were sympathetic towards cartels, but how did they respond to them?

In Germany the repercussions of losing the war and being declared responsible for it (Article 261, Versailles Treaty) were immense, and the country not only experienced substantial political turmoil as it moved from an ultra conservative monarchial system to a new democratic and republican order in the period after 1919, but was also confronted by a huge reparations bill and a much changed economic climate. Although much had changed in terms of the political and social landscape of the new Weimar Republic, some practices, and in this case cartels, remained undisturbed and intensified during the Weimar Republic. Many were the product of agreements to tackle and manage the overproduction of goods which still continued after the war and the drive for self-sufficiency. The number of cartels rose dramatically and had reached some 2500 by 1931 (Feldenkirchen, 1988: 116–8), and the figure would have been considerably higher if those cartels relating to banking, insurance and the free professions (doctors, dentists and architects) had been included. How is this increase to be explained? To understand why cartels flourished it is necessary to appreciate the changed economic and trading circumstances facing many German businesses after 1919. Much of Germany's pre-1914 links, export markets and other international connections, and especially those relating to the United States, had been severed by the First World War. The early post-war years saw both *Reich* governments and German business seeking to rebuild the economy and regain access to markets.

Apprehension abounded on several fronts. The German business community was wary about investing in other countries, partly amid concerns about possible expropriation and partly on account of their lack of finance. The realities of considerably larger US companies (see Berghahn, 1996: 37) also rocked business confidence about the perils of free market competition, as did the possibilities of companies with hard currency purchasing power acquiring German companies (given the falling value of the German currency in the early 1920s). German companies needed to locate and gain access to export markets and cartels were often the chosen vehicle towards greater security and stability. Moreover, the interwar period was marked by the constant growth of trade barriers between states. The pressure to maintain competitiveness in the latest technology fields of chemicals and electrical engineering culminated, for example, in agreements, and their creation followed a similar pattern that upon translation meant reaching an agreement with rival competitors in other states as a means of allocating markets and fixing prices. Cartellisation became an endemic feature of business activity (Barnikel, 1988: 13) in Germany, and although it found reflection in many other European states it never assumed the same velocity or depth as in Germany, which had become the 'land of the cartels'.

Faced with a series of political crises and attempted coups in the early 1920s the Weimar governments may have seemed ill-prepared for tackling the cartel issue, but the first major steps towards regulating cartels in Germany can be traced back to this period in the form of the *Kartellverordnung* (Cartel Regulation) of 1923.[8] There had been a growing degree of unease about cartel activity among sections of the wider public and especially from the SPD since the turn of the century. The real impetus for legislation at this particular moment owed much to the dire economic position facing the German government in the wake of an economic downturn which was exacerbated tremendously by the Belgian and French decisions to occupy the Ruhr coalfields as a means of extracting reparations and pushed the German economy to the brink of collapse and hyperinflation. Against this backdrop the *Reich* government under Chancellor Gustav Stresemann opted under emergency legislation (*Ermächtigungsgesetz* as provided for under the constitution) to monitor and control, where appropriate, the growing cartel industry. Two questions immediately arise. What was the purpose of this cartel regulation and how effective did it prove to be in operation? The regulation was drawn up by officials within the *Reich* Economics Ministry, and recognised the legality of cartels and centred on regulating the abusive exploitation of economic power (Liefmann, 1930: 207; Neumann, 1998: 44). The regulation placed ultimate responsibility for ensuring adherence to the law with two main actors, the *Reich* Economics Minister and a Cartel Court, and was designed primarily as a mechanism to catch those cartel agreements which threatened to damage the economy or public welfare through such practices as keeping prices high, limiting production and/or distribution.[9] Cartels which did so and thus threatened to undermine and endanger the economy could be deemed by the Economics Minister (under Section 4) to be null and void. In short, the regulation was constructed around the 'abuse principle' (*Mißbrauchsprinzip*) and provided legal protection for most cartels, but simultaneously established special legal norms and conditions beyond which cartels were not permissible. As such the basic aim of such legislation placed responsibility on the cartel members in the form of a self-regulation exercise to ensure their activities were within accepted parameters of the law.

Such aspirations and models of self-regulation to secure optimal economic behaviour may be laudable but were with hindsight simply too optimistic. Many of the issues raised in the previous chapter surface again here. Most cartels were created for immediate benefits, and the regulation did not lead to a decline in the number of cartels but the reverse, and gave further ammunition to the regime's critics. Most cartels, however, proved to be short-lived and as new entrants arrived in the market place so prices-often fell and so cartels often collapsed and reformed. The emergence and dissolution of cartel agreements provided a certain rhythm with the German business environment. The most enduring and hard-core cartels continued to prevail in the basic industries and deliberately sought to undermine the market by reducing production and showing scant interest in innovations and technological developments.

The cartel regulation certainly received attention in Germany but, as Harding and Joshua comment (2003: 74), aroused considerable criticism abroad and especially from American competition academics and practitioners. The fault-line of this German model centred specifically on the 'control' model of regulation rather then the US prohibition model. Fears expressed (Kronstein and Leighton, 1945) concerns about philosophical approaches and the degrees of business control. It cannot be denied that cartel members held the advantage from the start. Their power found representation in the hiring of gifted cartel lawyers and economists who helped to reinforce existing and positive perceptions of cartels and who were better placed and resourced to counter any opposition, for example, from consumer groups. There was a clear pro-cartel ethos at play, and one which was both mostly tolerated and encouraged by government for their own interests. Competition from foreign companies both pushed greater economic concentration and facilitated the rationale for cartellisation. IG Farben represents one of the most well known and largest of the mergers at the time. It was formed in 1925 following a merger between Badische Anilin und Sodafabriken, Bayer and Hoechst. It was, however, still dwarfed by the US giant, Du Pont. In this case the *Reich* government overlooked the company's nitrogen cartel arrangements as it enabled IG Farben to maximise profits and therefore to fund new research in oil and rubber.

Views on this specific form of cartel regulation have been somewhat mixed. On the one hand detractors might point to the growing number of cartels in the latter half of the 1920s and thus question the regulation's impact. Any such conclusions are largely unfair because the institutional arrangement needed time to bed down and develop. Unfortunately time was the one variable, in retrospect, which the Weimar regime did not have and the after shocks of the Wall Street Crash in October 1929 and the recalling of US loans plunged Germany into recession, major unemployment and signalled both the Weimar Republic's and the cartel regime's demise. For some critics (see Voigt, 1962: 180–1) the regime established under the cartel decree was simply too rigid and inflexible to work and had a limited impact on cartels. Positively it led some to terminate the agreements but it was powerless to prevent the tendency toward concentration. Some of the most spectacular mergers occurred, and these included IG Farben, Vereinigte Stahlwerke and Daimler-Benz (Rutherford, 1974: 23) in the 1920s. By the end of 1929 some 1800 cartels (Voigt, 181) existed in Germany.

Nevertheless, the Cartel Regulation was an ambitious marker and surpassed anything close to it in either France or Britain. It also represented an inspired move, as its framework of administrative supervision came to influence the shape of the European legislation that emerged after 1945. It was never truly, however, able to establish itself, given the onset of the depression after 1929 which led the government to change its tactics on the cartel front and pursue a policy akin to developments in the USA. As prices collapsed only cartels were in a position to keep markets in some order. The German authorities were pushed onto the defensive and issued a number of decrees to combat inflation and the collapse of business concerns. Compulsory cartels, which had prevailed in only a few selected economic sectors such as potash, became the new vehicle to defend and promote vulnerable industries such as milk, sugar and potato starch. The attitude of the state was not always consistent, and this partially explains a special cartel emergency decree to prevent 'uneconomic price fixing' (Voigt, 1946) in 1930. Cartels came to represent a form of economic and competitive nationalism. It was at this point that the *Reich* government obtained the power to outlaw price cartels completely when public welfare was threatened. The *Reich* Economics Minister's powers were enhanced and this figure became the most important individual in the German cartel policy when he replaced the Cartel Court and could both nullify cartel agreements and prevent the formation of cartels in his own right. Another decree ordered a drop in prices by 10 per cent where price agreements existed, although to little real effect. By 1930 an emergency cartel decree order (*Zwangkartellgesetz*) was put in place to assist declining industries and enabled the Economics Minister to create compulsory cartels. The prevalence of cartels just developed an extra dimension under National Socialist rule after January 1933. The Nazi administration went from being overtly hostile to cartels (under the original 25 Point party Programme of 1925) and abandoned practically all its original economic goals to actually encourage the formation of cartels (Gillingham, 1985). It went even further and effectively jettisoned the Cartel Court. The sudden slump and great depression after 1929 led to the implementation of a policy of forced cartellisation which was largely at the behest of German business circles. The new National Socialist administration responded to such calls with the promulgation of a new law in July 1933 which encouraged cartel formation (Feldenkirchen, 1985: 159). Some 2000 new cartels had appeared by December 1936. Together these developments initiated a new phase in cartel development in Germany. Whereas government had intervened before to tackle abusive behaviour which threatened public welfare, cartellisation now became a tool for government to pursue its own economic strategy and serve the needs of economic planning. Responsibility for creating and allowing cartels centred on the *Reich* Economics Minister. Of course, this law was intended to be a transitory development in times of economic difficulty, to be utilised only in special circumstances and with discretion by government. It had not been the intention of its drafters that the law would be used widely to change the nature of the economy itself.

By the late 1920s only Sweden and Norway had followed the German example and adopted specific competition legislation in 1925 and 1926 respectively. Although considerably later than developments in the US the idea of a cartel policy had been circulating in certain states (especially in Scandinavia) from the turn of the century. The Norwegian Law marks a significant step in the history of European competition policy in so far as it constitutes the most advanced and closest thing to developments post 1945. It established an independent agency to control cartel activity and centred on a Control Office which was headed by a senior judge (Gerber, 1998: 155–9). The Norwegian approach represented the first real juridical regime in Europe. It was, however, an exception, as most European states adopted the much more administrative based German model which was underpinned by ministerial discretion and overwhelmingly driven by a cartel friendly ethos. The German approach held that cartel conduct could be modified through cases of 'negotiated' control (Harding and Joshua, 2003: 75). The notion of control and the possibilities of discretion opened up room for considerable debates on the merits of individual cartel agreements. It is interesting to note the emergence of a growing number of specialist cartel lawyers who both welcomed and defended the control approach when working for the companies concerned.

Although arrangements between competitors had also shaped business practices in both France and the United Kingdom in the latter half of the nineteenth century, they had tended to form much looser forms of collusion such as gentlemen's agreements, and both countries opted not to pursue or seek any form of legal control. France, in particular, displayed a real reluctance towards any specific competition legislation, and none was enacted until after 1945. Although the French state had in 1926 introduced an amendment to its 1810 Penal Code, which sought to criminalise agreements which deliberately set out to boost business profits through price-fixing arrangements, the amendment was phrased in such vague terms as to be practically meaningless as a means of deterring cartellisation.

The British system was not shaped by any mass anti-trust movement, and while restrictive practices were far from uncommon in the UK, the prevailing view of the time was that cartels posed no particular cause for concern. In the absence of any legislation the courts felt ill-prepared to condemn, as the East Asian Shipping Agreement on 1890 demonstrated, 'peaceful and honest combination of capital for the purpose of trade competition' (see Martin, 2006: 122). So in practice the courts were not prepared to condemn cartels. Such attitudes quickly gave way to an explosion in the number of agreements. These and demands for higher tariffs were regarded as the best means to prevent any undesired collapse in prices. The onset of the depression just solidified the cartel movement. The tolerant British attitude towards cartels and concentration, particularly in the interwar period, stemmed at least in part from the belief that British industry was generally much more exposed to international competition than the US, and as such had little need for US-style legislation. Unlike the Americans, British public opinion was not preoccupied with notions of concentrated power. Social protest, which was certainly a feature of the times, rarely seemed to focus on the power wielded by big business. The UK was driven primarily by export markets and there was scant interest in competition related matters. However, as Germany began first to challenge the UK and then surpass the UK in the goods of the second industrial revolution, many UK firms sought recourse to agreements to limit the dangers of increased competition and entered cartel agreements.

Growing recognition of the problematic nature of cartels (and despite repeated protestations from business circles that the cartellisation process was helping to avert economic difficulties) led to the adoption of cartel laws in many European states (including Hungary, Czechoslovakia, Poland and Romania). Many were modelled on the German approach and required compulsory registration, and some pursued strategies of state led cartellisation as a means to regulate certain industries. Other states preferred other approaches to both protect and encourage other industries. In both the UK (coal mining) and France (coal and silk) laws were passed to prevent any newcomers coming into more sensitive markets by requiring state approval which could be withheld for a variety of reasons. There was an explosive expansion of British based cartels after 1920 (Freyer, 1992), and many received governmental encouragement. Many European states had come by the 1920s to appreciate the advantages of using cartels as an instrument of public policy. Some openly tolerated and some demanded greater cartellisation. In Mussolini's Italy, for example, and as a sign of things to come cartels were created as part of the state's corporatist economic structures. Cartels were very much encouraged, and especially in certain sectors such as silk and steel (Schröter, 1996: 136). Spain demanded the creation of cartels in a wide number of industrial sectors including wine, sugar, coal, lead and paper.

The different approaches across states reflected the very dissimilar starting points for each regime. In retrospect, it is possible to trace a slow but sure and growing recognition and concern from many European governments after 1919 about the nature and degree of cartellisation. The extent of cartellisation in the global economy was such that it has been estimated that somewhere between 40 and 50 per cent of international trade was affected by industrial agreements which extended across all leading European states. By way of example the Incandescent Lamp Cartel (Osram) represents one of the most infamous of the international cartels to emerge during the interwar period. Its origins lay in an agreement comprising only German manufacturers before this cartel was transformed into a fully blown international arrangement which included partners from Brazil, Canada, China, France, Italy, Hungary, Japan, Mexico and the Netherlands in 1925.

5. THE TREND TOWARDS INTERNATIONAL CARTELS

By the late 1920s there was an increasing recognition among politicians and governments about the depth of international cartellisation. These concerns were reflected by the League of Nations which sponsored a World Economic Conference in Geneva in 1927 and the 27th Conference of the Inter-Parliamentary Union in London in 1930. The Geneva meeting provided an excellent opportunity to discuss the issue of industrial agreements, and during the debates revealed the different perceptions and attitudes among the delegates towards such activity. France, for example, proposed the need for some form of regulation to control international cartels, but this proposal was rejected by Germany, Norway and the

United Kingdom. Cartels had survived regulation. The Geneva meeting concluded with a specific resolution on cartels which not only noted such differences between the states on the subject but called on the League of Nations to explore, analyse and make public 'these forms of international co-operation and their efforts upon technical progress, the development of production, conditions of labour, the situation as regards supplies and the movement of prices, seeking in this connection the collaboration of the various governments'. The resolution maintained 'that the publicity given in regard to the nature and operations of agreements constitutes one of the most effective means, on the one hand, of securing the support of public opinion to agreements which conduce to the general interest, and, on the other hand, of preventing the growth of abuses'. The conference was a missed opportunity, but it highlighted the dangers of cartellisation, and this in itself was a step forward.[10] The 27th Conference of the Inter-Parliamentary Union meeting in London in 1930 represented a more significant event and marks a more decisive watershed as it called for regulatory supervision and control of cartels. Delegates passed a resolution which stated 'that cartels, trusts and other analogous combines are natural phenomena of economic life towards which it is impossible to adopt an entirely negative attitude. Seeing, however, that those combines may have a harmful effect both as regards public interests and those of the state, it is necessary that they should be controlled' by 'the state' (Boserup and Schlichtkrull, 1946: 59). During the debates the different approaches on either side of the Atlantic were clearly visible. Whereas the American regime was based on the principle of prohibition and illegality, the general European approach allowed and tolerated cartels and other combinations so long as such agreements did not harm the wider public interest. Many US firms looked longingly at the lighter touch of the European form of cartel regulation, and even initiated a campaign (Levy, 1968) to remove the Sherman Act's prohibition clause.

The London resolution even referred to a special cartel commission to examine any agreements that were detrimental to the public interest. This commission was to 'be independent of government' and to include representatives from both consumers and workers. This commission was to investigate the facts and make recommendations to a central authority, which was entitled to open legal proceeding through the law courts in order to have certain agreements declared null and void. The model advocated by the London conference was considerably closer to the Norwegian system and reflected a more socialist-led thinking on cartels. In retrospect both these conferences provided an interesting template for future generations to consider when formulating the competition provisions of the later ECSC policy regime.

By the start of the Second World War it has been estimated that some 40 per cent of world trade was driven by cartels and the intensity of these arrangements scaled new heights during the war. The cartel movement had also witnessed the emergence of international cartels, especially in the saltpetre, copper, aluminium, plate glass, paper and textiles markets. Cartels certainly brought greater stability for the members of these cartels in tough economic circumstances. Defence and security were usually the principal driving factors behind cartellisation and proved a much easier course of action than any attempts to push expansion through competition. Some (Fear, 2006) argue that these cartels actually prevented the onset of trade wars which might have brought both greater instability and damage. In this sense cartellisation can be read as a response to globalisation, and it is both revealing and interesting to see it against the backdrop of a growing nationalism, both economic and political, within power politics. While political tensions and distrust between the major European powers intensified in the late 1930s the business communities from these same states found co-operation mutually beneficial. It should also be pointed out that both US and Japanese companies were also actively involved in the creation of international cartels.

The shift to international agreements reflects producers' objectives, rivalry and even geo-political diplomacy. Many excellent studies have been undertaken with regard to specific industries. The international steel cartel was probably one of the most high-profile cartels to emerge during the late 1920s.[11] Its aims were simply to stabilise the coal and steel market and to control prices. To understand the origins of this cartel it is first necessary to grasp some of the peculiarities of both sectors. Some 80 per cent of Europe's coal and iron deposits were located in France and Germany, with smaller amounts in Belgium and Luxembourg. Whereas Germany held considerable reserves of both coal and iron, France had limited coal reserves.[12] France's need for coal had led her temporarily to occupy the Ruhr, Germany's industrial heartland, in 1923 as a means of extracting reparations from Germany as awarded to France under the Treaty of Versailles. The situation facing both states was difficult. German companies had overproduced and were looking for ways to sell their surplus and cut production. The French companies were looking for more coke supplies. An agreement between companies from both states could solve the issues. Consequently the *Rohstahlgmeinschaft* (literally translated as raw Steel Community) was founded in 1926. This was a cartel in all but name and sought to limit production and set quotas for each company party to the agreement. Its membership widened in 1927 to include companies from Czechoslovakia, Austria and Hungary. Co-operation was not always straightforward, given the prevailing jealousies and aspirations, and it collapsed in 1931 before being re-established in 1933 with a new and reworked quota and price system. Membership widened further to incorporate the United Kingdom and many other European states, and the cartel evolved into a full fledged international concern when American companies became party to the agreement in 1938. The steel cartel provides an apt illustration of the power of a cartel, which in this case commanded control over 90 per cent of the world's steel exports. The only industrialised nation which was absent from the cartel's membership was Japan, and even Japanese companies might have joined had war not broken out in 1939 when the terms of the agreement were dissolved (Kiersch, 1963: 349). There were numerous other examples of European cartel activity covering sectors such as tin, nitrogen and dyestuffs. Cartels had become a basic staple part of business life and extended across the globe involving foodstuffs (cocoa, coffee, sugar, wheat (Hexner, 1946)) A rubber cartel underlines how first world countries had set up established cartels in the colonies and corporations (Stocking and Watkins, 1946: 56–117). By the late 1930s the steel and coke (founded in 1936) cartels had become connected to the appeasement policy pursued by both London and Paris in the hope that economic deals with Nazi Germany might have been sufficient to prevent the outbreak of a major European war.

6. CONCLUSIONS

This chapter has sought to display the history of the European cartel over the time frame from the unification of Germany in 1871 until the end of the Second World War some seventy years later. The task was certainly ambitious, but it was necessary fully to comprehend the magnitude of developments after 1945. Two key elements can be distilled from this overview: In the first period from 1871 to 1918 the advent of the cartel much fitted into the realities of rapid industrialisation, the freeing of world trade and the realities of greater international competition. Under these circumstances cartels were generally deemed not to be so problematic, and in many cases were recognised as almost natural forms of defence to secure the life span of indigenous industries against foreign competition. Social and political concerns about the side-effects of cartellisation were occasionally vented in public but were never strong enough to challenge the 'positive' aspects of cartel agreements.

In the second period from 1919 to 1945 the trend towards cartellisation on both the national and international fronts gathered pace, but this period also saw the emergence of the first domestic laws to regulate cartel activity. It was a beginning. Without the onset of war it might be interesting to speculate how European policy might have evolved. Certainly the eclipse of Europe by the two superpowers not only brought an end to 500 years of European hegemony on the world stage, but also provided the basis and influence of new economic thinking. It initiated a total transformation in attitudes to cartels. 'It took 60 years and two generations to thoroughly cartelize Europe up to the 1930s, and another 60 years for a complete change in policy in favour of intense de-cartellisation'. (Schröter, 1996: 153). As attitudes changed so cartels became identified as problematic for business, unsuitable for consumers and incompatible with democracy. How, who and in what manner they were to be regulated forms the core of the following chapter.

NOTES

1. For a comprehensive and shorter political historical overview of this period see N. Davies, *Europe: A History*, Pimlico, 1997 and especially chapter 10. Also see the now classic works by D. Thomson, *Europe since Napoleon*, Penguin, 1957 and also J. Joll, *Europe since 1870*, Penguin, 1973.
2. For further information on this period of industrialisation in Britain, France, Germany, Italy and Russia see R. Sylla and G. Toniolo, *Patterns of European Industrialization*, Routledge, 1992.
3. For centuries Germany had simply constituted a geographical expanse in the heart of Europe which contained some 300 states and city states. After the Napoleonic wars many of these smaller entities were merged to create 38 states. The leading three were Austria, Bavaria and Prussia, and all sought control of Germany. The battle for supremacy between the German states finally came to an end when Prussia defeated Austria in a war in 1866 and excluded Austria from the German Federation. Prussian dominance was further developed with its defeat of France and her allies (including Bavaria) in 1870 which enabled Prussia to unify all the German states (and excluded Austro-Hungary) into one federal political structure which was controlled by the largest and most economically powerful of the German states, Prussia (D. Blackbourn, *The Fontana History of Germany, 1780–1918*, Fontana, 1997; W. Carr, *The Origins of the Wars of German Unification,* Longman, 1991; and also G.A. Craig, *Germany 1866–1945*, OUP, 1981. The Prussian King in turn became German emperor. The emergence of Germany as a new and rapidly industrialised state upset the balance of power in Europe and led to a series of alliances and ententes between the major powers and ultimately bred rivalries and distrust and culminated in war in 1914.
4. For one example in the British contest see F. Scott Morton, 'Entry and Predation: British Shipping Cartels, 1879–1929' in *Journal of Economics and Management Strategy*, Vol. 6(4) (2004), 679–724.
5. See R.K. Massie, *Dreadnought: Britain, Germany and the Coming of the Great War*, Random House, 1991.
6. The creation of Canadian competition policy narrowly predates the onset of the American legislation by one year, but the former was rather symbolic and was quickly surpassed in terms of activity and depth by the US model. For further information on the Canadian model see Bruce G. Doern, 'Canadian Competition Policy: Institutions and Decision Processes' in Doern and Wilks (eds), *Comparative Competition Policy*, Clarendon Press, 1996.

7. See R.C. McGrath, *American Populism: A social History, 1877–1898*, Hill and Wang, 1993.
8. The full title of this legislation was the *Verordnung gegen Mißbrauch wirtschaftlicher Machtstellung* (Regulation against the Abuse of economic Market Power) of 2 November 1923.
9. This specialised cartel court or *Kartellgericht* was put in place to enforce the law (see Blum, 1933) but its impact is debatable as the number of cartels continued to increase from some 1,500 to 2,010 by 1930.
10. France remained committed to some form of regulation of the European economy and Aristide Briand, the French Foreign Minister, proposed the idea of a 'European Union' in 1929. Subsequent discussions considered the positive role that international cartels could play in a new and regulated economic system. The Briand Plan, which involved political as well as economic structures, was rejected by the League of Nations in 1932, but represented an attempt at a form of closer European co-operation and was a precursor of sorts to the later European integration process.
11. For further information see D. Barbezat, 'Competition and Rivalry in the International Steel Cartel, 1926–32', *Journal of Economic History*, 1989, 49(2), 435–447.
12. After Napoleon Bonaparte's final defeat at Waterloo in 1815 the Treaty of Vienna passed large parts of the Rhineland and the Ruhr area to Prussia and helped establish this state as the economic powerhouse of Germany.

4. The dawn of the competition principle in Western Europe, 1945–1957

The unconditional surrender of Nazi Germany on 8 May 1945 brought the Second World War in Europe to an end. The final two years had been waged at considerable economic and physical cost to Germany and the outcome radically changed the political map of Europe and heralded the slow demise of the former great West European empires as economic bankruptcy took its toll. Military might and power now transferred to the two new superpowers in the form of the United States of America (USA) and the Soviet Union (USSR). During the war both powers and their allies (primarily France and the United Kingdom) had shared a common goal in securing the defeat of Hitler's Germany, but little united these powers beyond this objective and little was said about what form the post-Hitler order would take. Indeed, different visions and approaches, given the incompatibility between capitalism and communism on the part of both new superpowers, ensured that the wartime coalition not only disintegrated very quickly but led to the onset of the Cold War and the division of Europe between East and West for over forty years.

The difficulties and tensions between the superpowers became pretty visible in their handling of policy towards Germany. Both Moscow and Washington may have sought the means to remould Germany into a democratic and peaceful state and agreement had been reached to divide Germany (shorn of its eastern territories of East Prussia, Silesia and East Pomerania) into four separate control zones of occupation prior to its re-unification. Definitions of democracy, however, differed tremendously and disagreements between primarily the Soviets on the one side and France, the United Kingdom and the United States on the other became all too evident in policy developments within their respective zones, and ultimately led to the creation of two states in Germany, namely the Federal Republic of Germany (West Germany with the fusing together of the American, British and French zones) and the German Democratic Republic (East Germany) in May 1949.

The aftermath of the world war also created a vacuum for new ideas about how the European economy, politics and society should be rebuilt. Although competition policy would surface as one of the new drivers, its future role and centrality were not immediately apparent. Surveying the European scene in 1945 what was striking according to Hofstadter (1964) was the complete absence of any commitment to the competition principle. Historical experience had demonstrated there was a clear distinction between the attitudes on both sides of the Atlantic over the issue of cartels. Indeed, any suggestions that the German cartellisation experience had proved detrimental to the growth of the German economy before 1939 must be open to real question and, had Germany won the war, then it is very unlikely that the competition principle, as we understand it today, would ever have emerged in Europe. Germany's military defeat and the ensuing Allied occupation brought new circumstances, a new context in which to frame economic and political developments and specific victor preferences which in retrospect enabled the development of anti-trust policy.

Western Europe was to follow a different path, and it is to this region that attention now turns. In retrospect, the American belief in competitive markets, the German pursuit of a social market economy and French preferences and planning were to help steer Europe towards the endorsement and adoption of European integration, and within it moves towards anti-trust policy, albeit initially for different reasons and objectives. Under the Soviet system and in the East German state cartel policy simply did not rise as an issue at all as the means of production had been brought under state control (Childs, 1986). Competition policy was regarded by the East German leadership as an element of the capitalist model to control and monitor abusive business activity which was not needed in the 'socialist' system of the Soviet Union and its satellites. The economy in these states was not constructed under any notion of competitive markets, but effectively managed by an inefficient and ultimately highly unpopular bartering system.

This chapter charts the emergence of the competition principle in Western Europe after 1945 up to the signing of the EEC Treaty in 1957. It is divided into four sections. The first continues the German experience and focuses on the Allied de-cartellisation plans for Germany and how the new economic order (or *Pax Americana*) which emerged after 1945 brought US influence to bear on the anti-trust arena. The second and third sections explore the ideas behind the Schuman Plan and the negotiations leading to the Treaty of Paris which established the European Coal and Steel Community respectively. Both sections also focus on the anti-cartel provisions. The final part explores the origins of the West German anti-trust experience and briefly refers to developments in other ECSC states.

1. ZERO HOUR IN GERMANY: FROM DE-CARTELLISATION TO THE FOUNDING OF THE WEST GERMAN STATE, 1945–1949

The surrender of Germany on 8 May 1945 brought the Second World War in Europe to an end. Unlike the situation in 1918, the Allies opted to occupy and administer Germany (albeit temporarily) in an effort to democratise the people and overcome any possible renewed Nazi resistance. From the American perspective in particular there was a determination from Washington to avoid reverting to her isolationist position as had occurred after 1918, and to involve herself directly and indirectly in restoring peace and stability. Allied intentions towards Germany were laid out in the report on the Tripartite Conference of Berlin and aimed that 'at the earliest practicable date, the German economy shall be decentralised for the purpose of eliminating the present excessive concentration of economic concerns as exemplified in particular by cartels, syndicates, trusts and other monopolistic arrangements (Eyre, 1999: 97).

This objective was far from surprising. After all, in America 'cartel policy had constituted more than just a theory and had 'practically become a way of life and creed' (Hofstadter, 195). The pursuit of a competition policy was deemed to bring benefits both to the overall economy through innovation and to society at large. Accordingly, the US authorities sought to export their vision of anti-trust legislation overseas, and it surfaced as much in their negotiations with the Japanese as it did with the West Europeans.[1] Towards the end of the war US president Franklin D. Roosevelt had expressed his desire that cartel practices which restrict the free flow of goods in foreign commerce would have to be curbed. He had envisaged the newly established United Nations as possible means to advance the arguments (Harding and Joshua, 2002: 89), but success was extremely limited. The US was well placed to shape European mentalities vis-à-vis cartel policy (Leucht, 2007) as the leading economic and political power in the Western hemisphere, but could it do so?

American policy towards Germany altered rapidly in the space of five years. Although initial plans, such as the infamous and punitive Morgenthau Plan which had sought effectively to transform Germany into an agricultural state as a means to prevent any possibility of the outbreak of World War III, were quickly discarded once the war had been won, US policy in the immediate period from 1945 to 1947 was still constructed negatively. De-cartellisation, for example, represented one of the major economic thrusts of US policy and had been outlined as an objective alongside de-nazification, re-education and democratisation in the Potsdam Agreement of August 1945.

Although Germany is often portrayed as the European state with the greatest predisposition towards cartellisation it would be foolish to deny similar, if less pronounced, moves before and after the Second World War in specific industrial sectors in other countries including the United Kingdom and France (Edwards, 1967). Cartels were conceived among the American administration in purely negative terms. The de-cartellisation agenda has often been underplayed in the literature of the immediate post-war history of West Germany and Europe, but in retrospect marks a hugely significant event.[2] The US document JCS 1067, *Directive to the Commander-in-Chief of the US Forces of Occupation Regarding the Military Government of Germany of April 1945*, epitomised the attitude of the immediate post-war period and explicitly forbade the Americans to maintain or strengthen the German economy and to 'prohibit all cartels and other private arrangements'.[3] The de-cartellisation agenda was often viewed in German business circles as a punishment and another example of the thinking that had created the Morgenthau Plan but it also represented an ideal opportunity (Gillingham, 2006) for the Allies to weaken the potential power of the German state. Initially, the aim of de-cartellisation in the period from 1945 to 1947 had little to do with creating a competitive environment, but was pursued solely as a means of weakening the German economy and hindering any German revival, both economic and military. The means of attaining these targets were to be realised through the Level of Industry Plan of March 1946, which sought to limit German industrial capacity to about 50 per cent of that of 1936, with the greatest reductions occurring in the chemicals, steel and heavy engineering sectors while other sectors of economic activity, such as armaments, aluminium, ammonia and ball bearings, were banned altogether. The outcome of such policies was felt rather quickly because the goods were used to produce a wide range of household items from bicycles to agricultural equipment.

Cartels were identified as problematic, and the US even endeavoured to make a direct link between the rise of the heavy industry cartels in the interwar period with the politics and aspirations of right-wing extremist parties. Indeed, the International Steel Cartel is often cited as an example (Gillingham, 1991: 1–44). De-cartellisation was to be targeted specifically in the coal, steel, iron, chemicals, plastics, heavy engineering and banking sectors. Some of the most noted examples included the dismembering of some of Germany's famous internationally renowned banks (the so-called *Großbanken*) to create thirty-three new banks (Djelic, 1998: 165) and the breaking up of companies such as IG Farben (Goyder, 1993: 17) into the three main successor companies of Bayer, Hoechst and BASF. How effective the policy would be in the longer term is often disputed, as the banking industry, for example, would quickly re-concentrate itself in the late 1950s (Van der Pijl, 1984: 164).

The de-cartellisation agenda never quite fully materialised as had been planned, and in order to understand why it is necessary to appreciate the economic, political and social background of the late 1940s. Firstly, western Allied economic policy had been running counter to the steps needed to ensure a German economic recovery, and this started to become problematic, for by the spring of 1947 Western Germany had edged ever closer to a state of economic collapse. The war had brought Germany to zero-hour (*Stunde Null*) and the economy rapidly collapsed and GDP levels fell back to pre-1936 levels. The perilous state of the economy was reflected also in France, Italy and Belgium. Food had become even scarcer in Western Germany than during the war. The situation was exacerbated by the severe winter of 1946–1947 and led to a practically worthless *Reichsmark* within a thriving black market economy. The conditions for serious political unrest were growing as relations with the Soviet Union were deteriorating. The American public became increasingly sympathetic to the media's images of the daily plight and hardships facing ordinary Germans. The American government became increasingly concerned that continuing economic hardship might propel Western Germany towards Communism, advance both Soviet interests and Moscow's sphere of influence and destabilise the political future of Western Europe, which was dependent on the vitality of Europe's industrial heartland, Germany. This market alone, it was recalled, had been a major American export market prior to 1939.

The US changed track and realised that recovery had to take precedence over reform. Consequently, the twin economic targets of de-concentration and de-cartellisation became of secondary importance. According to Giersch (1994) the essential steps necessary to avoid economic collapse included 'an incentive system for channelling manpower and physical resources into the most productive activities and for converting armaments production to the best civilian ones, an opportunity to expand industrial production and to export manufacture in exchange for food in line with the comparative advantages of Western Germany and lastly, a chance, to import capital, which . . . has become relatively scarce.' US foreign policy towards Germany altered almost overnight and transformed from a policy which sought the elimination of German war potential and the termination of the dominance of a few powerful entrepreneurs to one which pursued the restoration of a sound and democratic economy and was to be characterised by competition and fostering economic and political democracy (Diegmann,1993).

The heavy degree of cartellisation within German industry in the period up to 1945 cannot be underestimated, but just how deeply embedded were such ideas within German business circles and was it possible to eradicate such anti-competitive thinking and practices by injecting a pro-competition ethos? This was one of the core issues confronting the western Allies after May 1945. In retrospect, the American military administration adopted a tougher approach towards cartels and de-concentration than either France or the United Kingdom (which both had broadly similar decrees) in their zones of occupation. According to Harding and Joshua (2003) the US pro-actively pursued cartels and brought an end to over 1,000 cartel agreements in one year. The French approach did not prohibit cartels outright, but instead preferred to undertake an examination of any anti-competitive effect which arose from agreements, while the decartellisation agenda was never seriously pursued in the British zone although evidence reveals that the *Vereinigte Stakhlwerke* (United Steelworks) was broken up and reorganised. Strangely, industry really operated in much the same way as it had done before the war as cartels became a feature of Allied administration and allocated raw materials and established markets.

It should be noted in passing that the Soviet Union adopted a rather unique approach and opted physically to dismantle much of the existing and undamaged German industrial plants and shipped them back to the USSR for reconstruction as a means of reparations. Yet, the US found another and more persuasive means to advance its competition policy agenda which took the form of financial aid through its Marshall Plan (or European Recovery Programme) which served as the turning point in German recovery. In short, the US released considerable funds to western European states, but only where states were prepared to formulate an economic programme based on the free market economy. Anti-trust policy formed part of this mix and US officials were eager to disseminate their knowledge and expertise and encouraged an open discourse and facilitated training sessions with their counterparts in both France and West Germany.

For example, shortly after the creation of the Federal Republic of Germany (FRG) a group of academic experts and officials from several of the new West German ministries travelled to the US to learn more about the practices and operations of American antitrust. The training involved, for example, lectures from staff from the Fair Trade Commission and included a meeting with Heinrich Kronstein, an eminent law professor who had already established close links to a number of senior German academics, who in turn became hugely influential within the emerging European integration process and included, for example, both Walter Hallstein and Herman Moseler.[4] All three men were heavily involved in the discussion of competition policy and instrumental in its development within the FRG. In 1952 the Americans arranged a similar visit for French officials. Such discussions were to prove pivotal in shaping mindsets following the publication of the Schuman Plan in May 1950.

2. THE SCHUMAN PLAN OF 1950

The Schuman Plan marks a decisive moment in modern European history and politics and effectively launched the process of what is now known as European integration. This Plan sought the creation of a common market in coal, iron and steel, but the uniqueness of this project lay in the pooling of sovereignty over these economic sectors to a new supranational institution known as the High Authority. The seeds of the world's first supranational competition regime were contained in the negotiations which stemmed directly from the Schuman Plan and came to form a core aspect of the ECSC treaty, but how, why and when they did require some elaboration.

Coal and steel may not have seemed the most obvious choices to pursue integration but they were symbolically important as the means to make weapons of war. They were deliberately selected as an attempt to 'solve' the Ruhr question. The Ruhr region (and the ongoing sensitivities of *Ruhrpolitik*) had served as the industrial heartland of Germany. In the immediate post-war period responsibility for this area had been taken from Germany and placed under international control (International Ruhr Authority). This step had been devised as a purely temporary solution, and by the end of the 1940s both the Americans and the British were ready to hand control of this region back to the new West German government. Both states realised that the Ruhr was essential to Germany's longer term prosperity, but this recognition faced the French government with a dilemma.[5] France had ideally wanted to separate the Ruhr from Germany (Gillingham, 2006: 40) altogether and feared that the industries of any reinvigorated Ruhr area within Germany might again challenge French competitors. There was little Paris could do, and to avoid the potential dangers of a resurgent German coal and steel industry an alternative approach arose to tackle the issue of a German revival in the traditional war sectors and to keep the French with a degree of control over both sectors. It was housed in the Schuman Plan of 1950 amid notions of reconciliation and rapprochement between the two states.

The Schuman plan was actually the brainchild of Jean Monnet, a French-born civil servant who had devoted much of his life's work to fostering better transatlantic trading relations and had been charged with rebuilding the French economy after 1945. The latter remained one of his main priorities, but another was reconciliation with Germany. His American contacts which had been built up during the interwar years now gave him direct access to the American government, and his influence over developments cannot be underestimated in the period from 1945 to the announcement of the Schuman Plan on 9 May 1950. He sought a new means of anchoring peace and stability while maintaining French interests.

Monnet had been dismissive of both the Organisation of European Economic Cooperation (OEEC) and the Council of Europe's chances for success at boosting European harmony and real closer integration, given the various national interests at play. The OEEC had been established in 1948 initially to co-ordinate the allocation of Marshall Aid to Western Europe and to assist in the rebuilding of the western part of the continent. Although discussions of a customs union did take place at this point in time there was little political will for any form of supranational integration process and the nation states preferred to maintain a conference of sovereign states. This same mentality ensured that the Council of Europe, which was also constructed on an intergovernmental basis, was not the best vehicle for many European minded individuals to push closer European co-operation. Indeed, initial suggestions of a European legislative assembly to which some sovereign powers were to be transferred were quickly dropped. It had been the opposition primarily from the UK that effectively blocked any such possibility and the outcome of the meeting in The Hague in May 1948 disappointed many federalists. The Council became a forum for member state governments to exchange ideas and develop common approaches. Although the Council came to pioneer the issue of human rights it never really sought to involve itself with economic and industrial issues, with some exceptions. Indeed, one of its very first projects was a proposal to establish a European convention on the control of cartels (Council of Europe, 1951). This draft (March 1951) offered an ingenious, ambitious and new design of supranational regulation (Harding and Joshua, 2003: 93) in the form of a commission to receive complaints about cartel activity and to undertake investigations and negotiate settlements. The draft document even proposed the establishment of a European level court. Strong member state resistance and antagonism rendered the plans redundant and mirrored the difficulties being experienced on the wider international front at trying to reach agreement on transnational competition rules (see chapter 8).

Monnet combined his priorities for economic co-operation, French interests, better relations with Germany and recognising the American desires for closer European integration within his alternative of inter-state relationships. Monnet devised a plan which centred on the creation of a common market for iron, steel and coal in Western Europe by removing customs duties, tariffs and quotas. The project was innovative in itself at the time as no other attempt had been made at pursuing sectoral integration. Interestingly it seems that the firms in the different states had come to specialise in different types of steel (Adler, 1969). To today's readers these economic sectors may seem somewhat uninspiring and even dull, but the plan was a truly revolutionary proposal. There were fewer areas of pure symbolism and few as well suited to promote co-operation than coal, steel and iron. These had served as main ingredients of the German armaments industry, and the plan to internationalise these markets was an attempt to secure peace. The innovative nature and uniqueness of this plan centred on the pooling of the coal and steel industries of France and West Germany under a supranational joint High Authority. Monnet presented his idea to the French foreign minister, Robert Schuman, who seized the initiative, took it forward and announced what has become known as the Schuman Declaration on 9 May 1950. Although the Schuman Plan did not say anything specifically about cartel regulation (Wells, 2001: 163), Monnet was careful to point out to the national delegations that the project envisaged the elimination of cartel practices. The announcement was 'bold, simple, imaginative and disarming'. It should be noted that the UK was kept very much in the dark about these developments until after the French and West German governments had effectively agreed the moves in a deliberate effort to prevent any attempt by the UK to dilute this new European project. The UK Labour government of Clement Attlee opted not to participate in the venture.[6]

The project itself was as much about politics as it was about economics, and a reading of the short one-page document illustrates Monnet's drive to secure a rapprochement between France and Germany and was 'designed to end an ancient rivalry, prevent war and build a better world' (Gillingham, 1991: 231). It had originally been conceived as a bilateral treaty between France and the new West German state using the tools of co-operation and integration (Gillingham, 1991: 170), but was opened to other states and attracted the interest of Belgium, Italy, Luxembourg and the Netherlands. The addition of other states was welcomed but promised to make the negotiations which began in June 1950 more cumbersome. Negotiations on the text of the ECSC as a means to making war economically impossible and politically unthinkable (Monnet, 1978) proved both difficult and intense (for an excellent account see Gillingham, 1991: 228–98).

The proposal was not particularly generous to the Germans and did not say anything about ending the occupation of the Ruhr, but promised equality of treatment. The entire period from the announcement of the plan to the final agreement some eleven months later (and eight months longer than Monnet had originally deemed necessary) is marked by rivalry and disagreements between the French (and their American supporters) on the one side and the new West German government on the other. From the French perspective the main driving force was to deal with the Ruhr question and prevent the German *Konzerne* or cartels in the Ruhr region from regaining total control again and determining output, finding markets for lower grade French coal as France has substantially expanded its steel sector after 1945. The French were to be persistent advocates of a strong de-cartellisation agenda for West Germany.

From the West German perspective such French insistence could have been interpreted as simple protectionism (Willis, 1968). Indeed, Ludwig Erhard, who served as West Germany's Economics Minister from 1949 to 1963 told Monnet, 'We don't understand why the Allies insist on decartelising the industries of the Ruhr . . . it's as if you were deliberately trying to put German industry in an inferior competitive position vis-à-vis its partners' (Monnet, 1978: 351). What particularly incensed the German representatives was the emphasis of the anti-trust measures on West Germany and not on France. Whereas the Germans were prepared to strike a deal as a means of being welcomed into the western fold again they were not prepared to do so at any price and spent time trying to water down Monnet's original blueprint to reduce the powers of the High Authority and to prevent a stringent de-cartellisation drive.

It is possible to identify a Franco-American alliance in the negotiations leading up to the ECSC. The ideal solution for the French government encompassed two preferences: The first pushed the case for adoption of a de-cartellisation agenda for West German industry while the second opted for the creation of some form of international control of the Ruhr region. Both issues aroused both frustration and anger among the West German government and the steel and coal industry and were particularly sensitive. As the negotiations commenced the Korean War broke out in June 1950 and possessed all the potential to destroy any efforts at forging closer co-operation as defence rose rapidly up the political agenda and raised the particularly thorny issue of German rearmament. Monnet rushed to produce the ambitious (and unsuccessful) Pleven Plan which envisaged the forming of a European army that included a German contingent under supranational control.[7] The negotiations surrounding the ECSC must be understood against the backdrop of the wider international context and policy developments, and in this case the need to stabilise Western Europe economically and politically.

Konrad Adenauer, the West German chancellor, had welcomed the Schuman Plan enthusicastically and accepted Monnet's leadership, but had sufficient guile to realise that the political climate was changing in West Germany's favour and the longer the negotiations lasted the more they would benefit the FRG. For these reasons Adenauer was even prepared to give Monnet the right to approve of the key members of the German delegation. Indeed, Monnet rejected the first two West German government's nominations and settled on a largely unknown Frankfurt law professor, Walter Hallstein. Adenauer's own domestic difficulties should not be underestimated, but he managed to maintain control throughout over other leading German politicians and elite business groups who, like himself, all wanted an end of the occupation period and a return to normal business conditions and were sceptical of the anti-trust agenda.

Battle lines very quickly became apparent between the French and West German representatives. The Benelux delegations, and especially those from Belgium and Luxembourg, were broadly supportive of the integrationist ambitions of the treaty, though they did have some reservations about the anti-trust provisions (Buch-Hansen, 2008: 93). Monnet was the most senior French delegate and advocated a much more *dirigiste* direction from the start which clashed with Erhard's more free market emphasis. The latter was strongly influenced by the Ordo-liberal school, and they in turn had been influenced by Hayek's belief in open and competitive markets. The German representatives recognised the need to regulate cartel activity rather than to be a forum to look after sectoral business interests in the pending discussions. In order to secure successful completion and to avoid any unnecessary and undesirable outcome Adenauer took a personal interest in developments. Monnet's original *document de travail* (blueprint) was full of inadequacies (Gillingham, 1991: 239) and particularly with regard to the powers of the High Authority, which were watered down as the German government sought a much less intrusive institution with much more limited competences.

The French delegation was backed to an extent by the US administration and, ultimately, the newly installed West German government had little option but to accept the Franco-American drift towards decartellisation which was contained within the treaty. Indeed, Adenauer had written to Monnet with the intention of having a treaty text by the summer recess in July 1950. This reality should not mask the negotiations, arguments, mistrust and resentment that coloured every step of the way. It is certainly easy to miss these, and even Monnet devotes scant attention to the debates in his memoirs, but disagreements raged prior to the treaty being accepted. Difficulties persisted throughout and often centred on the competition provisions for the coal and steel industries and the two specific articles on competition threatened to derail the entire process and held up progress.

One of the main problems during the negotiations phase centred on France's determination to ensure that the old pre-war concentrations in the coal and steel industries in the Ruhr did not simply re-materialise, as indeed looked to be the case. The revival of the *Konzerne* or cartels threatened to destabilise any equilibrium as it would enable the coal and steel magnates to acquire their former commanding positions and usher in uncertainty. The United States too showed a distinct sensitivity and had sought to address this issue by insisting that the German Coal Sellers Association (*Deutscher Kohlenverkauf* or DKV) should lose its monopoly and arguing that the steel industries should no longer be allowed to own coalmines.

Opposition also existed among the coal and steel producers throughout the ECSC6 towards the *dirigiste* nature (read bureaucratic interference) of the treaty and towards the idea that they might be prevented by the new political institutions from undertaking a certain course of action. Steel industries across all six states were generally opposed to the anti-cartel provisions and much preferred a situation where they themselves could determine the market structure. The West German steel industry lobbied its government to oppose the anti-cartel aspects of the emerging treaty, and in France the very nature of the anti-trust agenda grew ever more contentious, especially the uncertainty that surrounded surrendering control to supranational institutions. It is generally assumed that the ECSC Treaty would have found more ready acceptance if the anti-trust rules had not been included at all (Ehrmann, 1954: 460). The French government was prepared to accept supranational control of the coal and steel sectors, which were deemed to be economic areas in France's development, as a means of maintaining a degree of power and control over German production.

Monnet was fully aware of such feelings and misapprehension, but these interest groups were not formally part of the negotiations. Indeed, Monnet even refused to consult with French steel interests. However, he did seek to garner support from other key sectors of the French economy, and especially the newly nationalised French coal and railway industries which proved instrumental in advancing his case. In Italy too, varying degrees of opposition from the steel companies (Assider and Ita) over the anti-trust provisions was also in evidence, and centred primarily on fears that the European rules would make the much needed concentration harder and led to an alliance of the coal and steel companies in an effort to resist moves to supranational *dirigiste* control. The opposition received their opportunity to give vent to their frustrations surrounding the treaty during the ratification process. France's *Chambre Syndicale de la Sidérurgie française* (national steel association) led an assortment of associations (from metal unions to small and medium sized concerns and even the main employers' union (*Conseil National du Patronat Français*) against the treaty. This opposition reflected the instability within the steel sector and the realisation of the actors involved that some form of restructuring through greater concentration or even through cartel type activities was going to be necessary to safeguard their economic viability.

Alongside these industry concerns degrees of scepticism and hostility towards the Schuman Plan also prevailed in the political arena. In West Germany the newly re-established Social Democratic Party ((SPD) and the main opposition to the Christian Democratic Union (CDU) led government voiced its concerns about the entire European integration process and opposed the treaty. Opposition also existed within sections of the Free Democratic Party (FDP or the Liberals), though they would actually endorse the treaty, while in France opposition to the ECSC project came from both extreme wings of political life (Haas, 1958). Opposition also found expression in Italy and the Benelux states.

In short, mistrust and hostility abounded on all sides. By 1950 German industrialists thought that enough had already been done and many sections of the Ruhr industries regarded the de-cartellisation as the last whiffs of the Morgenthau agenda. For many the seemingly anti-German direction and discriminatory demands were hard to reconcile with the new climate of fairness and peace and fuelled a German desire on several occasions to walk away from the talks. Erhard thought that some of the measures such as those which sought to limit production were absurd, and even though these limits were subsequently raised following the outbreak of the Korean War, they were still derided as being not only too low but a serious obstacle to future German expansion. Agreement on the text remained elusive, and by the start of December 1950 little concrete agreement had been reached. Adenauer had even suggested to Monnet that the West German government had considered the option of a partial nationalisation of the coal and steel industries. At this stage Monnet opted to place the fate of the Schuman Plan in the hands of the Americans by bringing them on board as an informal actor in the discussions. The French and the US governments remained firmly committed to de-cartellisation and especially in West Germany.

Even in the US doubts were expressed about the overall direction of the project, and concerns were voiced in some quarters about the objectives of the Schuman Plan, and even led the Secretary of State, Dean Acheson, to wonder whether the ECSC was an ingenious attempt to reinvent a European cartel (mirroring the form of the 1926 International Steel Cartel) masquerading under Schuman's cleverly articulated diplomatic language (Wigger, 2008). In a serious effort to dispel such notions Monnet sought support in drafting the competition rules from an American diplomat, Robert Bowie, who was serving as General Counsel to the US High Commissioner for Germany, John McCloy, who in turn was a close associate of Monnet. Bowie himself was a competition law specialist and Harvard professor, and applied his knowledge of the workings of the US system which he sought to extend to the ECSC. American coal and steel business interests were generally in favour of the ECSC plan as a means of safeguarding competition and fighting cartels and were well briefed about developments and were not unknown to try to influence debates if such debates seemed to be heading towards a more cartel tolerant position (Berghahn, 1986: 134).[8] Ongoing discussions on competition policy between the French delegation and the Americans were conducted also on an informal basis (see Leucht, 2008) as a means to provide advice and guidance.

However, Bowie effectively helped to draft the early versions of the ECSC competition provisions (in what became Articles 65 and 66; see Ball, 1973: 88; Bowie, 1989; Monnet, 1978: 352–3) although his text was reworked and worked into a more 'European idiom' by Maurice Lagrange (Gerber, 1998: 336–9) who was a member of the French *Conseil d'Etat* and later became one of the first Advocates General to the Court of Justice. It is important to stress that US influence was directly felt in the shaping of the ECSC's anti-trust provisions (Schulze and Hoeren, 2000), although the US authorities were keen to ensure that this US involvement was concealed as much as possible. The Americans were in reality much more than just casual 'advisers' and kept close watch on proceedings and meetings. The first full draft treaty introduced by the French delegation on 9 November 1950 contained two articles (Articles 41 and 42) which specifically addressed the problem of cartels, concentrations and market dominating companies.

Article 41 declared cartels invalid and, according to George Ball in a memorandum to Monnet (Ball, 1973), stated that this specific article was designed 'to prevent the fixing of prices, the control of production and the division of market by agreements'. The draft was in turn passed to Hallstein who endorsed the logic of the competition provisions, as did the US representatives at the Schuman Plan conference. Still, it was not too difficult to distil the different mindsets at work. Hallstein argued, 'free competition – I venture to say this with assurance – is indeed the economic core of the Schuman Plan. You should not compare its rules with American rules; it may contain too many governmental competences. But measured by European rules such as have prevailed up to now, it contains a drastic reduction of governmental competences' (Leucht, 2008). As negotiations intensified Adenauer even threatened to pull the German delegation out of the negotiations unless certain anti-trust measures contained in Law 27 were removed. Principally, this piece of Allied legislation was intended to break up the six leading steel companies, to ensure a break between the vertical integration of the coal and steel industries and, if enacted, would create some fifty new companies. Some twenty-seven would be steel companies and eleven would be allowed to run only coal mines. The German government was incensed and presented an alternative programme but to no avail, and the 'bashing of the Ruhr' (Gillingham, 2006: 71) commenced. The German delegation, for example, had sought to protect the DKV by suggesting in vain in the face of outright hostility from Paris that the company could have been administered by the High Authority. Hallstein responded to such French intransigence by bringing to an end the bilateral coal discussions. Bowie's negotiations with the West German representatives over Law 27 got bogged down in disagreements between the various parties over such issues as the calculation of total coal consumption, while the latter kept seeking to revisit the negotiations on Articles 60 and 61 in mid February 1951.

It was to be in the Ruhr area where most of the anti-trust measures would be most keenly felt, and although Adenauer had the backing of these companies to resist he was ultimately powerless. In the end the Americans had simply threatened to introduce their own anti-trust measures unless the German government co-operated. In one sense the Schuman Plan might have been in difficulty but, as West Germany was still subject to Allied rule and as the de-cartellisation agenda could still be implemented, the German government was simply playing for time and concessions. It was simply postponing the inevitable. There was little point in collapsing everything, especially as the Adenauer government wanted to see the restoration of full sovereignty to West Germany and the end of Allied controls. In reality, there was no other way forward. In any case Monnet had sent a letter to Hallstein basically saying that if the Germans did not sign the treaty then the Schuman plan and all notions of supranationalism in European sectors would be dead (quoted in Gillingham, 1991: 276).

Further pressure was brought to bear on Adenauer when the Americans under McCloy intervened and dictated the terms of the settlement under Law 27. This option proved rather straightforward, as the Germans delegation had conceded many of the main points already and had agreed to anti-trust provisions being in the treaty. Moreover, it had accepted the limitation of the coal–steel tie and the dissolution of the giant steel *Konzerne*. The West German government was ready to accept the anti-cartel provisions because they created a level playing field among the ECSC6 and meant the end of the Allied de-cartellisation laws. Of course, this is not to deny the tensions and the difficulties that had arisen over specific definitions.

McCloy argued that there was much political capital riding on the successful completion of the Schuman Plan, and that failure would impact on the ongoing European Defence Community (EDC) discussions (see Dinan, 2006) and the whole movement of Western integration. He even hinted that in the absence of any agreement the Americans might seek an 'Austrian' style solution (that is a neutralised state under four power occupation) as a model for the immediate future of Germany.

It may have taken some four months of bitter wrangling to settle the difficulties on the competition policy front, but Adenauer finally approved the Allied position on de-cartellisation on 14 March 1951 and the Paris conference came to an end on 20 March 1951. The treaty was signed on 18 April 1951 by the six foreign ministers. Agreement ensured that the DKV was to be dismantled by 1 October 1952 and to be replaced by twenty-seven steel companies which were no larger than any others among the 'Six' and allowed only eleven steel companies to maintain control of two coal mines. The ECSC Treaty was duly ratified by the six founding member states with degrees of relative ease. The parliamentary votes were closest in France and West Germany. In the former 376 deputies within the French National Assembly voted in favour (with 240 against), while 232 members of the German *Bundestag* approved the treaty (against 143 votes). In the other four states the outcome was far more decisively in favour. The Italian Chamber of Deputies, for example, voted 275 to ninety-eight votes in support of the ECSC Treaty, while the Benelux states gave almost unanimous endorsement to the plan (Haas, 1958: 134–51). Judging exactly why this treaty proved attractive leads us to consider a number of factors, but two are certainly worthy of greater research elsewhere. The first centres on the overwhelming support from the Christian Democratic parties in all six states and the second concerns the role (direct and indirect) played by the United States and how far it was a major 'federator' (Berghahn, 1986: 132). The UK government had declined participation in 1950 and observed developments as the 'Six' established the European Coal and Steel Community which came into effect in June 1952 (Gillingham, 1991: 293) and was scheduled to last for fifty years.[9] The 'Six' had effectively created a new legal entity with status in international law and attention now turns to what this treaty meant for cartels.

3. THE TREATY OF PARIS, 1951 AND THE FIRST STEPS TOWARDS SUPRANATIONAL CARTEL REGULATION

The most striking and revolutionary aspect of the ECSC Treaty lay with the institutional structure, and especially the role and powers conferred on the principal agent, the High Authority. The High Authority was conceived as a supranational institution and represented the exclusive source of executive power. The High Authority comprised nine members who were to be completely independent from the national states.[10] This body became the sole vehicle for taking policy decisions which, on the anti-trust front, were binding on the member states in relation to agreements between undertakings, restrictive practices (including cartels) and to control concentration. It also was equipped with the ability to impose fines. The treaty also established the Council of Ministers as a forum for the member state governments to have an input into the system, a Common Assembly to inject a form of democratic credentials into the institutional machinery and a Court of Justice to resolve any disputes between the member states and the ECSC institutions.[11] Jean Monnet was appointed to serve as the first president of the High Authority.

The ECSC Treaty comprised 100 articles, but from its very inception competition policy formed an integral aspect of its activity and created a competition regime (Diebold, 1959). Anti-trust exerted a strong influence throughout and surfaced in various parts of the treaty text. Article 4 explicitly identified a number of more general practices which were incompatible with the new market, such as import and export duties, measures which discriminated between producers and conditions which interfered with the purchaser's free choice of supplier; subsidies or aids granted by states and restrictive practices which tended towards the sharing or exploiting of markets.

Article 5 contained the reference to the safeguarding of competition and placed a clear obligation on the ECSC to secure normal competitive conditions. The High Authority was tasked with responsibility for carrying out its key objectives. It sought to ensure competition so long as supplies of these products were in reasonable balance. Where problems arose the High Authority was empowered to intervene directly within the market place to bring the market under control. The High Authority possessed powers to deal with restraints of trade within an individual member state and affected trade between member states. Article 58 enabled the High Authority to impose production quotas in response to crisis conditions and Article 61 allowed it to fix maximum and minimum prices if necessary.

The initial references to competition were given much greater substance in Articles 65 and 66 of the ECSC Treaty. Article 66 (see Buch-Hansen, 2008) dealt with mergers and the potential problems of concentration on these economic sectors, and paragraph 7 dealt with the problem of an undertaking, private or public, which held a dominant position in the market place. Agreements between undertakings, decisions by associations of undertakings, and concerted practices were prohibited if they tended directly or indirectly to prevent, restrict or distort 'normal' competition within the common market. Although this applied to all agreements and decisions the High Authority was particularly interested in tackling those agreements that opted to fix prices, restrict control of production, technical development or investment and sought to share markets and customers.

The now familiar format of Article 65 was both new and really revolutionary at the time, as it dealt with an issue where few member states had any experience. It also represented a mix of different traditions. On the one hand this particular article deployed a US style prohibition and penal sanctions, and as such was a clear descendant of Article 1 of the Sherman Act, which prohibits 'agreements among enterprises, all decisions of associations of enterprises, and all concerted practices which would tend, directly or indirectly, to prevent, restrict or impeded the normal operation of competition within the common market'. Paragraph 2, on the other hand, was unique and differed completely from the US model in so far as the EEC variant of anti-trust allowed for exemptions to the first paragraph. Such exceptions were subject to specific rules and these included the case of specialisation agreements where the arrangement provided for substantial improvement in production or distribution, was necessary to achieve results and was not liable to give undertakings power to determine prices or restrict production. The High Authority was empowered to exempt such agreements, but any such authorisation was intended to be of both a conditional and temporary nature only. The High Authority was also authorised to apply sanctions if agreements had not been approved under Article 65(2) and was capable of fining companies (up to 10 per cent of a company's annual turnover) for cartel activity. The ECSC cartel regime itself was constructed more on an administrative as opposed to a legal basis. The ECSC came into effect in July 1952 and has been described as a stalking horse of European integration (Martin, 2006: 135). Gerber is correct to argue that the real significance of the ECSC regime is that it served as a model and prototype for the later EEC competition regime (Gerber, 1998: 341–2).

4. THE WEST GERMAN EXPERIENCE; ECONOMIC MIRACLE AND THE ADOPTION OF CARTEL LAWS, 1949–1957

Writing in the early 1950s Franz Boehm presented a picture of Allied determination to deploy and enforce radical and consistent laws and a scenario which the new *Land* (regional) governments were ill-equipped to resist. He argued that the new competition ethos had made an impact and dissuaded many companies from engaging in restrictive arrangements. However, most authors now concede (Gerber, 1998) that these laws were not widely enforced. Paradoxically, the new West German government was intent on building an efficient cartel policy as a central element of its new economic framework. Ludwig Erhard is credited with creating the correct environment to launch the German economic miracle. His economic philosophy stemmed directly from his contacts and links with the Freiburg School of Ordo-liberalism and its ideas as advanced by individuals such as Alfred Mueller-Armack, Alexander Boehm, Wilhelm Roepke and Wilhelm Eucken (see Gerber, 1998 for a greater discussion).[12] All sought a new philosophy to secure the growth and stability of post-war Germany and engineered what they deemed to constitute a third way between Manchester 'laissez-faire' capitalism and the centrally planned economy (Peacock and Willgerodt, 1989). The aspects of social justice and individual freedom were built into Ordo-liberalism, but at the heart of the 'social market economy' lay the conviction in the competitive order, i.e. that the state was to be charged with bringing about competition through prohibition of cartels and a de-concentration policy (Eucken, 1952; Grosser, 1985). The Ordo-liberals were particularly concerned about the dangers of economic concentration and economic power, and argued that competition had to be fostered and especially to ensure the creation of many smaller firms. In short, any efforts to establish a successful economy required the adoption of a rigorous competition policy.

Erhard enthusiastically backed this economic philosophy and was ready to 'declare war against all efforts to form cartels and against those aiming at a limitation of competition of whatever kind . . . I regard all such attempts as a crime against the sanctity of life, whose inner meaning is change, movement and progress, and therefore cannot respond to the uncouth methods of planning regulation and stabilisation' (Erhard, 1957). His opposition was directed equally to all forms of industrial collusion and state planning. Attitudes towards the competition principle were far from universal and attempts to develop a West German anti-trust policy were anything but harmonious and led to repeated scuffles.

The first serious though stillborn effort at enacting West German cartel policy was contained within the Josten competition law draft of 1949, and promised a radical departure from earlier practices to contained provision for a total ban on cartels, the creation of a monopolies office and the introduction of merger control. The draft legislation sparked off disagreements between the Ordo-liberals and industrial and business groups. Erhard's preaching of the new faith of competition fell on deaf ears of large sections of the German business world and many remained wedded to the old orthodoxy. For example, vocal opposition was loudest from the German business groups which maintained that any attempt at dissolving concentrations threatened to undermine economic development and impede West Germany's ability to compete with her European rivals.

Erhard's crusade was also hampered from within the German cabinet and in particular from both the agricultural and transport ministries, and also significantly from a rather unenthusiastic Konrad Adenauer who sided in a more diplomatic fashion with his close friend, *Bundesverband Deutscher Industrie* (DBI or the German Employers' Federation) president Fritz Berg. In short, opposition to a German competition policy was formidable, and both the Josten draft and thirteen other anti-trust proposals were also unsuccessful. But eventually and after Erhard's threat to resign, American threats of imposing a competition regime and much industrial lobbing, a watered down competition law was finally agreed and passed. The outcome of the seven year cartel war (*siebenjährige Kartellschlacht*) culminated in the adoption of the *Gesetz gegen Wettbewerbsbeschränkungen* (Law against Restraints on Competition or GWB) in 1957 which came into force in 1958 (McGowan, 1993). The GWB at one stroke replaced the Allied cartel laws, and as such was widely accepted as a welcome achievement.

Judged positively the GWB's passing marked a decisive landmark in the evolution of German and European competition policy. It created the *Bundeskartellamt* (Federal Cartel office or BKartA) which was authorised to prohibit cartels, though there were grounds for possible exemption for certain forms of restraint. The business community had been successful at both delaying a German law and watering down its original and harsher provisions and omitted all mention of the problems of economic concentration and merger control. In terms of cartels the GWB laid the first real basis for a substantive anti-cartel policy. The BKartA was empowered to prohibit cartels, but the new law also provided for a number of exemptions from the competition rules on prevailing grounds of the greater public good. Certain sectors (such as agriculture, banking and finance) were exempted from its reach. This institutional arrangement differed strikingly from the truly independent standing of the Bundesbank and its role in determining monetary policy (Marsh, 1992). Yet, cartel policy emerged as one of the core pillars of the social market economy and reflected the real dawn of the competition principle in continental Europe.

The development of cartel policy in West Germany and the EEC heralded a major sea change in governments' approach to cartels after 1945. These developments in the antitrust field were replicated by the adoption of similar competition provisions across most Western European states (although there were some notable omissions such as Italy and Portugal) over the next thirty years. Isolating exactly which factors and what types of thinking reinforced such change is relatively straightforward and have been identified (Edwards, 1967) as a greater awareness of the potential problems arising from cartellisation, particularly in relation to higher prices and poorer choice products for consumers. Moreover, the existence of cartels was increasingly being viewed as an obstacle to removing barriers to international trade and forms of activity that often in practice actually discouraged greater economic efficiencies and higher productivity. Economic thinking towards cartels had changed. How much is put down to the US experience and American influence is a matter for conjecture, but there can be little doubt that there was indeed a US factor at play in the spread of the anti-trust idea in Europe after 1945, and certainly evident in the cases of the EEC, West Germany and even the UK.

Cartel policy may have been making its appearance but it was emerging at different speeds and in different forms. Outside West Germany and the EEC the antitrust policies of most other European states were more influenced and built around the outcome of an agreement rather than its conduct. In other words, most national authorities focused on controlling only those arrangements which were deemed to have harmful effects. This is where toleration crept in and where national authorities recognised that there could be economic and political advantages in cartellisation. This attitude had echoes of the situation prior to 1939, and it continued to linger with the result that some domestic competition laws (where they emerged) were blurrier and of a softer style and substance than the US version; many were more cautious and discretionary in design, and most were usually administrative in form rather than judicial (Harding and Joshua, 2003: 98).

France affords the best illustration, but even the French state was not immune to cartel policy developments elsewhere and was slowly being ushered in the direction of its own competition policy. The French economy flourished from the second half of the 1950s but had been constructed and developed on a different model from that in neighbouring West Germany. Whereas the government of the West German state was trying to create the framework to ensure a successful economy, the French approach favoured a much more interventionist stance and degree of state planning. This *dirigiste* model had been pursued under the *Commissariat Général du Plan* (Planning Board) which had been created by Monnet after 1945. It certainly favoured greater economic concentration but also overlooked cartellisation at home at any rate. On paper a government decree from 1953 (53–704) enabled the state to control prices and ensure the maintenance of free competition, but this was not pursued with any real vigour and in any case there were a multitude of exemptions (Hall, 1986). Cartels would be tolerated even if not always in the public interest, and this position did not change until the French government adopted its anti-cartel legislation in 1977. The Benelux states had also lacked any anti-trust tradition and what legislation existed, as in the form of, for example, the Economic Competition Act (*Wet economische mededeling*) of 1956 in the Netherlands was never really enforced (Goyder, 1993: 30). In time, however, cartel legislation would not only be adopted across Western Europe, but would ultimately converge on the European model. The seeds of these future developments can be traced back to the 1950s.

5. CONCLUSIONS

Efforts at reconstructing the countries of Western Europe after 1945 ran directly in parallel with steps to foster greater European integration through a myriad of new institutions. In terms of cartel policy European regional co-operation would lead to the emergence of a highly developed and sophisticated model of supranational regulation. It is important to stress that a European cartel regime was far from a foregone conclusion. Indeed, initial moves in European co-operation in the form of the Organisation for European Economic Co-operation (OEEC) and the Council of Europe were deeply disappointing for US competition policy enthusiasts. The arrival and acceptance of European anti-trust initially owes much to US influence and changing economic philosophies.

The adoption of the ECSC rules marks a quite radical departure in approach, but the impact of the ECSC's cartel policy was anything but impressive. The anti-trust rules were not widely used and the 1950s heralded a new phase of greater economic concentration in the coal and steel industries (Buch-Hansen, 2008: 98) and especially in West Germany, to the frustration of the rival French industries. Progress was not much better in relation to cartelbusting (Leucht and Seidel, 2007). The High Authority only deployed its provisions to a very limited extent (Gerber, 1998: 342).

In retrospect, coal and steel were arguably not the best sectors in which to seek integration from an economic perspective (Bebr, 1953; Martin, 2004), but the project was conceived and driven as a political vehicle and towards political ends. Monnet was the architect and driver and had little knowledge of either coal or steel (Milward, 1992). Both economic sectors were largely unsuitable and economically very different, and the integration model threatened to produce greater disequilibrium and a number of difficult problems. These involved such issues as freight costs which tended to separate markets, structure of ownership, the history of concerted practices, cases of strong governmental control and the labour intensive (Lister, 1960: 403) nature of the coal, iron and steel industries. Adjustment proved difficult and the coal industry started an almost terminal decline from the mid 1950s, while steel followed the same downward trajectory from the mid 1970s. The steel industry itself in Europe provides an apt illustration of some of the problems facing the competition regulators and became a recipient of state aids and even led to a number of crisis cartels.

Monnet had set out to solve the Ruhr problem by controlling German industrial power and protecting French interests, but ultimately the centrepiece of Monnet's grand vision produced a regulatory code which was influenced by US antitrust ideas. However, although a general consensus was emerging in Europe for some form of legal regulation after 1945 it developed differently and came initially to be built upon an administrative process of scrutiny that took account of the public interest and stood in somewhat marked contrast to the harsher US model of probation, court orders and litigation (Harding and Joshua, 2003: 86). The Schuman Plan introduced the competition principle. The ECSC may have become increasingly irrelevant as the 1950s and 1960s passed by, but it had partially solved the German problem and represents a stepping stone in the integration project which leads to later European treaties and a truly genuine system of supranational competition governance.

NOTES

1. For a fuller discussion of the Japanese system see Kenji Sanekata's chapter in Bruce G. Doern and Stephen Wilks (eds), *Comparative Competition Policy: National Institutions in a Global Market*, Oxford: Clarendon Press, 1996.
2. For a solid discussion of the economic and political condition of immediate post war West Germany see A. Grosser, *Geschichte Deutschlands seit 1945: Eine Bilanz, Deutscher Taschenbuch Verlag*, 1974 and translated into English as *Germany in Our Time* by Alfred Grosser and Paul Stephenson, Pall Mall Press, 1971.
3. The JCS 1067 Directive to the Commander in Chief of US Forces in Germany (from April 1945) laid down the basic principles guiding the American occupation of Germany and these tougher conditions and restrictions that lasted until July 1947. These included denazification measures, aimed to ensure that renewed political activity was only allowed with American permission, and sought to keep a firm grip on the reopening of educational facilities. For further information see http://germanhistorydocs.ghi-dc.org/sub_document.cfm.document_id=2297.
4. Kronstein left his mark on anti-trust thinking: see H. Kronstein and Gertrude Leighton, 'Cartel Control: A Record of Failure', 56 *Yale Law Journal* (1946), 297.
5. The French government also controlled the Saarland which Paris had annexed from Germany after the war. This smaller region which bordered France represented the other main coal and steel making region within western Germany. The French had long sought control of this area and had also annexed it after World War I before it returned to Germany after a plebiscite in 1935. The same area voted in a referendum to return to (West) Germany in 1957. Both episodes illustrate the sensitivities of these sectors.

6. This episode marked the beginnings of the UK's problematic relationship with the European integration project. The problem lay not so much in the idea of a common market, but rather in the creation of the supranational institutional structures. The UK still perceived itself as a global power. It had won the Second World War, was the leading economic power in Western Europe until the mid 1950s and still possessed on accepted and unchallenged political system which dated back to 1066. Consequently, the UK government of the late 1940s and 1950s did not feel the same attraction towards European Integration. The troubled relationship is considered in depth in Stephen George, *An Awkward Partner, Britain in the European Community*, OUP, 1998, 3rd edition. See also Oliver Daddow, *Britain and Europe since 1945: Historical perspectives on Integration*, Manchester University Press, 2004.
7. The Pleven Plan led to negotiations and Member State agreement among the ECSC6 for a European Defence Community. This project was overlooked by the British government and the treaty failed to be ratified in the French National Assembly in 1954 and was duly aborted.
8. According to Berghahn (1986: 144), 'it is certain that Washington, represented by McCloy and . . . Bowie . . . insisted more than once on a particular wording of individual articles'.
9. The ECSC Treaty expired in 2002 and the issues of coal and steel were transferred to the EC Treaty.
10. The nine members were appointed by the respective ECSC6 Member States and comprised two individuals from France, Italy and West Germany and one each from the Benelux states. These individuals were not to take instruction from their national governments. (See Nugent, 2006.)
11. The Council was established at the insistence of the Benelux States which wanted some degree of supervisory monitoring of the High Authority in case it became too powerful. The Common Assembly was established as an advisory body only and comprised delegates from the 6 national parliaments.
12. See also Franz Böhm, 'Monopoly and Competition in Western Germany' in Edward E. Chamberlain (ed.), *Monopoly and Competition and their Regulation*, Macmillan, 1954.

5. Establishing the architecture of EU cartel governance, 1958–1962

In retrospect, the place of competition policy in the history of EU integration seems a somewhat accepted fact. It is now generally recognised as one of the central columns of European governance and some authors have even identified the competition rules as the 'economic constitution of the EU' (McGowan, 1997; Wilks, 2009). Strangely, few observers could have predicted some fifty years ago the actual development and success of the EU competition governance regime, given the divergent positions on anti-trust among the original EEC member states. For that matter, few could have predicted the trajectory, evolution and expansion of the entire European integration project. For many ardent 'integrationalists' including Monnet (1978) the EEC Treaty seemed to represent a much watered down and looser form of integration which contained fewer supranational characteristics and even appeared to signal the revival of more nationally determined policy preferences. Yet, the overwhelming economics related provisions of the EEC Treaty and the drive for a single market contained the seeds of significant later policy developments from a European space with no barriers for business to one which looks after its workers' needs and from the promotion of free movement of people to justice and home affairs (Church and Phinnemore, 2002).

Competition policy played its part and was identified as one of the few policy objectives in the EEC Treaty base from the outset, and would gradually emerge as arguably the best example of a supranational policy in operation and one which displayed 'federal' characteristics.[1] The next three chapters demonstrate this change and account for the evolution of cartel policy. The first of these chapters sets out to provide an overview of the key articles which came to serve as the foundation stones for the emergence of the EU competition regime. This chapter traces the origins of the EEC Treaty's competition provisions and focuses specifically on the content and objectives of Article 81 (on restrictive practices/cartels). It explains how the Six came to reach agreement in spite of some major differences between member states on the institutional design and structures of the European competition regime. It also explains how and why agreement was reached on Regulation 17 to create the procedural mechanisms to achieve their anti-cartel policy aspirations.

1. INTRODUCTION: DEEPENING EUROPEAN INTEGRATION AT ROME

The euphoria surrounding the ECSC as a model of supranational integration proved short-lived and a severe reality check took hold once the plans for a European Defence Community (EDC) were rejected in the French National Assembly in 1954. Monnet's disappointment at the turn of events and defeat for deeper integration led to his resignation as president of the High Authority, and his spirit was not lifted by the idea of creating a general (as opposed to sector specific) customs union. The idea for the latter emerged from Belgium and the so-called Benelux memorandum which formed the launch pad for what became known as the European Economic Community. The concept attracted the interest of the Adenauer government, which welcomed such liberalisation and placed emphasis on the necessity of the inclusion of competition rules in order to establish normal market conditions. This initial support quickly led to a meeting of the Foreign Ministers of the 'Six' in Messina in May 1955 to discuss the possibility of extending the principles of the ECSC further. In the final conference resolution (Messina, 1955) the ministers pledged their support for closer integration, the creation of a common market which, amongst other things, would require rules to ensure undistorted competition and paved the way for the preparation of two ensuing treaties, one on the common market and another on an atomic energy community.

To make further progress on the common market treaty a committee of representatives from the ECSC member state governments was created under the chairmanship of Paul-Henri Spaak. Hans von der Groeben and Pierre Uri were appointed as two of Spaak's experts. Both men not only represented the West German and French governments respectively but took a particular interest in the competition clauses, and this issue found reflection in the Spaak Report.[2] Paragraph 55 provided the detailed requirements for a competition policy and duly recognised the problem of monopolists and their threat to the creation of a common market. It deemed action necessary to prevent 'a division of markets by agreement between enterprises, since this would be tantamount to re-establishing the compartmentalisation of the market; agreements to limit production or limit progress because they would run counter to progress and productivity'. The Spaak Report was accepted without any major amendments by the Foreign Ministers of the Six in May 1956. The detailed negotiations then commenced over the next ten months prior to the signature of the Treaty of Rome on 27 March 1957.

The European Economic Community Treaty (EEC) came into force on 1 January 1958 and its objectives of pursuing closer economic integration and creating a common market profoundly and positively have further transformed relations between its member states in the years ever since (Bomberg, Peterson and Stubb, 2008; Cini, 2007; Nugent, 2005) and created the EU political system (Hix, 2005). Any critical dissection of the EEC Treaty readily reveals that it is a product which reflected the priorities and sensitivities of the member states. Real differences certainly existed among the 'Six' and especially between France and West Germany over economic policy making. These differences epitomised fundamental distinct approaches (Maes, 2004) to post-war economic policy. Whereas France placed its emphasis on the sovereign state as the source of legitimacy and saw the state as the director of economic policy, the new Federal Republic of Germany stressed the advantages of decentralised power and an ardent belief in the virtues of a social market economy.[3] It is interesting to note how the economic recovery in both states in the 1950s, as represented by 'Le Plan' and the economic miracle (*Wirtschaftswunder*) respectively fitted each state's preferred model and both worked.[4] Such differences characterised the positions of both states and made the negotiations about the EEC Treaty at times quite problematic.

The German representatives had sought to create a new European economic system on the direct structure and foundations of the newly developed West German model, namely on the principles of a market economy which included a liberal trade policy and strong competition rules. Paris, on the other hand, had a preference for a much more active involvement of the state in economic matters. This major distinction coloured much of the debate. Notably the French government was particularly concerned about just how far French companies were in a position to compete directly with their German rivals within a common market. Consequently, competition policy emerged as one of the issues of conflict, but it was one which was resolved as part of the wider negotiations on European integration. Indeed, the only credible solution to the national differences necessitated substantial 'give and take' between the states and the ability to trade certain nationally based preferences off against those of others. In the end compromise was agreed. Thus, the French government was prepared to accept the German model of competition in return for West German agreement on the creation (and funding) of the French favoured European Atomic Energy Community Treaty or EURATOM which also came into force on 1 January 1958 and formed the second Treaty of Rome.[5] French concerns were also placated with the inclusion of agriculture in the EEC Treaty and, it is worth noting, this policy's specific exemption from the competition rules. Both agriculture and energy reflected strong French interests. In return the West German government ensured that the common market was constructed on the free movement of capital, goods, people and services and included a strong competition policy.

The overall 'settlement' was reflected in the original Article 2 which stated that 'the Community shall have as its task, by establishing a common market and progressively approximating the economic policies of the member States, to promote throughout the Community, a harmonious development of economic activities, a continuous and balanced expansion, an increase in stability, an accelerated raising of the standard of living and closer relations between the states belonging to it'. This article set out the main objectives, which were given greater specificity in Article 3. The original Article 3(f) sought the creation of a system ensuring that competition in the common market was not 'distorted' and formed the basis of the competition rules in the EEC Treaty.[6]

Understanding the origins of these rules and their distinct character necessitates, according to Gerber (1998), the recognition of a long European tradition in competition issues at national level. This is an interesting interpretation and challenges the almost canonical vision that the rules were largely the product of a process of Americanisation after 1945. Europeans, as discussed in chapter 3, had certainly considered and dealt with competition issues from at least the end of the nineteenth century. The original domestic legislation enacted in the German speaking states found replication to varying degrees across many states in Europe, and at the very least had enabled and initiated a debate about the purpose and characteristics of competition law. These ideas helped shape the mindsets that looked at how the European economies could be rebuilt after 1945, and especially in West Germany where a group of Ordo-liberal reformers pursued a belief in a market economy which afforded competition policy a special status as the economic constitution and also tie in notions of social justice. Although all are true, care must be taken not to diminish the power and influence of the United States. How was agreement reached on the EEC Treaty anti-trust provisions and why and how were its institutional architecture and mechanics created in the way that they were to establish supranational cartel governance?

2. NEGOTIATING THE COMPETITION RULES WITHIN THE EEC TREATY

Ultimately the EEC Treaty was to prove in time a much more successful vehicle for deepening integration than its immediate forerunner, but at the time it seemed as if the EEC was simply a lighter shade of integration than the ECSC. Pursuing a customs union free of customs duties and quotas, the removal of tariff barriers, the erection of a common external tariff and the adoption of the competition principle proved more decisive. The importance of the competition principle was clearly embedded in the treaty from the outset. According to one senior Commission official, 'It is no exaggeration to state that economically, the Rome Treaty is basically a Treaty for more competition . . . [competition] has been considered as one of the principal pillars on which our building rests' (Mussard, 1962). Yet, caution should be applied because the inclusion of these same competition provisions had been preceded by intense debate about the role, purpose and enforcement of competition policy in the common market.[7] Competition policy had not lost any of its controversy over the wording and scope of the cartel clauses, as the discussions preceding agreement on the provisions of the EEC Treaty revealed. Indeed it became more controversial once its reach was going to be extended to cover many more economic sectors.

It should be emphasised that the US was not as decisive an actor at the time of the negotiations on the EEC Treaty, though it warmly endorsed moves to include competition provisions. The two key really important protagonists in the actual anti-trust debates were once again the French and West German governments (Goyder, 2003: 23). Indeed, some observers have gone as far as to state that 'once Guy Mollet [French Prime Minister] and Adenauer had laid out the path for the rest of the negotiations, the smaller countries simply had to take what was handed down to them by the French and the Germans' (Milward, 2000: 217–8). There is a strong degree of truth in this. The French and German positions reflected their own very different ideas on government/industry relations. Whereas the French government leaned heavily towards state planning and *dirigiste* intervention, the Bonn government held firm in ordered market capitalism. The issues of competition and cartel policy proved controversial and cannot be divorced easily from geo-political considerations. Once again the United Kingdom government absented itself from all discussions over the EEC Treaty.[8]

The French and West German governments held divergent views on what exactly the objectives of competition policy should be and on the structure and powers of any European authority to apply and enforce them. Interestingly, the positions of both states had somersaulted from the stances adopted in the negotiations leading up to the ECSC. Whereas the French government had been ready earlier to call for tougher prohibitive rules on the breaking up of German coal, iron and steel companies, France was growing resistant to the extension of such a system to cover many other economic sectors. This position reflected the lack of any French tradition in competition policy, but also the French state's preferences for working in close co-operation with French industries. The West German government adopted a much more active position and its delegation included two figures who later became prominent European regulators in the form of Walther Hallstein and Hans von der Groeben and welcomed the setting up of a prohibition system where all type of co-operative agreements had to be notified to the supranational competition authority.

This vision meant the creation of an authorisation system based on *ex ante* notification and an independent competition authority to review all the notifications. The optimum position for Paris was a much looser system where a number of clearly defined abuses would be subject to legal control. The French model envisaged an *ex post* abuse system which was not built on a notification system and would apply only to the specifically defined abuses. The French government was keen to resist moves towards a fully fledged system based on law and sought a more lenient and malleable system where the national competition authorities held most power and where any supranational competition authority's powers were limited and designed to facilitate co-ordination across the EEC (Warzoulet, 2005: 66). The Guy Mollet government in Paris (1955–1957) had been much more eager to harmonise social regulations and to promote the integration of industrial policy (Scharpf, 2002: 648) than pursue a competition policy. Its position was supported by Monnet. Indeed, the French delegates voiced their opposition to the idea of a law based market economy based on stringent competition laws. In response the German delegates were not receptive to the French vision as they feared it would enable more protectionist minded states (i.e. France and Italy) to limit competition and work to the detriment of German companies.

The West German government, and especially the Economics Minister, Ludwig Erhard, strongly supported an Ordo-liberal inspired regime which had strong constitutional status, was independent and able to take decisions on its own. The German negotiators were supported by their Dutch counterparts. The West German *Bundeskartellamt* (Federal Cartel Office) or BKartA in Berlin (McGowan, 1994; Sturm, 1996) became an ideal prototype (Gerber, 1998: 343) for a flexible system which could take various issues into account when making decisions. This was important because an economic upswing required a very different type of cartel policy from a downturn. The German position was endorsed by the Benelux states and left France with Italy to mount a degree of opposition to the others. After prolonged debate and numerous drafts the final text reflected the German approach which centred on an *ex ante* notification scheme with the possibility of exemption.

Free trade may have been the target, but it could be only partially realised with the lifting of customs duties and the removal of quotas. In themselves both could not guarantee success or the creation of a competitive market. Logic may argue that as companies face greater competition the least inefficient will have to adapt or die as well as reorganise and innovate to enable greater specialisation and efficiency. This may be true, but were companies going to respect the new-found belief in the powers of competition or would inefficient and equally efficient companies seek means to resist and thwart any competition? According to Hallstein, 'besides the best known economic and social advantages, an economic order based on competition has the decisive political advantage that it guarantees personal freedom to an extent not attainable in any other economic order' (Hallstein, 1962: 8). In other words in a free enterprise economy competition is deemed to epitomise the best guarantee of personal freedom, but it depends on the willingness of business to compete. This assumption cannot be taken for granted, as some firms will resist the competitive process and seek to engage in cartellisation. Competitive markets cannot be assumed to occur and require regulation.

The inclusion of competition rules within the EEC Treaty was a demand which had originated within the West German delegation at the Messina negotiations. The influence of Ordo-liberalism found voice in both Hallstein and von der Groeben. Both figures were actively supported by Ludwig Erhard and both were highly instrumental in shaping the EEC competition regime and steering its direction until the late 1960s. The French delegation was spearheaded by Pierre Uri (Ramirez, 2007: 3) and its discussions on competition policy were influenced by a variety of facts which included the ECSC rules, the French (and failed) attempts at introducing an anti-cartel law in 1949 and the lengthy struggles in Germany to enact a national competition policy in 1957. It is important to stress that outside West Germany and France none of the other four ECSC member states represented at Messina had any great interest in competition, and thus the subsequent discussions involved Bonn and Paris.

Another interesting aspect of the negotiations, and one which stands in sharp contrast to the ECSC experience, was the very limited involvement of business concerns in either trying to influence national government positions or actively running any campaign to attack the anti-trust elements of the EEC Treaty. This somewhat surprising reality finds explanation in three factors (McLachlan and Swann, 1967: 82). Firstly, the ardent opposition to the ECSC provisions had reflected the propensity of the coal and steel industries to engage in cartellisation, but this same hostility did not seem to extend to other business sectors. This may have been the case because, secondly, business had had time by this stage to observe the High Authority in action and, as the regulator had never really enforced the anti-trust rules, business had come to the conclusion that the extension of similar anti-trust rules to other economic sectors would simply follow the same pattern. Finally, the actual wording of the competition chapter was rather vague, seemed relatively harmless and completely excluded any reference to European merger control. Few at this point in time could have predicted a different trajectory and the emergence of a puissant European cartel regime!

The competition rules as established in the EEC Treaty covered four main areas; restrictive practices including cartels (Article 85, and now 81); abusive monopolies (Article 86, and now 82), state aids (Articles 92–94, and now 87–89) and an aspiration to open publicly owned monopolies to greater competition (Article 90, and now 86). All developed over time. Merger control was deliberately omitted from the EEC provisions and would not fall under Directorate General IV's (DG for competition) remit until 1990 (Büthe and Swank, 2007; Cini and McGowan, 2008; Buch-Hansen, 2008).

The focus of DGIV's activity came to centre on restrictive practices, and this area, given its complexity and often lengthy investigative processes, was to consume most of the competition directorate's resources and time. DGIV developed expertise in this core area and gradually emerged as one of the most highly competent and focused parts of the entire Commission. Cartel policy, although not immediately appreciated, came to encompass a fascinating study of supranational regulation and represent an apt narrative of the pulls and logic of the European integration process as DGIV came to deploy ever more skilful and innovative methods in its ongoing cartel wars. These are examined in chapters 6 and 7. The outcome of Article 81 deliberations in the end lay closer to the German Ordo-liberal position than the French one, but did not entirely reflect such values. All the articles were rather vague in design, and for some commentators it was 'difficult to see exactly what the objectives of competition policy were for those who drafted the Treaty of Rome' (Motta, 2004: 14). The vague language of the articles reflected the differing standpoints of the authors and in effect left the detailed rules to be established later. As such the articles did not quite embrace Ordo-liberalism in their entirety because there was not any mention of merger control, monopolies were subject to scrutiny only if they were deemed to have abused their position and restrictive agreements could be exempted. Some commentators suggest that these articles look remarkably similar to the French model (Buch-Hansen, 2008: 102). Again there is an element of truth here and many observers were looking to see just how these articles were going to be implemented and enforced. Article 81 reflected an emerging European model of legal control which was based on an administrative procedure of evaluation of cartels. But would the anti-cartel measures be enforced? Much depended on the institutional structure that was created. This chapter now turns to Article 81 which has formed the backbone of EC competition policy. It begins by introducing the structure and personalities at the helm of the European regime before providing the necessary background on the legal base and the accompanying regulations which ushered in this puissant anti-cartel regime.

3. THE EUROPEAN COMPETITION REGULATOR

The very first European Commission took office in January 1958. It comprised two distinct wings: a political executive wing and the much larger administrative wing. The former comprised the nine European commissioners (two each from France, Italy and West Germany and one each from Belgium, Luxembourg and the Netherlands) and their cabinets (or private offices). Each Commissioner was handed responsibility for a specific policy area which fell within the Commission's competences under the EEC Treaty. The treaty cast the Commission in the role of policy initiator and not as the decision taker, as the High Authority had been under the ECSC Treaty. Under the Rome disposition power was to reside with the Council of Ministers which responded to Commission proposals and consulted the Assembly (European Parliament).[9] The division of responsibilities within the Commission to a large degree reflected both the size and economic power of the member state and its particular policy preferences which they hoped to develop, shape and defend where necessary. This initial style of sharing and carving up policy portfolios has often given ammunition to critics that the European integration project has largely been driven by a Franco-German hegemony. There is an element of truth here. The very first president of the EAEC was the Frenchman, Louis Armand, while the first president of the Commission of the EEC was the German Walter Hallstein. The 'sharing' of the services followed a similar pattern as member states sought to maintain a strong voice in certain areas. The West German delegation took charge of the competition policy portfolio under Hans von der Groeben and also external trade issues,

Table 5.1 The First College of Commissioners

Policy Portfolio	Commissioner	Director-General
President	Walter Hallstein (D)	Emile Noel (F)
Economic/Financial Affairs	Robert Marjolin (F)	Franco Bobba (I)
Competition	Hans Von der Groeben (D)	Verloren van Themaat (NL)
Internal Market	Pierro Malvestiti (I)	François-Xavier Ortoli (F)
Agriculture	Sicco Mansholt (NL)	Jacques Rabot (F)
Overseas Countries	Robert Lemaignen (F)	Eric Allardt (D)
External Affairs	Jean Rey (Bel)	Guenther Seeliger (D)
Social Affairs	Giuseppi Petrilli (I)	Jean De Muyinck (Bel)
Transport	Michel Rasquin (Lux)	Mario Renzetti (I)

while the French took the lead in macro-economic policy and agriculture (see table 5.1).

The Commission's first directorate general to handle competition policy was established in 1960. It is interesting to note that the original DGIV was handed responsibility for four sectors. In retrospect, two of these, namely restrictive practices and monopoly policy and state aid policy, were not so surprising, but it also possessed authority for another two areas, namely taxation and the approximation of laws.

The relationship between the Commissioner and DG Competition has not always been so easy to fathom. On the one hand, the Commissioner and the cabinet may be viewed as the political-executive arm of the DG, introducing a novel dimension into the legal-economic investigations of the competition officials. On the other hand, the Commissioner and cabinet are more akin to a political cap, directing and controlling the work of the DG from the top of the hierarchy. However, executive and administrative functions can rarely be so easily separated. It would certainly be naïve to imagine that political/ideological questions do not enter into the decision making of the DG. Likewise, although the Commissioner is clearly subject to external political (national, sectional and ideological) pressures, the need to ensure legal certainty, consistency and respect for the rules remains crucial at this stage in the decision making process. The provisions of the EEC Treaty followed the conclusions of the Spaak Report and also created two other bodies to assist and work with the Commission in the competition policy arena. These were, firstly, a consultative committee (to allow a member state input) and the European Court of Justice (a specialised chamber of lawyers to review Commission decisions).

4. UNPACKING ARTICLE 81

The drafters of the EEC rules were all too aware of differing approaches (or even the complete lack of any domestic competition legislation in Italy, Luxembourg and Belgium) between the states and sought in the first instance to agree to a set of common goals that could be subsequently fleshed out. France's competition provisions at this time were skewed heavily towards vertical agreements and preventing refusals to deal, while the Netherlands had only a fledgling Economic Competition Act which required registration of restrictive practices but granted exemptions on a liberal basis. Only West Germany had anything comparable to a comprehensive competition regime in place, which incidentally came into force on the same day as the EEC rules on 1 January 1958. German preferences and debates had influenced and shaped, to a large extent though not completely, the European rules and would continue to do so. It is interesting to speculate whether there would have been any competition rules at all in the EEC Treaty if the West German delegation had not insisted upon it or at best a much vaguer system.

Framed in very general terms Article 81 TEC (formerly Article 85 EEC) comprised three paragraphs and sets out to cover both those anti-competitive agreements between direct competitors (horizontal restraints), and those agreements between firms involved in different stages of the production/distribution/marketing process within a particular market (vertical restraints). The central question which arose for the regulator centred on whether or not a particular agreement had been designed to prevent, restrict or distort competition. The first paragraph of Article 81 established the type and characteristics of anti-competitive activities which were not permissible, and to this end prohibited agreements which affected trade between states, especially where such agreements aimed to effect the prevention, restriction or distortion of competition within the common (or single) market. The article declared that certain agreements were simply incompatible with the common market, and these included: those agreements that directly or indirectly fixed purchase or selling prices or any other trading conditions; those agreements that limited or controlled production, markets, technical development or investment; those agreements that shared out markets or sources of supply; those agreements that applied dissimilar conditions to equivalent transactions with other trading parties, thereby placing them at a competitive disadvantage; and those agreements that made the conclusion of contracts subject to acceptance by the other parties of supplementary obligations which by their nature or according to commercial usage, had no connection with the subject of such contracts.

Article 81(1) was ambitious in its scope and applied to both concerted practices which were agreed informally, where little documentary evidence existed to establish collusion, and to well-documented cases of concerted parallelism.

The second paragraph (Article 81(2)) declared that agreements or decisions that ran counter to Article 81(1) were prohibited and automatically void. At first sight this looked very much like the system of *per se* rule which has operated in the US anti-trust context and particularly since the 1960s, and where basically all named anti-competitive agreements were categorised as illegal, with no exceptions to the rule. This reflected the US regime's aversion to the concentration of economic power. Arguments in favour of the introduction of a US-style rule of reason approach had certainly existed within European anti-trust circles. The principle of prohibition reflected the US approach and the Ordo-liberal position but, it should be stressed, was very much a new and at times alien concept for many European states which had taken a more lenient position towards cartellisation in the past. By forming hard core cartel agreements the firms involved were deliberately attempting to keep their agreements as secret as possible and away from the attention of the Commission. Yet in reality EEC policy was not as strict as the US approach because this seemingly *per se* prohibition of cartels and restrictive practices under Article 81(1) was accompanied by an exemption clause, the third paragraph of Article 81.

Article 81(3) declared that Article 81(1) may be inapplicable where an agreement 'contributes to improving the production or distribution of goods or [promotes] technical or economic progress, whilst allowing consumers a fair share of the resulting benefit, and which does not (a) impose on the undertakings concerned restrictions which are not indispensable to the attainment of these objectives; [or] (b) afford such undertakings the possibility of eliminating competition in respect of a substantial part of the products in question'. Thus, four conditions were laid down if an agreement were to be granted: the agreement had to benefit the EU as a whole and its advantages had to outweigh its disadvantages; it had to produce a fair share of the benefits to consumers; any restriction to competition had to be indispensable in order to attain the objectives sought; and there had to be no substantial elimination of competition (Sufrin and Jones, 2004). In many ways contrasting the prohibitive rule in Article 81(1) against the exemption clauses in Article 81(3) demonstrates aptly the flexibility of the EU's cartel provisions. Indeed, Article 81 introduced a complex balancing process.

To ensure that the competition logic transpired into more than just rhetoric it was no coincidence that the German government selected a pro-competition individual to take responsibility for the competition policy brief. The selection of Hans von der Groeben as the first EU Competition Commissioner was a skilful move, given his background and experience, and in part also reflected the 'carving up' of the Commission's key portfolios by the member states to secure their fellow nationals in those areas of particular member state sensitivity. Von der Groeben's task was further aided by the selection of Walter Hallstein as president of the European Commission. Both shared a similar vision and had been strongly influenced by the Freiburg school.

The Ordo-liberal influence within this DG was further strengthened with the appointments of Ernst Albrecht as Von der Groeben's *chef du cabinet* and Ernst-Joachim Mestmäcker's arrival as principal legal advisor. In short, von der Groeben was ideally placed to steer, develop and anchor the competition policy logic, which he did for nearly a decade from 1958 to 1967. Von der Groeben's team regarded a rule of reason approach as a necessary component, and claimed that exemptions from the rule under Article 81(3) provided enough of a safety valve for pro-competitive agreements, such as those involving research and development and intellectual property.

The von der Groeben 'team' were determined to establish the principle of a *Wettberwerbsordnung* (competition principle), to ensure that competition policy was propelled as the foundation stone of the common market and simultaneously to promote integration and realise the goals of the EEC Treaty. As such competition policy was perceived as an economic constitution. These individuals were not on a crusade to unleash a '*bellum omnium contra omnes*' (Hambloch, 2007) or a state of perfect competition, but to secure a state of workable competition where free market access was secured. Competition policy was not conceived as an end in itself, but a means to achieve faster growth and accelerated integration of the six economies. Equipped with a team of officials (some 100 strong) who all agreed on the need for fair and effective competition to create a common market and who appreciated the necessity of preventing the restriction or distortion of competition. According to von der Groeben, 'we must therefore endeavour to put into practice that degree of competition which is feasible under the conditions of the market concerned' (European parliamentary debates, 19 October 1961). For the competition commissioner and DGIV staff there was not any contradiction between innovation and competition as they were inextricably linked.

The size of the task ahead of von der Groeben and his staff should not be underestimated as there were many questions over whether and exactly how the competition principle could be realised, let alone enforced. How was Article 81 even going to be interpreted? Were the treaty provisions fully fledged legal instruments or merely designed for administrative decision making? From an Ordo-liberal perspective there was never any doubt that they formed a quasi-economic constitution the principles of which would be followed. For the Germans the answer was again in the positive, but there were issues of how well other states (with historically weaker or no experience of competition policy) might apply them. The French were less convinced of such an approach and were more inclined to regard Article 81 not as an enforceable law but rather as policy statements that should guide the Commission's administrative behaviour. It should be borne in mind that other policy priorities such as energy and transport (and despite their treaty status) turned out to be major disappointments (Gillingham, 2003: 62) as member states deliberately obstructed Commission activities in these areas. Anti-trust policy could have shared a similar fate had not the institutional mechanics developed in a very different fashion though this actual route was not set out in the Treaty of Rome.

The EEC Treaty had not provided specific answers as to how the new competition regime would be realised and put into practice, what type of powers it would possess and it left open the distribution of competences between national authorities and the new EEC institutions. Article 211 EEC, however, did establish the Commission as the basic executive agency for carrying out the implementation of the treaty. This was a starting point and was reinforced by Article 89 EEC, which placed responsibility on the Commission for investigating suspected infringements. Overall responsibility for creating a fully functioning competition regime under Article 87 (EEC) fell ultimately onto the Council of Ministers, which was tasked with agreeing upon regulations and directives to give effect to Article 81 (and 82), and within three years of the Treaty coming into force. Article 87(2) explicitly stated that the relationship between the Commission and the national competition authorities would be established in regulations and directives adopted by the Council acting unanimously on proposals from the Commission and having consulted the Assembly (European Parliament). It is interesting to note that total unanimity among the 'Six' states was deemed essential. To push matters forward and to prevent any prevarication and vacillation on behalf of the 'Six' failure to agree by the end of this time frame allowed the Council to determine procedural rules by qualified majority vote. This certainly focused minds.

Responsibility for drawing up a draft proposal to resolve these issues thus fell onto the Commission, and specifically the newly created Competition Directorate (DGIV). Not surprisingly the minds of DGIV's officials in the early years were focused on adding flesh to the skeletal outline of the treaty provisions and preparing a proposal which would provide answers as to how the machinery would operate. To this end DGIV examined the few existing national competition laws in place. There was constant interaction between the staff from the Competition Directorate and senior officials from the member states and particularly in the early summer of 1961. In terms of inter-institutional dialogue and as part of the wider external consultation process discussions were held with delegates from both the European Assembly (which had the right to be consulted) as well as the views of the European Economic and Social Committee (EESC) and representatives from the academic community, leading anti-trust experts and also trade union and employers' associations.[10] The Commission organised a number of conferences between senior officials from the EEC6 in Brussels to discuss, for example, on 30 June 1961 cartel issues, and held others to work through a number of definitional issues such as what constituted an undertaking.

Negotiations were intense and drawn out and encountered a number of legal and political difficulties. The Commission recognised the amount of work and welcomed member state co-operation, but it also recognised the need to hold onto a monopoly of the exemption procedure for fear of losing a grip of the system. Several positions were on display at the commencement of discussions. These can be summarised as the Dutch, the French and the German positions.

Whereas the Dutch suggested that all restrictive agreements should require Commission authorisation as a necessary condition for their presumptive legality, the French government was more disposed to a system where business would regulate itself and ensure that its agreements did not breach the competition rules. This French position can certainly be described as an even more lenient approach and envisaged a role for the Commission to challenge any anti-competitive agreements which ran counter to these rules but very much after the event. The final position advanced by West Germany clung to the Ordo-liberal position and placed its emphasis on a system with preventative controls (as under the ECSC provisions), where pre-authorisation was necessary and where only the Commission held the right both to approve agreements and also to exempt those agreements that met the conditions laid down under Article 81(3). An emerging coalition took shape which included West Germany, the Netherlands and Italy favoured an authorisation system, while the other three states preferred the route of a legal exemption system. France and Luxembourg were particularly united in their vision of joint decisions being made by the Commission with the relevant member state authority as a means of preventing the Commission from 'undermining industrial policies' (Buch-Hansen, 2008: 107).

It is important to stress the interest of multinational business in the design of the then future administrative rules. One of the more powerful voices from within this group belonged to the International Chamber of Commerce. This organisation had been based in Paris since its creation in 1919 and had its own committee on international business agreements affecting competition. It is often tempting to overlook the role of both the Assembly and the Economic and Social Committee (EESC) in competition policy matters for most of the last fifty years, given their non-involvement in actual decision making, but there have been times when it has actually impacted on the shape of the fledgling European competition regime. These early days proved to constitute one such time, as the Commission's draft was reviewed by both institutions. The EESC was the first to respond formally to the Commission's draft proposal on 28 March 1961. The EESC had been deliberately created under the EEC Treaty as a non-political body to enable interests in economic and social fields to voice opinions on European policy formulation. It had a purely advisory function. These so-called other interests fell under three general headings, namely employers, employees and others (such as agricultural interests and consumer interests).

Attitudes towards the notification of agreements were evenly divided within the EESC. Forty-one opted for formal notification while forty-one opted against such a move and preferred a system where the Commission initiated its own investigations. There were ten abstentions. It is interesting to note that the two main groups within the EESC divided by designation because the employers overwhelmingly opposed the obligatory notification system, whereas the employees openly supported it. The employers' representatives argued that any moves towards a notification system would effectively paralyse the Commission because it would be overburdened with cases. This initial assessment was to prove correct (see chapter 6). Nevertheless, the EESC supported the competition principle within the EEC Treaty with the proviso that all Commission decisions were subject to an appeal process and that the member states were drawn into the process through some form of formal consultative process.

Within the Assembly, the issue of competition policy fell under the remit of its twenty-four strong internal market committee. The *rapporteur* was Arved Deringer, a renowned German competition law specialist and member of the Christian Democratic Union (CDU). The Assembly (as the EP was known at the time) was composed of self-selected individuals from the national parliaments, and the vast majority of these belonged to parties of the centre right. The internal market committee contained fourteen Christian Democrats, five Liberals (including Gaston Thorn, the later Commission president, 1979–1984) and five Socialists (including Helmut Schmidt, the later West German Chancellor, 1974–1982). The Deringer report included a careful exploration of the three possible approaches for the Commission to adopt in order to implement Article 81. In effect, the Committee shared the Commission's viewpoint that all restrictions on competition were in principle incompatible with the common market and did agree on the inclusion of possible exemptions. It supported the idea of obligatory notification and a retroactive system, that is from the moment a notification was lodged. The committee sought four main objectives. These were to establish the simplest possible machinery and highly flexible administrative practices; to ensure that no firm was left in any doubt about who was affected by competition law; to signal its support for the Commission to become the competition regulator and to advocate the necessity of financial sanctions for breaches of European competition law.

The Deringer report had added some more minor but significant refinements to DGIV's proposal. For example, it suggested that Article 82 (abusive monopolies) should also be brought within the terms of the regulation. The committee also suggested the inclusion of a negative clearance procedure (which interestingly did not exist under West German law). This innovative suggestion would enable the Commission to state that any agreement that did not fall within the scope of Article 81 did not run counter to European law. The Internal Market committee approved the Deringer report on 11 July 1961 and passed the issue for further discussion to the plenary session in October 1961. The EP formally debated Deringer's report on 19 October 1961 and produced the resolution which the Council had requested on 8 December 1960. The EP had effectively recognised the advantages of a co-ordinated competition policy and the development of European law in this area.

Meanwhile Council/Commission deliberations had continued throughout the autumn of 1961. These negotiations were 'extremely tense' (von der Groeben, 1987: 108). A further conference, for example, between officials from both institutions had met on 14 September to clarify and discuss ongoing different styles, concepts and approaches. Once again, differing interpretations on issues such as 'enterprise' and 'concerted practices' illustrated the diverse approaches and views on anti-trust and business activity. The major point of division at this time had centred on the different form and type of regime preferred by both West Germany and France. The former was set on a general cartel ban with prior authorisation for exemptions. The German approach contrasted sharply with the French position. The French '*Commission Technique des Ententes*' on the other hand wanted to screen cartels and only have those deemed to have been bad to change their contracts to avoid sanctions. In the end, however, the Council finally agreed on an authorisation system but on the condition that any final interpretation or ruling would rest with the Court of Justice.

On the issue of exemptions it was decided that the Commission would itself determine which agreements could be allowed, but again only upon request (i.e. notification). German influence certainly found its stamp in this regard and the German competition authority supported Commission competence over Article 81, as did the EP's committee on the common market. France had given way in exchange for a more favourable deal in the simultaneous discussions over the framing and operations and funding of the CAP (Warzoulet, 2005: 67) and the exemption for certain economic sectors (most noticeably agriculture) from the entire remit of the competition rules (Neven et al., 1998: 5). Not for the first time did the governments in Bonn and Paris reach an accord when positions seemed diametrically opposed. That the French government eventually agreed to the final form of the regulation may be more surprising, but the answer to this seeming conundrum owes much to the fact that Paris had assumed that competition policy would play very much a limited role at the EU level as the policy did within the member states (Gerber, 1998: 348). It would be going too far to point to French naïvety because in all reality few people at the time seemed to appreciate the powers contained within the Regulation and its implications and how they could transform the Commission.

5. EMPOWERING THE COMMISSION THROUGH REGULATION 17

The draft proposal of a text on how to administer Articles 81 and 82 was first approved by the full Commission (College). Agreement was reached on a final text in Council by unanimity, after taking on board the positions of both the EP and the EESC, on 6 February 1962 and it became effective on 13 March 1962. The regulation was a triumph for the German negotiators and expressed their views of how an efficient competition system could be created. That it largely reflected the hallmark of a strong German Ordo-liberal influence is not surprising. The German flavour reflected the realities, the expertise and the time and effort the West German government had spent since the late 1940s on their own domestic cartel law.

Agreement on Regulation 17 marks a very important milestone in the historical development of European competition policy. The regulation itself has been described as 'one of the most important ever enacted' (Wilks and Bartel, 2002: 164). Indeed, its enactment represents one of the very few occasions when the member state governments were prepared to restrict their own competence in favour of the Commission (Kon, 1980: 156). Regulation 17 laid down the administrative procedure for handling all cases under Article 81 (and also Article 86). At first sight the anti-trust provisions of the EEC Treaty looked very much like a replica of Article 65 ECSC, but the ECSC and EEC treaties were very different and distinct creations. Whereas the ECSC granted exclusive authority to the High Authority the EEC Treaty provided for the sharing of jurisdiction between the Commission and the member state authorities, with the latter in control until the necessary regulations had been passed. This change in emphasis reflected the broader, less supranational structure of the EEC Treaty, where the main decision making powers were vested in the Council of Ministers. Regulation 17 served as the 'procedural bible' of the EU competition regime, provided a unique form of institutional framework and remained in place (subject only to a few minor tweaks) for over forty years until 2004 (see chapter 7). In terms of both institutional involvement and the supranational enforcement of European cartel policy Regulation 17 demonstrated a highly radical shift in power dynamics and would be reinforced some forty years later in Regulation 1/2003 (see chapter 7). The most striking aspect of this later regulation in terms of day to day decision making, and in contrast to most other policy areas (both past and present), was the central position conferred upon the Commission. It was handed far reaching powers and its decisions were subject to review only by the Court of Justice (Article 9). In retrospect, Regulation 17 had created the foundations of a puissant competition authority which was going to be largely free from member state interference and provided the business community with one institution. DGIV incorporated the roles of investigator, judge, jury and executioner all in one. The Council and the European Parliament were involved neither in the investigations nor with the decision making. These two institutions were effectively confined to the margins of competition policy, although the former had the power to make changes to the administrative procedure through new regulations and the latter had the ability to discuss and debate competition issues. The Competition Directorate had been placed firmly in the driving seat and set on a predestined route. How the European competition regulator would utilise and expand its powers was unknown.

With the instruments of decision making almost exclusively in the hands of the Commission, both of the legislating bodies are clearly on the margins of competition policy making. European cartel policy is *de facto* a Commission policy. It was the Commission which determined what the policy was and how it was to be implemented on the ground. It was the Commission which identified a breach of the rules, which undertook any investigation and which decided whether to take a formal decision. And it was the Commission which fined, and even established the level of the penalty.

Regulation 17 had been constructed along the lines of the West German enforcement system, and elaborated and spelt out the powers of the Commission. Articles 1–9 of the regulation provided for the procedural machinery under which agreements were to be notified and brought to the attention of the Commission. The regulation (Articles 4 and 5) established a framework for the notification of all agreements that might restrict competition and it remained largely unchanged until 1999 (Regulation 1216/99). Companies were entitled (Article 2) to receive confirmation that their agreement did not infringe competition rules through the possibility of negative clearance, while the Commission was empowered (under Article 3) to dispose of complaints by means of informal negotiation. Originally it had been intended under Article 81 to include a timetable mechanism, as advocated in the Deringer report, to state that all agreements notified which were not opposed by the Commission within a period of six months from notification remained lawful. This so-called 'opposition procedure' reflected German practices and, although both attractive and convenient, was not adopted by the Commission. Regulation 17 empowered the Commission to grant negative clearances (an opinion that a particular practice does not infringe Article 81 and, thus, there are no grounds for Commission intervention) and also to decide whether an exemption (Articles 6 and 8) should be granted under the terms of Article 81(3).

Articles 10–14 focused directly on the Commission's substantial powers. Article 14 equipped the Commission with powers to undertake its investigations, empowering its officials to examine books and other documentation, to take and make copies of such relevant materials, to request oral interviews from the undertakings concerned and to enter premises or vehicles or land belonging to the undertaking. These so-called dawn raids have frequently made headlines. During the investigations the Commission was compelled (Article 11) to liaise with and keep the existing national competition authorities fully informed and to forward copies of all necessary documentation relating to the case in question. Member state support was needed when premises were searched. However, there were no powers for the Commission to summon CEOs to Brussels and, unlike in the American antitrust tradition, violations of Article 81 were deemed to be administrative offences rather than criminal offences. Finally, Articles 15–25 centred on administrative processes. The Commission was authorised (Articles 15 and 16) to levy fines of up to 10 per cent of the company's annual turnover for infringements and was also requested under Article 19 to publish its decisions (be it formal decisions, negative clearances or exemptions) in the EU's Official Journal. In short, Regulation 17 had established the rules for the EU competition regime and actors.

6. LOCATING THE INSTITUTIONAL ARCHITECTURE OF EUROPEAN CARTEL POLICY

The Commission had been handed three main instruments with which to detect the existence of anti-competitive agreements and behaviour. These took the form of notifications from firms, complaints by third parties and the Commission's own powers to investigate specific cases on its own (*ex officio*) initiative. Notification became the foundation stone of the Commission's restrictive practices policy. Under the competition rules, firms were advised to register their agreements or practices on a voluntary basis to ensure they did not breach the competition rules. The procedural process is illustrated in Table 5.2. The benefits for firms following this course of action included immunity from fines (at least from the date of notification) and the possibility that the Commission would give its blessing to, or at least state its lack of interest in, the case and allow agreement to continue. Indeed the notification route also provided the only means to allow an anti-competitive agreement to be exempted from the pull of Article 81. The existence of an exemption route within the European rules was a welcome addition, but it required resources (in terms of time, money and staff) for any company which sought to follow this particular route. For some firms cartel arrangements provided a much better, if much riskier, course of action and one that depended just on the companies concerned. Indeed, failure to notify an agreement became something of a gamble for some firms because ultimately, if the practice were detected, it could result in substantial fines. However, the unearthing of cartels was never going to prove easy for the regulator, and feeling reasonably safe in the knowledge that cartels had to be identified in the first place and that the Competition Directorate was inundated with notifications, a number of companies took the gamble and deliberately sought to escape Commission detection altogether. The new European system of anti-trust would certainly be tested by the realities of cartellisation and its impact,

Table 5.2 The five stages of administrative procedure in Article 81 proceedings as established under Regulation 17

Stage 1	Investigative Stage – request for information
Stage 2	Initiation of Proceedings – Statement of Objections sent to the parties
Stage 3	Access to file and Objections from Third Parties
Stage 4	Consultation of the Advisory Committee
Stage 5	Adoption of a Formal Decision in the form of a negative clearance, an exemption or a prohibition with the possibility of a fine.

and success would depend very much on how well it was able to uncover cartels. The Commission's task was certainly ambitious, and to be successful needed to overcome past business tradition and culture. For the new European system to deliver it was going to prove essential to establish an efficient institutional structure and an effective administrative process. In retrospect, the system came to place too much emphasis on the notification system, which came to consume much of DGIV's rather limited resources. To understand why this occurred it is necessary to understand the drawbacks in the form of substantial administrative bureaucracy and paperwork which accompanied the notification system

It is understandable why the introduction of a compulsory notification system was deemed desirable, and in practice it provided two possible routes to escape the EEC rules: firstly, in the form of an application for a negative clearance, and, secondly, in the form of an application for an exemption.[11] A negative clearance was granted if the Commission judged that there was no competition case to answer. Exemptions were also allowed under Article 81(3) so long as their pro-competitive effects outweighed their anti-competitive effects. The notification system was, however, time-consuming and would very quickly consume most of DG Competition's resources and manpower. The process commenced with the opening of a file which was allocated to a specific unit and individual (the *rapporteur*) within the DG who began an informal analysis of the case. At this stage in the process, the Commission's formal powers of investigation were rarely used. More informal sources were tapped, such as records and reports held in the DGIV library, all background information to hand, and past cases involving the firms under scrutiny. Each notification received by the Commission was acknowledged and copied as a matter of course to all member state governments or national competition authorities. If the *rapporteur* considered a negative clearance or an exemption appropriate, a Notice was published in the EEC's Official Journal. Cartel agreements did not feature as part of either process, as they were not going to follow either the clearance or the exemption routes. Cartels were deliberately constructed to conceal their activities and were often going to prove difficult for the regulator to detect.

Complaints by third parties certainly came to be an essential aspect of uncovering cartels. Making a complaint has always represented a relatively cost-free route for firms which wished to involve themselves in the Commission's formal proceedings. If convinced of a case's importance, the Commission took up the matter on their behalf, carrying the burden of any costs incurred. It was the responsibility of DGIV to decide whether a case should be pursued or dropped. Complaints could be thrown out for a wide variety of reasons such as non-application of the competition rules, the lack of substantial evidence, limited investigatory resources available; or, even where the rules were breached, agreements were not deemed important enough to warrant a full investigation (Vesterdorf, 1994: 101).

Questions asked in the Assembly/European Parliament, newspaper articles, information from member state representations, interest group contacts and documentation in company reports all provided respectable routes through which the Commission could be informed about possible breaches of the competition rules. 'Own initiative' investigations could also be launched. The Commission was also in a position to conduct general enquiries into particular sectors of the economy when it considered that a particularly harmful distortion of competition existed. Once any case had been opened the operational unit and the *rapporteur* possessed a significant degree of discretion. DGIV was equipped under Regulation 17 with two distinct legal tools at its disposal (under Article 11) to extract further information. The first enabled competition officials to request (and subsequently to demand) written documentation and information about a particular case. Where the response was incomplete the Commission was empowered to levy fines of up to ECU 5,000. Where no response to the informal request for information was forthcoming, the Commission was in a position to demand the information backed by the threat of heavier fines.

The second weapon assigned to DGIV (under Article 14 of Regulation 17) allowed for on-the-spot investigations of firms' offices. These could take place without any prior notification if the Commission believed such course of action to be justified. Such 'raids' were particularly best suited to 'obtain direct evidence of hard-core infringements such as cartels' (Ritter et al., 1991: 632). These surprise visits, or 'dawn raids' as they are often referred to by the media, were a particularly useful tool at the investigators' disposal, both as a 'precaution' and as a way of countering certain weaknesses in the Commission's fact-finding procedures. This was especially true where there was some suspicion that the firm might try to hide evidence, or if there was some prior experience of unhelpfulness. Use of this 'element of surprise' (Joshua, 1986) was left entirely up to the Commission. If the firm opted to agree to the investigation, the Commission was empowered to take copies of 'books and other business records' and ask for 'oral explanations on the spot'. This was to be used as an additional device, though it could give the firm's representatives an opportunity to put their case and enable DGIV staff to enter premises and even search vehicles belonging to the company or companies in question (Ritter et al., 1991: 637).

The national authorities had always to be kept informed (in advance) of all investigations. National officials were usually present. As a matter of procedure, the investigators identified themselves by their staff cards at the reception and asked to see the most senior manager present, to whom they presented the warrant or order. At this stage they could explain the procedure to those present. In the case of a warrant, refusal to submit to the investigation was recorded and the investigators withdrew. With an order in hand, the situation was quite different, as a refusal to submit could lead Commission officials to call upon their national counterparts to force the firm (perhaps even with the help of the police, or at least with the assistance of a court order) to open their doors. The Commission itself had no means of direct enforcement and had to rely on co-operation from the national authorities. A firm refusing access could be susceptible to larger fines.

Once the informal preliminary investigation had ended the Commission had to choose whether to issue a formal decision or not. Where it opted to open formal proceedings the Commission sent the companies concerned a Statement of Objections. This statement was effectively the charge made against the firms accused of breaching the competition rules. It contained a concise and preliminary assessment of the case, stating why DGIV thought that there was a case to answer. Normally, it also provided further information on the course of action that the Commission intended to take. This was generally divided into two sections, dealing with the facts of the case (as seen by the Commission) and legal assessment, demonstrating how the agreement had allegedly breached Article 81 (or 82). Documents used by the Commission in making this preliminary assessment were usually attached to the statement, with a covering explanatory letter signed by the Director-General for Competition.

The proceedings following the arrival of the Statement of Objections were usually conducted in writing, with the submission of a written defence and further documentation provided by the accused firms. The Commission normally fixed a date for the submission of written evidence, usually between six weeks and two months after the Statement of Objections had been sent out, and it might even provisionally establish the timing of the oral hearing, although the Commission was fairly flexible in extending deadlines where there was good reason.

Once the written procedure had finished, an oral hearing could be held if the firms involved so wished it (Kerse, 1988: 42). Officially this stage of the process gave the defendants an opportunity to clarify matters which had not already been settled. It was intended to be entirely administrative and non-adversarial, although this may not always have been apparent from the behaviour of parties. Matters raised in the Statement of Objections were reviewed here, with oral representations made by senior representatives of the firms involved, by their lawyers, and possibly also by economists

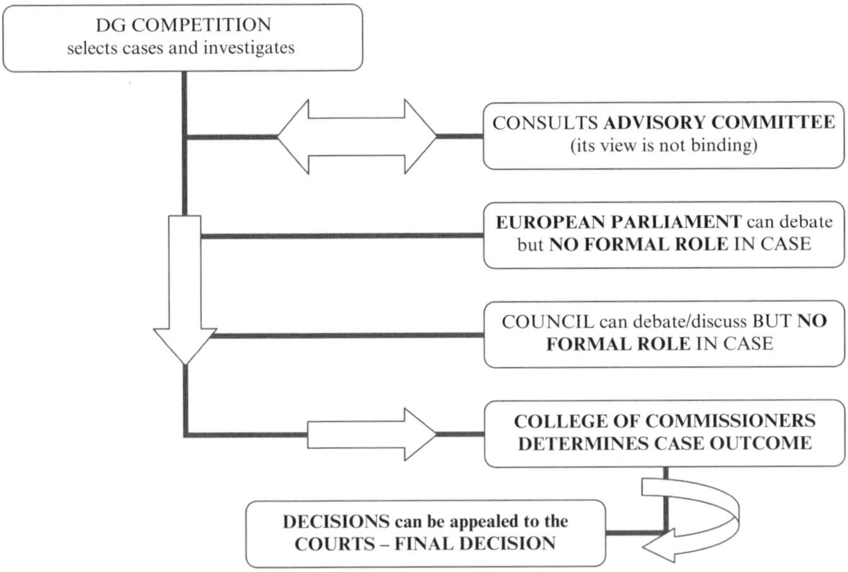

Figure 5.1 Actors and decision-making under Article 81 cases

and expert witnesses. The actual procedures for collecting oral evidence were further facilitated with the creation of the post of Hearing Officer in 1982. This position within DGIV was designed to counter criticism of the Competition Directorate's administrative procedure. The Hearing Officer supervised all aspects of the hearing, including the dates, location and documentation, the chairing of the hearing, the orchestration of its structure and content, and also did a fair amount of the groundwork for each case. In a sense the Hearing Officer's role was to act as a sort of independent arbiter between the accused firms and the Commission. To this end the Hearing Officer sought to ensure that the firms' rights of defence were protected, but also protected the position and rights of the Commission.

After the oral hearing, the Hearing Officer circulated the minutes and transcript for comment and correction and drafted a report which was passed on to the Director-General and to the *cabinet* of the Competition Commissioner. At this point in the proceedings, the Commission had a legal obligation to consult representatives of the member states' competent authorities within the Advisory Committee on Restrictive Practices and Monopolies (illustrated in table 5.1). This was intended as a final safeguard and allowed the member states a check, if a limited one, on DG Competition cases. The aim at this stage in the proceedings was to ensure that the Commission's decisions had been taken in a reasonable and consistent way, and that the procedure had been fair. It is important to stress that the Advisory Committee was created as a purely consultative forum only and held no veto power as the French government had originally wanted. Indeed, there was no requirement that the Commission had to take on board the recommendations of the Committee.

Comfort letters also came to form an essential aspect of the notification scheme. They were administrative letters which were issued by DGIV (and were usually signed by the Director-General) to the firms involved in a potential breach of the competition rules and at an early stage of the investigative process. The comfort letter notified the firm(s) in question that their agreement did not fall under Article 81 and was allowed to continue. Used as a way of speeding up decision-making in light of an ever increasing backlog of cases and limited resources, the legal status of the comfort letter remained ambiguous. In brief, comfort letters were not legally binding and they failed to take into account the interests of third parties. This was clearly a problem for lawyers and judges, as a letter of this sort did not possess the status of a decision (Stevens, 1994: 82).

At the end of the formal proceedings a formal decision had to be taken. This usually translated into a decision which either authorised the agreement or one which forbade it. Into the former category came negative clearance and exemption decisions. Decisions of this sort often included time constraints, and were usually conditional. By contrast, negative decisions, or those which condemned an agreement, were often labelled 'cease-and-desist orders'. In the harder cases, the draft decisions were often considered first by the special *chefs*, which in this context is the meeting of cabinet members responsible for competition matters, and then by the *chefs de cabinet*. If the decision still lay unresolved, the matter was referred to the College, although in more straightforward cases the Commissioners merely rubber-stamped what had in effect already been informally decided. When issues did come formally to the College then decisions were taken by simple majority vote.

When substantive rules had been broken the Commission enjoyed considerable discretionary powers and was able to impose fines which ranged originally from one thousand to one million units of account, or a sum in excess thereof but not exceeding 10 per cent of the turnover in the preceding year for each of the undertakings participating in the infringement. There has always been some controversy about the extent to which the Commission can use its discretion in setting fines, and, indeed, about whether a prosecuting body should even have the authority to fine in the first place. Regulation 17, Article 15(1) and (2) provides some (though not a great deal of) assistance in stating at what level fines should be set. Additional penalty payments (under Article 16) of between ECU

50 and 1000 per day could also be imposed on those companies, which failed or refused to comply with an actual Commission antitrust decision. By the middle of 1962 the actors and the rules were in place to attack cartellisation.

7. CONCLUSIONS

In outlining the competition provisions within the EEC Treaty this chapter has shown the controversial nature of the area as seen in the differing positions adopted and pursued by the EEC6 founding member states. The decision by the six founding EEC member states to commit themselves to competition discipline and simultaneously recognise the logic of a supranational dimension is significant, given the unfamiliarity of the majority with antitrust. This chapter maintains that the agreement on a European tier of competition governance, where power came to reside with the two foremost supranational actors (the Commission and the Court of Justice), marks a critical moment in the history of not only the European integration process but also the development of European antitrust. In retrospect it is fairly straightforward to identify the adoption of Regulation 17 as a major stepping stone, but at the time the actual trajectory of this unique (*sui generis*) form of supranational antitrust regime was far from assured. How would DG Competition work in practice? Would it attract competent and a sufficient number of high quality staff? How would it devise its workload? How would the European regulator interpret the rules, and was there any possibility of lingering state protectionism always going to trump the competition principle? Would the business world be prepared to co-operate? Only time and experience would tell, but the cartels wars had begun.

NOTES

1. Apart from the emphasis on the free movement of people, goods, capital and services, the creation of a customs union and a limited social policy, the EEC Treaty included specific reference to only three policy areas; namely agriculture, transport and competition policy.
2. The Spaak Report of 21 April 1956 set the context post-Messina for the formal start to the intergovernmental negotiations between the ECSC6 at Val Duchesse. The document was over 150 pages long and can be read in full at http://www.ena.lukspaak_report-020102534.html.
3. For further information see D. Grosser, T. Lange, A. Müller-Armack and B. Neuss, *Soziale Marktwirtschaft*, Verlag BW. Kohlhammer, 1988. Also W. Eucken, *Grundsätze der Wirtschaftspolitik*, Mohr/Siebeck, 1990, For a much shorter overview of the

German economy see R. Overy, 'The Economy of the Federal Republic since 1949' in K Larres and P. Panayi (eds), *The Federal Republic of Germany since 1945*, Longman, 1996,

4. See J. Ardagh, *France Today*, Penguin, 1995, and especially chapter 2 'the Economy modernised but menaced'.
5. The European Atomic Energy Community (EAEC) Treaty was also signed on the same day as the EEC Treaty. It was designed to create another specialist market, this time in nuclear power. The French government was the most vocal supporter of such a Community as a means of sharing costs and funding research for the drive towards cheaper nuclear power. This Euratom treaty was signed by the same six states which had signed both the ECSC and the EEC Treaties. It has never been revised and its provisions have been fully integrated into the structure of the European Union.
6. The Article became 3g under the 1992 Treaty on European Union.
7. Indeed the EEC treaty rules, as Buch-Hansen argues, were actually harder to establish than those for the ECSC.
8. The United Kingdom was invited to take part in the discussions in Messina which ultimately led to the EEC Treaty. The UK accepted the request to participate. However, although the UK government welcomed moves towards freer trade it objected strongly to the institutional model being created and specifically the supranational characteristics of this particular project. As a consequence the British delegation withdrew from the Messina talks and opted instead to take a leading role in the creation of the European Free Trade Association (EFTA). For further reading begin with Unwin, 1992 or Dinan, 2006 for developments.
9. The Assembly had been created as one of the four main institutions within the EEC Treaty. Its members renamed it the European Parliament in 1962 (see Judge and Earnshaw, 2008). The original idea behind this Assembly was to provide parliamentarians from the member states (and they selected themselves from the national parliaments) with an opportunity to express their views on European developments. There were no direct elections to the Assembly/EP and none would occur until 1979.
10. The Economic and Social Committee rebranded itself as the European Economic and Social Committee at the turn of the millennium. Prior to this renaming it was usually referred to under the acronym of the ESC or ECOSOC. For consistency this work refers to the EESC throughout.
11. Notification later provided another means to secure exemption under one of the Commission's block exemptions which are discussed in the following chapter.

6. European cartel policy: deployment and combat, 1963–1998

With the institutional and administrative machinery in place to deal with restrictive practices (and also monopolies) the Commission found itself embarking on a radical experiment in supranational governance, and one which attracted the first generation of European integration researchers (Haas, 1958; Lindberg, 1963). Many questions were posed at this time about how regional integration would both function and develop and how it could be explained in theoretical terms. Haas devised his theory of neo-functionalism as an attempt to explain and account for the political integration process which emerged in its unique form in Western Europe in the 1950s. For Haas regional integration was the process of 'how and why states cease to be wholly sovereign, how and why they voluntarily mingle, merge and mix with their neighbours so as to lose the factual attributes of sovereignty while acquiring new techniques for resolving conflict themselves' (Haas, 1970: 610). For neo-functionalists the available evidence as manifest in the European Coal and Steel Community (ECSC), the European Economic Community (EEC) and the EURATOM treaties seemed to suggest that the nation state was becoming redundant as an authoritative source of governance. In this European laboratory powers and sovereignty were being transfered from the nation states to a set of new supranational institutions. Supranationalism appeared to offer a new and definitive answer to resolving conflict through the pooling of sovereignty and the beginnings of a new Europe, but could a model explain what was happening in such advanced countries and what were the dynamics pushing the process onward?

Neo-functionalism placed its emphasis on the principal agents of change, which were identified primarily as technocratic elites, politicians, supranational interest groups and other lobbies. It was assumed that these actors pursued their own interests, and in doing so provided the dynamics for further integration. According to Haas, 'political integration is the process whereby political actors in several distinct national settings are persuaded to shift their loyalties, expectations and political activities to a new centre, whose institutions possess or demand jurisdiction over pre-existing national states. The end result is a new political community, superimposed over the existing ones' (Haas, 1958: 16). Neo-functionalism came under increasing scrutiny and attack from the mid-1960s for downgrading the role of the member state governments, and this theory's overall relevance has been severely tarnished ever since. However, it is interesting to reflect on the degree to which it aptly explained developments in the competition policy arena (McGowan, 2007), given that power resided with the Commission and not the Council.

The Commission was very much an unknown quantity at the outset, as much to its own staff as it was to the outside world. It was commencing from a position of ground zero and needed time to adjust to its role, develop its relations with the other European institutions and identify its priorities. The Commission needed time to identify the main obstacles that threatened to undermine the creation of a common market and foster market integration in line with the objectives of the EEC Treaty. The Directorate General for Competition faced all these issues, and arguably its position was even more difficult as its staff came from the six member states where divergent views existed about the role of competition policy and its place in the economy. Such difficulties and obstacles confronted the European competition regulator as it sought to acclimatise to its new surroundings and relationship with the member states before it could push forward with the competition principle. The DG for Competition's success was always going to depend on a number of both internal and external variables. It was going to be judged on and included issues such as leadership from within the Commission and DG Competition, the ability to recruit capable and well-resourced staff, the acceptance of the competition principle and the correct economic philosophies, and a reliance on case law and legal interpretations. With hindsight it was going to take time to bring all these factors into some form of alignment, but from the position of the early 1960s the future trajectory of policy was far from certain.

The history of EU cartel policy provides a fascinating narrative of institutional development and how the Commission has become not only increasingly proactive but increasingly combative. In terms of principal/agency theory EU cartel policy presents an area where the Commission (as the agent) has been able to push the boundaries of its power and activity (and especially through a series of Notices and Guidelines) well beyond its initial remit and the intention of the principal actors (the member states). This chapter illustrates the development of EU cartel policy over the four decades from the 1960s to the 1990s. It explains how DG Competition emerged over this time from a relatively 'sleepy administrative backwater' (Wilks and McGowan, 1996) and matured into one of the main and most influential DGs, takes account of the above variables and discusses how competition policy developed as the policy area where integration has proceeded furthest and where a genuine supranational (read federal in all but name) regime gradually emerged from the foundation stones of the 1950s.

1. INTRODUCTION: DECLARING 'WAR' ON THE CARTELS

The origins of EU cartel policy have to be understood in the context of three factors: the imperative of the drive for the realisation of a single market, the historical context which shaped policy after 1945 and the influence of the US experience on the European regimes (Leucht, 2008). Cartels had been identified as an immediate target from the outset when Article 85 (now 81) of the European Economic Community (EEC) Treaty specifically prohibited all agreements 'which may affect trade between member states and which have as their object the prevention, restriction or distortion of competition within the common market'.[1] Nevertheless, as Chapter 5 illustrated, political consensus was reached on the inclusion of competition policy in the EEC Treaty, and further agreement in the Council established DG Competition's legal competence to operate as an autonomous and quasi-judicial policy making institution under Regulation 17. More significantly in terms of governance, Regulation 17 identified the Commission as the principal actor in the administration and implementation of competition policy decision making and assigned it the roles of judge, jury and executioner. In hindsight the member states had created a powerful supranational agent (Seidel, 2007) which has continually advanced its power through the adoption of guidelines and notices, and in so doing has altered the terms of the principal/agent relationship (Lehmkuhl, 2008).

From the outset the EU regime was developed as a regulatory rather than a confrontational model, and one which laid more emphasis on economic analyses than moral considerations, in contrast to the older more established (in 1890) US competition regime. However, 'it is interesting to note how a more adversarial and combative system of enforcement (in some senses a quasi-criminal law model) has gradually been created and grafted over time onto a seemingly "softer" more administrative culture of regulation' (Harding and Joshua, 2003: 3) and this issue will be explored in this chapter. The decision to initiate an EU competition regime heralded the advance of a Community legal order which would in time ensure strong degrees of convergence on the realisation of a European cartel policy.[2]

Although cartels were identified over fifty years ago by the EEC Treaty as the first and primary target of the EU's competition policy order, the

EU cartel regime took time to form, and its enforcement until the 1980s can be described as hesitant, patchy and largely ineffectual. The number of cartels which were unearthed and penalised rarely surpassed more than three at best a year during first decades of EU cartel policy. It is never a straightforward task to pinpoint specific chronological turning points or periods in any policy's development, but these next two chapters suggest four periods of development for EU cartel policy. In each the position of DG Competition and cartel policy developments can be examined with reference to both the substantive and the procedural regimes. Accounting for internal changes is one aspect of competition policy which is generally well covered (Wilks and McGowan, 1996), whereas there has been considerably less attention paid to the external variables. Any examination of the evolution of EU cartel policy cannot be completely separated from developments at member state level. This allows recognition of the varieties of capitalism literature (Albert, 1993) which emphasises the spectrum of capitalist models across Europe and the variable impact of each on the role of national competition policy (see Wigger, 2008) on liberal, coordinated, state and transitional economies. This literature is not explored here, but policy development needs to be considered against changes and events in the wider economic and societal spheres. Wigger (2008) does this in an innovative manner by adopting a critical economy perspective to the development of EU competition policy, in which she traces the impact of Ordo-liberalism, embedded liberalism and neo-liberalism on the evolution of the competition regime and especially on Commission thinking (Wigger and Nölke, 2007). Given the variety of approaches questions could indeed be raised over whether the Commission really operates a single cartel policy when so many different cartel traditions have prevailed and continue to exist at member state level. EU cartel policy can be divided into four separate phases (table 6.1). The first phase of the Commission's anticartel activity can be located to the 1960s and early 1970s. This period was largely exploratory in nature as the Commission sought to bed in, appreciate its powers and gain experience. The second was on one level a continuation of the first, but on another level required the Commission to readjust its thinking in the face of the economic downturn and recession which covered the years from 1973 until the mid 1980s. The third extends from the 're-launch' of the integration process through the Single European Act of 1987 and specifically the single market project until the end of the 1990s. The fourth and current phase focuses on developments in the period after 1999 when we see the first serious discussions about the reform, decentralisation and modernisation of European Union cartel policy. These debates led to the quiet revolution which was encapsulated within Regulation 1/2003 and reflected a new dynamism within DG Competition to combat

Table 6.1 The four incremental phases of the Commission's anti-cartel engagement

Period 1: 1962–1972, Surveying the Terrain and the 'Phoney War' (Reg17, move to own initiative investigations, first fines) Commission style: Hesitant, patchy response but growing signs of activity
Period 2: 1973–1984, Forays and Stalemate First use of dawn raids, further cartels discovered, crisis cartels Commission style: still hesitant and some retrenchment
Period 3: 1985–1998, Seizing the Initiative Fines increasing, Leniency Programme Commission style: Leadership, comes of age, increasingly active
Period 4: 1999–present, Modernisation and Combat (*Decussis Mirabilis*) Reg1/2003, Decentralisation, Modernisation, revised Guidelines for Setting Fines, New Settlement Procedure, Green and White Papers on Private Actions, Internal reorganisation Commission style: Pro-active and increasingly innovative

cartels more effectively through, for example, the levying of higher fines and a series of policy innovations. This fourth phase is arguably the most important and becomes the exclusive subject of the next chapter. The current chapter provides an overview of the first three periods.

Council agreement on Regulation 17 marked a critical juncture in the overall history of EU competition policy. It not only placed the European Commission very much centre stage in the day to day decision making process, but ensured that the daily operation of competition policy affecting trade between states had become a European competence. With power delegated to the Commission, DG Competition was relatively in a free position to begin carving out its role, delineating its responsibilities and building a solid identity. But could it meet expectations? DG Competition faced a sizeable challenge. The Commission's freedom proved all the greater as the possibility of interference from both the Council and the EP diminished almost altogether, as the attention of both institutions switched from such more minor technical policy areas in the case of the Council to confront a number of issues which threatened any further developments on the integration project. These included the decision by the French president, General Charles de Gaulle, to reject two UK applications to accede to the EEC in 1963 and 1967 respectively and the French government's decision in 1965 to withdraw its nationals from the EU institutions (from June 1965 until January 1966) as a powerful means to express its protest against the financing of the Common Agricultural Policy, the onset of majority voting in the Council and any expansion to the Commission's powers as sought by Walther Hallstein. This so-called 'empty chair' crisis was resolved only with the infamous Luxembourg Compromise, which allowed member states to use a veto in Council to protect their national interests. The European Parliament meanwhile became ever more embroiled in attempts to persuade the member state governments to allow for direct elections. The resistance of the French government towards further supranational identity of the EU severely undermined Hallstein, who had remained a committed federalist and had continued to advance the Ordo-liberal agenda. These events, however, illustrated the power of the member states to disrupt integration, and for political theorists reinforced the intergovernmental aspect of integration (Hoffmann, 1966) to the detriment of the neo-functionalist interpretation. To an extent the former were correct in their assumptions, but in focusing on areas of 'high politics' (e.g. foreign and defence policy), they completely missed and underplayed developments at the lower (technical) policy level, as the emergence of European competition policy revealed. It is very striking from today's perspective how the Commission's initiatives on the competition policy front were simply largely overlooked by the member states.

Admittedly, the very early years of EU competition policy have been described as a 'calm period' (Goyder, 2003: 522) as the Commission adjusted to the new circumstances and practicalities of European integration. This should not be read as a negative, as this early period of institution building was vital to the future course of competition law enforcement (Wigger, 2008: 155). DG Competition has been compared to a small and unremarkable part of a supranational administration (Goyder, 2003: 31). Yet, officials were in fact and largely unnoticed by many already sowing the seeds for its future trajectory as DG Competition embarked on a steep learning curve which came to shape the emerging European model of cartel policy. It is certainly true that the first decade of EU competition policy focused more on administrative reform than any substantive reform. DG Competition's evolution during its first decade in existence occurred against a favourable economic and business backdrop with continuing prosperity, a rising standard of living, greater economic growth and the realisation of a customs union in 1968. During this period the Commission extended its control of this policy area through a series of Notices and Guidelines which became a hallmark of the daily functioning of competition governance. These measures were usually presented as administrative tools and mechanisms to both simplify and facilitate the work of DG Competition and the demands placed on business undertakings. How well some of these worked is open for discussion, but they never quite managed to tackle some of the more voiced and long-running criticisms of the EU cartel regime over issues such as case delays and Commission overload. These issues are explored below.

Article 81 (TEC) had identified policy priorities and presented the Commission with considerable powers of interpretation to determine, for example, when agreements affected trade between member states, when an agreement restricted competition and what was a fair share for consumers (Neven, Papandopoulos and Seabright, 1998: 5). The pursuit of Article 81 focused DG Competition's energies on agreements which 'directly or indirectly fix purchase or selling prices or any other trading conditions'. Although examples of such anti-competitive activity can be displayed in vertical arrangements, most cases that primarily fall under part deal primarily with agreements or concerted practices made between horizontally related competitors, and usually centre on fixing prices, dividing markets and conditions of sale (Goyder, 2003: 142).

DG Competition slowly set about fulfilling its remit under the competition provisions of the EEC Treaty, i.e. to protect and promote the competition principle within the marketplace. It was not seeking some model of perfect competition but striving for a state of 'workable competition' and free market access for all. Interestingly, the original structure and purpose of DG Competition had a wider brief which incorporated regional policy and in particular regional state subsidies, and was also tasked with harmonising national regulations over excise taxes and VAT. Restrictive practices took centre stage and the Commission was charged 'to bring the totality of restrictive practices affecting inter-member state trade within the scope of administrative surveillance, to enable their economic evaluation' (Harding and Joshua, 2003:109). The Treaty had effectively cast a very wide net to catch many anti-competitive arrangements. As discussed above, many potentially anti-competitive agreeements had to be notified to the Commission where it was hoped they would be cleared.

Cartels, of course, by their very nature were highly unlikely to notify. Consequently any cartelbusting agenda required time, effort and expert knowledge of each individual product market. DG Competition's main concern and priority in the early years of the 1960s centred on forms of vertical integration/relationships rather than the horizontal variety. In fact in trying to establish a common market the Commission became very much concerned with the structure of this regional market and the extent of trade flows across its internal (member state) borders. During its first five years the Commission received almost 40 000 notifications, and the vast majority of these (some 25 000) were of a vertical nature (Commission, 1980: 15). Many were structured around exclusive dealing arrangements and were usually managed through national trading associations and very much embedded in the national context (Harding and Joshua, 2003: 119).

From the Commission's perspective such vertically based agreements seriously affected trade between the member states, created barriers to trade and distorted the realisation of a genuine common market. For this reason DG Competition focused much of its resources on vertical restraints in the distribution and licensing schemes. In *Grundig-Consten* ([1964] CMLR 489), the Commission was concerned about the German company Grundig and its trading relationship with its French distributor Consten. The latter had been granted the exclusive right to sell Grundig's products in France (see Goyder, 2003; Whish, 2009). It had initially been thought that Article 81 did not cover vertical restraints, but this view was contradicted by the ECJ (Case 56/64 [1966] CMLR 418). This case represented the very first infringement prosecution in the history of EU competition law and accurately displayed the problem of vertical agreements and how they damaged competition within the market. The case centred on the German company Grundig and its trading relationship with its French distributor Consten where the latter was granted the exclusive right to sell Grundig's products in France (see Goyder, 2003). The Commission rejected the possibility of an exemption, whereupon its decision was appealed, unsuccessfully from Grundig's perspective, to the Court of Justice. This example of a vertical arrangement represented a familiar, if undesirable, aspect of business activity and the Commission took action against a number of similarly styled arrangements in the mid 1960s. By focusing on this type of agreement the Commission faced intense criticism (especially from US observers) over its priorities and failing to tackle the main form of anti-competitive activity. Such accusations of policy failure/misdirection compelled the Commission to conceive ways of dealing with the more pressing and contentious issue of carrels as opposed to the more 'mundane' vertical agreements.

Rather ironically DG Competition's problems stemmed directly from Regulation 17. It may have provided the tools but it also gave rise to some problems, and foremost amongst these was the requirement to submit notifications. No matter how desirable the notification was as a mechanism, it severely stretched DG Competition and practically signalled the collapse of the system. The types of agreement being notified in the hope of an exemption can be classified under three headings: harmless, some with minor but solvable problems, and harmful. The notification problem was compounded by an insufficient number of staff in DG Competition and a staff which was unfamiliar with the new rules. It needed time to bed down and appreciate its roles and powers. It possessed a handful of 'A' grade officials at the outset, and by the end of 1964 had only seventy-eight members in total (see table 6.2). Commission requests for further staff to alleviate the difficulty were ignored by the Council. Although numbers

Table 6.2 Charting DG Competition staff levels, 1964–2009

Year	Staff	'A' Grade
1964	78	25
1970s	300	140
1992	411	210
1998	450	225
2008	650	320

Sources: Cini and McGowan, 2009; Commission, 1992; Goyder, 1993; von der Groeben, 1965.

would increase over time they never rose sufficiently. Indeed, the issue of inadequate staffing levels with DG Competition has long been one of the constant criticisms of the EU regime as its staff have struggled to deal with the expanding competition brief.

To compound matters even more nearly three quarters of these some 40 000 notifications related to exclusive dealing agreements. All these issues hindered progress on cartel policy. To tackle the problem of being overburdened with less serious cases the Commission opted to exclude certain types of agreement from the EEC competition rules altogether through the adoption of block exemptions and its addition of *de minimis* thresholds. The block exemption was designed as a response by DG Competition to the huge number of notifications. The Council enacted the first block exemption in 1965, but it did not make any real inroad into the accumulating backlog of cases and opted instead to delegate major responsibility for future block exemptions to the Commission itself. In retrospect, the Council's decision reflected its unwillingness, given its range of responsibilities, to become embroiled in such technical and mundane areas and the Council did not fully appreciate the power it was passing to the Commission. This decision marks another important milestone in the early years of EU competition governance, and placed DG Competition in the enviable position of being able to influence and steer competition issues in a specific direction, to determine what could be exempted and where it should focus its efforts. The block exemption instrument, which has since become a distinctive feature of European-level competition enforcement, allowed certain economic sectors to be exempted from the competition rules for a period of time. Where block exemptions applied, there would be no need for firms to obtain an individual Article 81(3) exemption. Block exemptions provide some legal certainty for firms and have particularly benefited small and medium-sized enterprises (SMEs). Block exemption regulations are frequently renewed and updated to take on board the latest data and to build upon DG Competition's experience in specific areas. The application of the block exemption regulations has not been entirely problem-free, however. The relationship between national and European competition law is only one of the areas which have been problematic. For example, do national authorities have the right to override a block exemption if the agreement falls under the provisions of a national competition rule? As yet the Commission has failed to tackle this question, although it would be unwise for a national authority to intervene and apply its own stricter standards should such a case arise. It is important to stress that the EC rules apply in the first instance only to agreements which threaten to have a detrimental impact on intra-European markets. In other words agreements that are deemed to be of 'minor importance' and fall under the so-called *de minimis* rule are automatically cleared. The *de minimis* rule was established by the European Court of Justice (ECJ) in its *Völk v Vervaecke* ruling in 1969 which stated that 'an agreement falls outside the prohibition in Article 81(1) where it has only an insignificant effect on the market, taking into account the weak position which the persons concerned have on the market of the product in question' (Case 5/69, [1969] ECR 295). This ruling was extremely important as it meant that small-scale agreements would be excluded from the notification requirement. In a sense, the *de minimis* rule marks the dividing line between agreements that are to be dealt with at European level, that is, those that are likely to have an impact on the common market, and those that remain the responsibility of national authorities. Guidelines in the form of a Commission Notice were produced in 1986 (OJ 1986 C231/2) and have been amended on several occasions since. The purpose of the *de minimis* notice is to enable the Commission to focus its activities on the more problematic cases. The 2001 notice therefore applies only to firms which possess more than 1.5 per cent of the market share Agreements which fall below these new thresholds do not fall under Article 81. In short, such agreements that fall below these new thresholds are judged not to possess even a minimum degree of market power and do not fall under Article 81.[3]

These two additions proved valuable and the number of notifications fell back sharply and consequently the Commission was able to re-focus its activities and divert more resources to horizontal agreements and cartelbusting by the end of the decade. By this time the Commission had already investigated a small number of cartels in the mid-1960s. However, these cases were largely the product of actual notifications and were based largely on national players who were restricting intra-EU trade as in detergents, natural sand, rubber, steel processing, pesticides, plaster, cement and timber. At this time the Commission was not yet fully engaged as a proactive regulator (Harding and Joshua, 2003). Indeed, the striking aspect of these early cases was the Commission's much softer approach towards business actors and its strong preference for a negotiated administrative settlement (i.e. to amend problematic practices) between the Commission and the firms involved, and a tendency to eschew the imposition of fines. Publicity about such cases was at best minimal and at worse practically non-existent. This reality led one commentator to comment rather negatively about the Commission's practices and its vagueness over either what the problems were or what remedies were suggested. At times even the names of the companies concerned were not made public even in the EEC bulletin (Edwards, 1967). Without outsiders/observers being able to fathom the rationale behind developments it became practically impossible for cases to set precedents and for onlookers to learn anything at all. This initial reticence from the fledgling regulator (DG Competition) arguably reflected a degree of doubt and uncertainty about its procedures and forms of analysis, and it would take time to alter. However, by 1967 the Commission had started to take its first more meaningful strides against hard core cartels.

The Quinine cartel became the very first Commission 'own initiative' case. Quinine is extracted from the bark of the cinchoma tree, which grows in a number of developing countries and is used to make medicinal compounds that are used principally to make drugs to combat malaria. There had been a long tradition of co-operative agreements between companies based in France, Germany and the Netherlands in this particular sector which can be traced back to the start of the twentieth century. The aim of these agreements had largely been to ensure supplies and to stabilise markets. However, after 1945 the situation for the main companies concerned deteriorated, with a steep decline in prices as more of this product was being produced. Supply was simply outstripping demand. The increasing availability of cinchoma bark owed much to the new supply chains from the plantations in the Congo and Indonesia, but it also arose after the United States opted to throw much of its accumulated stocks of this bark onto the world market. In response a series of European companies formed a defensive cartel in 1958 which involved sharing territorial markets, fixing prices and establishing a series of quotas for sale on export markets. This cartel, as in all cases, was internally policed by the leading cartel member (the Dutch chemical giant, Nedchem) and was scheduled to last for at least five years. It involved frequent meetings and the sharing of information on prices among the cartel members. The cartel was formally wound up in 1965.

However, during its operation prices for cinchoma bark had risen throughout Western Europe while prices had been falling on the world market. The Commission suspected collusion in this case and launched a two year investigation in 1967. This decision post-dated an earlier American move against the same cartel group after prices had risen, and particularly as the bark was now needed to meet the growing demand for malaria treatment at the full height of the Vietnam War. The US authorities found the parties guilty of anti-competitive practices, forced the cartel's dissolution in 1965 and imposed a financial penalty. The Commission followed the American lead and imposed fines of some 210000 units of account and 190000 units of account on the Dutch and German members respectively.

Quinine represents the first major, landmark case in EU cartelbusting. It was a success for the Commission. This case decision was supported by the ECJ on appeal and provided a useful illustration of both business thinking and strategy as the members had deliberately set out to avoid notification and conceal their activities. The anti-cartel provisions in the EEC Treaty had not in themselves acted as a deterrent to cartel formation. The fines imposed seem insignificant by today's standards, but the important thing to note is that they established a benchmark against which all cartels would be examined.

Quickly on Quinine's heels followed a series of cartel cases (see table 6.3). One of the more notorious cases was situated again in the chemicals sector but on this occasion focused specifically on dyes. Both cartel cases were export cartels which had been pulled together to protect national markets and both were based around price fixing arrangements. The chemicals industry has displayed a long tradition of, and a seeming fascination for, engaging in co-operative and collusive arrangements. Dyestuffs introduced the Commission to a number of actors who have since been involved in further cartel activity. In *Dyestuffs* the actual evidence was on the face of it much more circumstantial than it had been in *Quinine* and it rested on the assertion that similar price changes were indicative of a concerted practice. The Commission had been alerted to this particular case by a number of third parties (such as business associations, consumer groups and rival competitors) on account of a series of similar price rises between 1964 and 1967. The actual agreement between ten companies operated within an oligopolistic market, but in contrast to *Quinine*, which had centred on a very small number of medicinal products, *Dyestuffs* involved several thousand different dyes. This case was potentially more complicated for DG Competition to tackle. The companies under suspicion rejected the Commission's price-fixing allegations and argued that any similarity in prices merely reflected a hugely sensitive market where all the other players followed the price leader. This defence was accepted neither by the Commission nor by the Court on appeal. The Commission's final decision accused nine companies in Europe (including the UK and

Table 6.3 Other major Commission Cartel decisions by sector, 1964–1983

Year	Specific Sector
1964	Belgian Tiles
1969	Belgian, Dutch and German Cement
1970	German Ceramic Tiles
1970	Belgium Perfumes Syndicate
1972	Belgian Central Heating
	Dutch Sanitary Ware
	Dutch Cement
1973	Dutch Gas Heaters
1974	Belgian Wallpapers
1975	Dutch Stove and Heaters
	Dutch Toiletry
	Glass Containers
	Aluminium
1976	Dutch and Belgian Paper
1978	Dutch Bicycles
	Belgian Tobacco
	Belgian Spices
1979	Dutch Pharmaceuticals
1980	Dutch Plywood
	German Natural Stone
	Sulphuric Acid
	Italian Cast Glass
1981	Italian Flat Glass
1982	Dutch and Belgian Publishers
1983	Belgian Newspaper Publishers
	Tobacco Retailers

Switzerland) of anti-competitive practices and once again imposed fines of some 50,000 units of account on the producers of aniline dyes.[4] The companies launched an appeal, but the Court of Justice confirmed the Commission's earlier decision and identification of a concerted practice in a 1972 ruling. However, it also signalled some issues which would arise in the future over degrees of proof and evidence to support the Commission's decisions.

Another example of the drive to restrict competition found illustration in the *European Sugar Cartel* which represented the last of the three major cartel cases during this initial phase of activity. The Commission had once again been alerted to suspicious activity in this sector by consumer groups and earlier enquiries on the part of the (West) German Federal Cartel Office and had opened its own investigations in 1969. The *European Sugar*

Cartel case was somewhat more complicated than the previous two cases, as the Commission had opted to open up a war on two different fronts by pursuing the companies concerned under both Articles 81 and 82 (for abusing their dominant position), but uncovered the existence of a market where prices had been pre-determined by members of the cartel. The Commission's 1973 decision condemned the practices of some twenty-two companies which had been involved with the cartel and levied a fine of over nine million units of account on sixteen of them. The Commission's decision was immediately, though unsuccessfully, appealed to the Court of Justice in 1975. The Court's confirmation of the Commission's decision instilled further confidence in DG Competition (Goyder, 1998: 162–163). It is extremely important to underscore not only the role of the Commission but also the relationship between the Commission and the Court of Justice (and after 1989 the Court of First Instance (CFI)), and in particular the latter's attitude towards the former's analysis. This relationship was going to prove vital and pivotal in the shaping of European cartel policy. By this stage it became possible to identify a more confident DG Competition and one which was developing a growing reputation that was based on its analyses and relationship with the Court, but appreciating its own role and wide discretion to define concerted practices, which in turn fuelled the Commission to bring forward new cases.

Still, it is also possible to identify even at this early stage a hardening of approach from the Court towards what was expected from the Commission's analysis in order to prove cartel activity. In *Belgian Wallpaper* the Court sought greater economic analysis and more concrete proof (Harding and Joshua, 2003: 127), and this less accommodating attitude was the precursor to the next decade of cartel policy, the onset of economic difficulties and a renewed interest among member state governments in the aims and directions of cartel policy.

2. FORAYS AND STALEMATE, 1973–1984

The 1970s began positively for the evolution of the EU as negotiations were successfully concluded on its first enlargement and the subsequent arrival of Denmark, Ireland and the UK as the newest member states in January 1973.[5] On the competition front the Commission published its first annual competition policy report in 1972 in an effort to inject a degree of greater transparency and provide publicly available information on the issues facing the Commission and on the cases settled in the previous calendar year. The very first report clearly laid down the objectives. Among these the Commission identified the 'need to take action with special rigour against restrictions on competition and practices jeopardising the unity of the Common Market, notably sharing markets, allocating customers and collective exclusive dealing arrangements, and preventing agreement which indirectly resulted in concentrating demand on particular producers' (Commission, 1973). These reports have been written by officials within DG Competition and have provided useful information on DG Competition's thinking. The reports also demonstrated a growing self-assuredness on the part of the European regulator which it was going to need as the competition principle came under attack. Even as Denmark, Ireland and the UK acceded to the EU the warning signs of economic downturn were already in the air. The collapse of the Bretton Woods system in August 1971 brought to an end the financial order of the convertibility of the US dollar to gold and floating exchange rates, and ushered in major changes to the financial landscape. The decision by OPEC in 1973 to raise the price of oil per barrel impacted directly on the economies of the Western world as costs soared, unemployment returned and inflation soared. If the 1950s and the 1960s had been the time of higher economic growth and greater prosperity, the 1970s were hit by recession, doubt and Eurosclerosis. In response member state governments scrambled to protect their national industries and thereby maintain employment. They did not do this in any co-ordinated or co-operative fashion, but sought refuge and protectionism in the erection and maintenance of a range of non-tariff barriers which included state subsidies to industry, imposition of quotas, incomes policies and preferential treatment for national companies. Where was competition policy situated in this transformed economy? Was competition the problem or the solution and how would DG Competition respond?

This second phase of cartel policy covers the period from 1973 to 1984 and is set against an unsuitable climate for any persistent offensive action. Overall the entire Commission did not respond very well to the economic downturn (Cini and McGowan, 2009). The story of EU cartel policy during the 1970s presents a picture of some incremental growth, but also displays a consideration for the plight of more sensitive economic sectors. The Commission certainly maintained its anti-cartel drive and prosecuted a number of important cartels during this period, but it demonstrated considerable flexibility and adjusted to meet the changed economic circumstances (Commission, 1977: 9). It recognised that certain industries, such as shipbuilding, were becoming more uncompetitive in the face of cheaper competition from abroad while others, such as coal and steel, faced a future of longer term decline. DG Competition remained wedded to its objectives and emphasised the advantages of the competitive process, but it was not the best or the correct time to pursue any dogmatic advancement of the competition principle in the face of both external and internal opposition. The former existed in the guise of the member state governments, whereas the internal opposition found voice amongst other DGs, most notably those dealing with industrial policy and regional policy. DG Competition was one voice among many and had not won a majority over to support the competition principle. As a result it advanced more slowly than many of its officials would have liked.

For these reasons DG Competition opted to maintain a less interventionist stance until economic conditions were more favourably disposed towards competition. In adopting a more light handed approach (Wigger, 2008: 175) the Commission was willing to turn a blind eye to state aid, but also showed its readiness to assist industries in decline and consider measures to alleviate unnecessary rises in unemployment, such as the support for structural crisis cartel. These emergency cartels where firms engage in reciprocal reductions in capacity and output were encouraged in the short term in the hope that they would spur recovery and enhance technological development. The Commission has been willing to sacrifice the competition principle 'to avoid the social costs that industry restructuring left to the market would cause' (Motta, 2007: 14). This softer approach was evident in the Commission's support of, for example, the sulphuric acid cartel. Few agreements were actually terminated and only a few of the Commission's decisions were appealed to the ECJ (*Belgian Wallpaper*, *Belgian Tobacco*). Such crisis cartels were, however, very much envisaged as temporary measures (European Commission, 1977), although in reality many of these cartels lasted until the mid 1980s. It is tempting to label this period of the 1970s and early 1980s as one of retrenchment in the case of competition policy, but it would not be totally correct because DG Competition was making progress, uncovering cartels and even conducting its first 'dawn raids' during this period. The story of EU cartel policy during this second period presents a picture of incremental growth, and one in which the Commission was becoming more assertive but also one where simultaneously many cartels intensified their efforts to cover their own tracks from the Commission's gaze.

3. SEIZING THE INITIATIVE AND ADVANCING, 1985–1999

At the start of the 1980s few could have predicted how the appointment of Jacques Delors and his Commission's drive to achieve a genuine single market programme would kick-start the European integration project, and in doing so would very much anchor the competition rules as a core policy. Concerns about global competitiveness had come increasingly to the fore. Viewed from the position of the early 1980s the longer term prospects seemed pretty bleak as European industries looked vulnerable to the growing rise of high tech industries (such as telecommunications, information technology and biotechnology) and fuelled fears that Western Europe was largely dependent on manufacturing the goods of the Second Industrial Revolution and, even worse, looked like becoming dependent on Japanese and US exports. The *Economist* magazine used the opportunity of the twenty-fifth anniversary of the EEC to depict it on its front cover with a headstone and the three letters RIP. Such concerns forced a reappraisal of the state of European economic integration and led to the recognition that too many non-tariff barriers (physical, technical and fiscal) prevented the full benefits of a genuine single market. In response the Commission drafted its now infamous White Paper (Commission, 1985) on 'Completing the Internal Market' which specifically addressed the issue of the Non Tariff Barriers (NTBs). The paper met with full scale agreement of the then ten member state governments (and ushered in a period of positive developments after the resolution of the lengthy saga of budgetary contributions and the UK rebate which had dominated European Council summits since 1980).[6] The actual content of the White Paper was the brainchild of the senior British Commissioner, Lord Arthur Cockfield, and identified 282 areas where progress was needed to secure the reality of a genuine single market. These proposals were expected to provide economies of scale, boost employment, increase member state GDP and attract foreign direct investment, and necessitated legislation which was to be put in place by the end of December 1992 (Cecchini, 1988).

Timing and leadership were both going to prove pivotal in the development of antitrust, and this was particularly the case with the growing neo-liberal turn in policy focus which came to transform notions about the role of competition in the market, and the application and enforcement of antitrust rapidly emerged as a necessary tool in the Commission's strategy to realise the SEM. The actual timing from DG Competition's perspective could not have been more fortuitous and coincided with the arrival of the ultra-liberal and highly competent Leon Brittan as competition Commissioner. Indeed, the changed economic circumstances enabled the Commission to defrost Hallstein's ideas which had been put on ice some twenty years earlier and to continue the process which the Ordo-liberals had commenced (Gehler and von der Groeben, 2002: 53). External developments on the economic philosophy front fused with internal ambitions, and in the space of a few years had utterly transformed DG Competition's reputation. The Commission was finally emerging as a fully fledged and powerful competition regulator. Positively, DG Competition's remit

Table 6.4 Assessing the record and determination of all EU Competition Commissioners against cartels, 1958–present

Commissioner	*National of*	*Office Term*	*Assessment*
Hans von der Groeben	West Germany	1958–66	passive
Emanuel Sassen	Netherlands	1966–70	active
Albert Borchette	Luxembourg	1970–76	passive
Raymond Vouel	Luxembourg	1977–80	passive
Frans Andriessen	Netherlands	1980–84	less passive
Peter Sutherland	Ireland	1985–89	aware
Leon Brittan	United Kingdom	1989–93	active
Karel Van Miert	Belgium	1993–99	active
Mario Monti	Italy	1999–2004	active
Neelie Kroes	Netherlands	2004–09	active

extended to cover mergers in 1989 and led to its increasing activism on the liberalisation of the former public utilities (energy, airlines and telecommunications). As DG Competition's fortunes rose in the late 1980s so it became more assertive on the cartel front as well and placed ever greater priority on the need finally to combat cartels. This anti-cartel agenda has fuelled the priorities, as so frequently stated in speeches, of every Competition Commissioner from Leon Brittan to Neelie Kroes (see Table 6.4) since. The role of personality in the transformation of DG Competition cannot be underestimated. However, on the down side it should be recognised that the more the single market took shape the more DG Competition felt itself further constrained and pressured on the cartel front, as it was compelled to shift some of its limited and much needed resources away from cartel-busting. In short, aspirations and ambitions did not necessarily correlate with a successful pursuit of policy.

The Commission's desire to combat cartels was beset with difficulties. Finding cartels was far from straightforward, and especially when those companies engaged in such activity went to considerable lengths to conceal such agreements. Even when they were unearthed the onus fell on DG Competition to prove the existence of the cartel. Cartel arrangements are often complex constructions, and those of a longer duration are more awkward to regulate because they see considerable change over time as some members, for example, take the lead while others may leave and return, and in so doing be subject to certain aspects of the cartel agreement at certain times only and not others, or party to different aspects throughout. By the mid 1980s the Commission had responded to this real difficulty through its identification of the 'single overall agreement' which placed responsibility on all members of the cartel (Whish, 2003: 93).

Beyond the rhetoric, however, the Commission's determination was also often thwarted, not only by the readiness of many businesses to engage in covert agreements, but also by the resistance or lack of interest in some member states on the issue and its own limited powers for manoeuvre. Regulation 17 had provided a valuable weapon in granting the Commission the power to impose fines on companies which deliberately opted to breach Article 81, but were the fines being set at a high enough level and what exactly constituted a high fine? In order to deter cartellisation the Commission first of all recognised the need to re-examine its fining policy and to raise the bar towards ever higher fines. This realisation reflected growing DG Competition confidence and determination, and from the mid-1980s it is possible to detect (see table 6.5) an upward trend in the severity of fines being imposed (McGowan, 2000). For example, the *Polypropylene* (OJ 1986 L230/1) and *PVC* (OJ 1989 L74/1, 4 CMLR 345) cases in 1986 and 1989 saw for the time the highest recorded fines of ECU 58 million and ECU 23.1 million respectively being imposed.[7]

The Commission's growing conviction that restrictive practices in the form of secret agreements were undoubtedly the most destructive form of anti-competitive practice reinforced its anti-cartel activities in the 1990s. Any doubt that van Miert was going to pursue a more tolerant approach to competition policy in general, given his political background as a Flemish socialist, on taking up the post of Competition Commissioner in 1993 were quickly dashed, and maybe it was this particular background that propelled him on the contrary to intensify the cartel crusade (see table 6.6). At the time, 1994 turned out to be a momentous year in antitrust policy. It was marked by the Commission's imposition of the highest ever annual fines to that point in the history of EU competition policy. This year saw fines totalling some ECU 535 million being levied against *Steel Beams*,[8] *Cartonboard*[9] and *Ciment*[10] cartels. Four years later the Commission recorded another historic result when it imposed new record fines of ECU 560 million on *inter alia* the following four offending cartels:

i) In *British Sugar* (OJ 1999 L76/1) four sugar producers (British Sugar, Tate & Lyle, Napier Brown and James Budgett) which together controlled over 90 per cent of the granulated sugar market in the United Kingdom were fined ECU 50.2 million. This collusive arrangement had adopted a collaborative strategy of higher pricing for sugar on both the industrial and retail markets.
ii) In *Preinsulated Pipes* (OJ 1999 L24/1) ten companies across the European Union were fined ECU 92.21 million for engaging in a series of anti-competitive activities. These included price fixing, market sharing and bid rigging. This cartel particularly displeased

Table 6.5 The imposition of fines for cartel infringements: major cases from the Sutherland and Brittan Years, 1985–92[1]

Decision	Date	Reference	Size of Fine in euros (m)	No. of under-takings
Woodpulp	1984	OJ 1985 L85/1	4.125	36
AKZO	1985	OJ 1985 L374/1	10	1
Polypropylene[2]	1986	OJ 1986 L230/1	57.850	15
Meldoc	1986	OJ 1986 L348/50	6.565	4
Belgian Roofing Felt	1986	OJ 1986 L232/15	1	3
PVC[3]	1988	OJ 1989 L74/1	23.5	14
Italian Flatglass	1988	OJ 1989 L33/44	13.4	3
LdPE	1986	OJ 1989 L74/21	37	17
Welded Steel Mesh	1989	OJ 1989 L260/1	9.5	5
SodaAsh-Solvay[4]	1990	OJ 1991 L152/21	48	2
Eurocheque Helsinki	1992	OJ 1992 L95/20	6	3
Building and Construction Industry NL	1992	OJ 1992 L92/1	22.5	–

Notes:
[1] One of the immediate difficulties for researchers of EU cartel policy has been the time taken by the Commission to publish the decisions against major cartels in the Official Journal. This issue arises because the Commission has to ensure that all business related confidential information has been removed before publication. There is also the issue of translating the decision into twenty-three languages.
[2] This arrangement represented the classic form of a cartel and had endeavoured to distort the market, restrict competition and set agreed prices.
[3] This complex cartel was constructed around a series of artificially high prices and involved a second Commission decision against the same companies in *PVCII* (OJ 1989 L74/1) where DG Competition applied its concept of the 'single overall agreement'. In this case the Commission maintained that the members of the cartel had formed an agreement or concerted practice. The companies involved appealed the case to the CFI but the Court upheld the Commission's earlier decision (OJ 1994 1239/14).
[4] The Commission imposed a fine of €20 million on this cartel which had abused both Articles 81 and 82. It had been in existence for decades, and although the original written agreement ended with the UK's accession to the EEC, the agreement continued and effectively divided up the European market between the UK and Ireland (ICI) and Continental Europe (Solvay).

Sources: Montag (1996), 430–32; and Whish (1993), 460–64.

the Commission as the anti-competitive agreement was sustained for a further nine months after the Commission had become aware of its existence.

iii) In *Greek Ferries* the Commission imposed a fine of ECU 9.12 million

Table 6.6 The imposition of ever higher fines against cartel agreements: the major decisions during the van Miert years, 1993–1999

Decision	Date	Reference	Size of Fine (ECU)
Euro beam producers	1994	OJ 1994 L116/1	104 million
Cartonboard	1994	OJ 1994 L243/1	132 million
Cement	1994	OJ 1994 L343/1	248 million
Far Eastern Freight Conference	1994	OJ 1994 L378/17	130000
Tretorn and others	1994	OJ 1997 L378/41	640000
PVC*	1995	OJ 1994 L239/14	25 million
Dutch Mobile Cranes	1995	OJ 1995 L312/79	11.8 million
Ferry Operators	1996	OJ 1997 L26/23	645000
Alloy Surcharge	1998	OJ 1998 L100/55	27.3 million
Brit Sugar/Tate & Lyle	1998	OJ 1999 L76/1	50.2 million
Preinsulated Pipes	1998	OJ 1999 L24/1	92.21 million
Greek Ferry Operators	1998	OJ 1999 L109/24	9.12 million
Dutch Electronic Equipment	1999	OJ 2000 L39/1	6.55 million

Note: This particular decision was the re-adoption by the Commission of its earlier December 1988 decision following a rejection by the Courts of the *PVC* appeal.

Sources: European Commission Annual Competition Policy Reports, 1993–99, Luxembourg.

on seven Greek ferry operators and one Italian operator. All parties to this agreement had regularly held meetings and exchanged correspondence to determine the fixing of prices for passengers and vehicles. Despite the seriousness of the charge and blatant anti-competitive activities the fine was to all intents and purposes rather modest on account of this cartel's fairly limited impact on the market.

iv) Finally, in *Alloy Surcharge* (OJ 1998 L100/559), six stainless-steel flat producers who accounted for over 80 per cent of European production of stainless-steel finished products were fined ECU 27.3 million for deliberately engaging in price fixing practices.[11]

Did such fines matter? The use of the seemingly powerful weapon of financial penalties certainly proved to be contentious, because until the 1990s published decisions in the *Official Journal* provided the only source of guidance as to the Commission's likely practice. Moreover the fining regime was often accompanied by doubts over impartiality and the way in which the Commission had handled the case, particularly where the wording of the final decision to impose a fine largely resembled the wording of the earlier Statement of Objections. In other words, for many undertakings and their legal advisers it often seemed that DG Competition was simply not interested in company defences and ignored their views and any justifications of the arrangements in question. In practice, the problem lay directly with the rules of procedure as dictated by Regulation 17, where certain individuals within DG Competition, acting in a series of guises of prosecutor, judge and jury, are responsible for a case from its inception to its conclusion (McGowan and Wilks, 1995).[12] The use of fines also proved problematic on two further counts: the first problem centred on the Commission and its reluctance to provide any substantial reasoning for how it arrived at individual fining decisions. This position had led to growing disenchantment and strong criticism from the Court of First Instance. The second criticism concerned the absence of a fines tariff (to enable companies to judge the financial penalties for certain activities), as is the case with regard to the practice in national courts in criminal proceedings.

It was increasingly argued that from a public policy viewpoint some form of tarification system was required to inject greater transparency into the Commission's policy making process. Traditionally, however, the Commission had displayed considerable reluctance to move in this direction and had argued '[t]hat the complexity of the factors to be weighed means that the assessment of fines, rather than being a mathematical exercise based on an abstract formula, involves a legal and economic appraisal of each case' (Commission, 1984). Some opponents of a tarification system argued that the introduction of such a system would simply eliminate the deterrent, for it would enable firms to engage in a cost-benefit analysis of any anti-competitive action. In contrast such views were castigated by others who countered that the basic assumption underlying all attempts to deter infringements by imposing fines is that companies indeed operate a cost-benefit analysis. If deterrence works, it does so by altering the potential offender's balance of expected cost and benefit in such a way as to induce him to refrain from the undesirable action. Tarification thus rather served the deterrence argument, so long as the tariff is either sufficiently detailed or sufficiently flexible (see Wils, 1998: 256–7). All in all, what this actually meant in practice was that these doubts translated into a 'low rate of acceptance of Commission decisions and a correspondingly high rate of court actions' (Montag, 1996: 433) with regard the Commission's fining policy.

Such disaffection was only further fuelled by the unacceptable length of infringement proceedings, and was further augmented by a growing number of Court judgments which criticised the Commission's interpretation as flawed. Statistics indicate that by mid 1998 the Commission had issued thirty-two decisions imposing fines of more than ECU 3 million on one or more undertakings. The reaction to such fines is very revealing. Of the twenty-nine such cases up to the end of 1996 only five were implemented without being challenged. In other words, twenty-four of the twenty-nine cases were appealed to the European Courts. Twelve actions for an annulment of the Commission decision proved highly successful as the fines were either lifted or quashed, and in a further two cases the levied fines were reduced. The lessons for any undertakings seem clear. On these statistics alone the Commission displayed a rather poor record in reaching decisions that were generally accepted, but this should not be so surprising. More alarmingly for the Commission the Courts had shown a readinesss to strike down any Commission decisions which the judges in Luxembourg held to lack sufficient evidence of alleged infringements, and often the inability of DG Competition staff to respect the correct administrative procedure. Indeed, massive fines imposed on European chemical companies by the Commission at the end of the 1980s had still not been paid a decade later as the firms have opened appeals to the Court of Justice. In *ICI–Solvay* (Case C–200/92 [1999] ECR I–4399), for example, the undertakings successfully appealed to the CFI to have their fines of ECU 27 million and ECU 27 million respectively overturned.

External criticism of DG Competition's procedure has been a customary given, but when exerted from the European Courts it shook the foundations of the Avenue de Cortenberg where the DG was based for most of the 1990s. For example, in its first year of operation the CFI annulled a Commission decision in the *LdPE* (low density polyethylene) cartel case (OJ 1989 L74/21) and, even worse, compelled the Commission to pay the legal costs for all seventeen legal teams. In its now infamous interpretation of the *Wood Pulp* cartel (both I and II), for example, the Court of Justice (Case 89/85 [1988] ECR 5193) ruled that the system of quarterly price announcements by producers identified by the Commission did not amount to concertation. It maintained on the contrary that this particular situation had evolved because both buyers and sellers had wanted to create a more stable environment, and this by necessity involved the need to limit commercial risks. More seriously, however, the Commission was condemned for its procedure and method of analysis. The Court went further and exposed DG Competition's reliance on material and on evidence obtained after the statement of objections had been sent, and a complete failure adequately to explain allegations in its statement of objections. *Wood Pulp* has forced the Competition Directorate to produce a 'firm, precise and consistent body of evidence of concertation' if it is to succeed in establishing such practices. However, that said, in general both the Court of Justice from the *Pioneer* decision in 1980 (OJ 1980 L60/1) and even the more aggressive CFI displayed a great deal of reluctance when it came to reducing by any large margins the Commission's discretion with respect to fines. Such cases severely tarnished DG Competition's credibility. Still, growing unease from the business community over the Commission's power to levy fines (Korah, 2007; van Bael, 1995; Gyselen, 1993), as well as increasing criticism of its own methods and procedures from the European courts, finally compelled the Commission to re-examine its procedures. This led to its January 1998 Notice (OJ 1998 C9/3) on its New Method for Calculating Fines in Antitrust Cases. In short, this Notice (which applied to cases falling under Article 81) aimed to increase the transparency and coherence of the Commission's decisions by setting out the different steps involved in the Commission's determination of a specific fine and by providing the ranges of this fine. To this end it abandoned the earlier practice of calculating fines as a percentage of the relevant turnover (when there never had been any good reason for fines to be proportional to turnover). Instead it opted in favour of a far more straightforward approach, in terms of both Commission decision-making and review by the Courts, by focusing more directly on the nature of the infringement.

This move marked a significant development, and meant that from this point onwards all reviews to be conducted by the CFI were not to focus on the choice of the relevant turnover figure (as in the past), but rather on the nature of the infringement. The 1998 Notice represented an earnest attempt by the Commission to improve its handling of competition cases and provided for a radically new four-stage procedure.[13] Infringements were now to be classified as minor, serious or very serious. In order to assess the gravity of the infringement, account had to be taken of the nature of the infringement and its actual impact on the market. DG Competition calculated the actual level of the fines within these parameters, which naturally varied from case to case, and on the nature of the particular infringement. In effect, it must be emphasised that this Notice did not herald any change in the general level of fines and merely reflected the Commission's practice throughout the 1990s, though it does not exclude possible future increases. Where more than one company was concerned it was the responsibility of DG Competition to decide where the level of blame lay and to differentiate between the participants' actions and involvement where necessary and fine accordingly.

A key element in any Commission decision under this Notice surrounded the new emphasis on the duration of the specific agreement.[14] Again these new rules made distinctions between 'short duration' (less than one year), 'medium duration' (one to five years) and 'long duration' (more

Table 6.7 Understanding the origins of DG Competition's workload under Article 81

Year	Notifications	Complaints	Own Initiative	Total
1980	190	58	51	299
1985	213	66	25	304
1990	201	97	75	373
1991	282	83	23	388
1992	246	110	43	399
1993	264	110	26	401
1994	235	170	21	426
1995	360	114	47	521
1996	206	159	82	467
1997	221	177	101	499
1998	216	192	101	509

Source: Office for Official Publications of the European Communities, Annual Community Competition Reports, 1988–1999, Luxembourg.

than five years). In the first instance the base amount for gravity remained unchanged, but in cases of medium duration the Commission opted to be in a position to increase the fine by up to 50 per cent, and in cases of long duration by 10 per cent per year. Essentially, by adapting and redesigning its approach the Commission hoped to provide a greater deterrent by making an explicit link between the duration of an infringement and the size of the fine. Once both the gravity and the duration of a particular infringement had been established, the next step in DG Competition's calculation was the consideration of any aggravating or attenuating circumstances (as listed under the Notice). This was followed (according to section 4 of the Notice) by consideration of the Commission's 1996 Notice on the Non-Imposition or Reduction of Fines in Cartel Cases (OJ 1996 C207/4).

The Commission's caseload had certainly got more manageable, but still remained somewhat problematic as notifications continued to provide the majority of DG Competition's workload under Article 81 (see table 6.7) and did not centre on hard-core cartels. Although a minority of third party complaints continued to draw Commission attention to potential cartel activity the Commission required other measures to assist its staff. The adoption of the 'Leniency' Notice in 1996 (discussed in chapter 7) illustrated the onset of a more proactive Commission response. Although novel as far as European competition experience was concerned, the leniency initiative reflected practice which had been

Table 6.8 Number of cases closed under Article 81 by the Commission, 1988–1998

Year	Formal Decisions	Informal	Total
1988	25	455	480
1989	11	567	578
1990	13	864	877
1991	21	814	835
1992	34	90	124
1993	14	792	806
1994	33	495	528
1995	14	403	417
1996	21	367	388
1997	27	490	517
1998	42	539	582

Source: Office for Official Publications of the European Communities, Annual Community Competition Reports, 1988–99, Luxembourg.

established by the Antitrust division of the Department of Justice (DOJ) in the United States in 1979.[15] The programme was essentially designed to de-stabilise cartels, which the Commission hoped to do though inducements and sweeteners in the form of substantially reduced fines, and even total immunity from fines if cartel members broke cover and informed on their colleagues. This initiative recognised the unstable nature of many cartels and deliberately sought to exploit this particular characteristic. Complete immunity under the leniency programme was only available for the first informant who provided sufficient information for the Commission to launch an inspection of premises, and so long as it continued to co-operate throughout the investigation. The Commission wielded considerable discretion throughout, and any applications for immunity which were deemed not to have provided sufficient information could be denied. Leniency was a useful innovation in theory, but again would it work in practice? The Commission publicly indicated that this practice was proving a productive mechanism to ease its burdens and cited the *Sugar* case of 1998 as an example (Commission, 1999). As a tool it was a means of deterring cartels, but few saw it as a means of preventing cartellisation, and the Commission was forced to contemplate a series of complementary measures to enhance its abilities both to focus on more cartels and simultaneously further to dissuade the emergence of such practices. Could it deliver?

4. CONCLUSIONS

Cartel agreements truly represent the most damaging forms of anti-competitive activity. It may be somewhat surprising therefore to learn that the Commission's pursuit of cartels has often been overshadowed by other policy commitments and has also been distracted by other notifications which fell under Article 81. The majority of formal decisions under Article 81 concerned exemptions rather than cartels (see Table 6.8). The fight against cartels took time to develop, though even by the end of the 1990s fewer than ten were formally detected in any given year. The number for most of these four decades was considerably lower than even this. In part this reality reflected the difficulty of detecting and establishing the existence of cartels and in part reflected the limited resources and the expanding brief of DG Competition. Progress, however, was being made as policy was being shaped in an incremental fashion.

This chapter has shown how the Commission's cartel wars developed and intensified from the early 1960s. As the Commission gained both experience and confidence it came to place greater emphasis on cartel activity. The move towards a tougher fining policy brought consequences. One of the most immediate repercussions was a rise in the number of challenges against Commission decisions being brought by the businesses concerned before the European Courts. The symbiotic relationship between the Commission and the European Courts has long represented one of the most crucial dynamics behind individual EU cartel case outcomes. The Commission's credibility has always been tested by appeals to the Courts. A degree of relative harmony had existed almost undisturbed between the two supranational institutions in the promotion of integration (from the earliest cases such as *Aniline Dyes*, *European Sugar Cartel* and *Quinine*) until the Court of First Instance emerged in 1989 with an altogether more independent and critical approach to the Commission's degree of analysis and argument. Relations between the Commission and the Courts, however, grew fraught during the 1990s when the CFI overturned a number of Commission decisions on the grounds of a supposedly flawed analysis which often rested on the absence of clear proof and documentary evidence that cartels were actually in existence. The *Woodpulp* case fully illustrated the tensions and soured relations between the institutions. The Commission was going to have to find a way to deal with the Courts and to provide greater evidence of anti-competitive wrongdoing. Fighting cartels was both stressful and very time-engaging and led the Commission to consider new and more innovative measures and to design new strategies to combat cartellisation, and set the backdrop to the fourth phase of the Commission's cartel wars which commenced in 1999 with the arrival of a new Competition Commissioner and the first real effort to overhaul and modernise the administrative mechanics behind the operationalisation of Article 81. The new century was to usher in the *decussis mirabilis* (glorious decade) of cartelbusting.

NOTES

1. It should be noted that some types of agreement (and this to some extent reflects earlier more sympathetic perceptions) were entitled to exemptions from the EU competition rules where they contributed to improving the production or distribution of goods, promoted technical and economic progress or ensured that consumers reaped considerable benefits. Prior to 1 May 2004 such exemptions under Article 81(3) were solely at the Commission's discretion to bestow if an agreement's beneficial effects were judged to outweigh any detrimental impact on competition.
2. See recital 1, Council Regulation (EC) No 1/2003 on the Implementation of the Rules laid down in Articles 81 and 82 of the Treaty, *Official Journal 2003*, L1/1.
3. In a sense, the *de minimis* rule marks the dividing line between agreements that are to be dealt with at European level, that is, those that are likely to have an impact on the common market, and those that remain the responsibility of national authorities. The latest Notice, published in 2001 (OJ 2001 C 368), served part of the Commission's modernisation agenda (see Peeperkorn, 2001) and aimed to reduce the compliance burden for smaller companies the agreements of which, by the nature of their size and impact, did not restrict competition. This move also allowed DG Competition to focus its energies on the much more problematic agreements. The amended Notice raised the *de minimis* level to a 10 per cent market share for agreements between competitors and to 15 per cent for agreements between non-competitors. In short, agreements which fall below these new thresholds are judged not to possess even a minimum degree of market power and do not fall under Article 81. The Notice states that agreements between small and medium sized enterprises are rarely capable of affecting trade between the member states and do not fall under EU scrutiny.
4. The European unit of account (EUA) was created through the Treaty of Rome for the purpose of providing a unit of account for the EU institutions. It was a monetary unit which was replaced in March 1979 by the ECU (European currency unit), which itself was the immediate predecessor of the euro.
5. The United Kingdom acceded to the EEC under the premiership of Edward Heath in January 1973 and some twenty-five years after the Treaty of Rome had come into force. The existing competition policy provisions had not factored at all as part of the negotiations as entry alone had become the utmost priority of successive UK governments (and the business community) since the very early 1960s.
6. Greece joined the European Economic Community in January 1981 and the Mediterranean push would be followed by the accession of both Portugal and Spain in 1986.
7. It is simply not possible, given space restraints, to provide background information on all of the cases mentioned in the text, and readers are strongly encouraged to check some of the leading legal texts as provided, for example, by Goyder, 2003; Sufrin and Jones, 2008; Whish, 2003, and should also check the excellent *European Competition Law Review*.
8. In February a group (from across the EU) of seventeen steel-beam suppliers were fined ECU 104 million (£78.9 million) for operating a cartel in the production of steel beams for use in the construction industry. In fixing the fine the Commission took account of the length, gravity and accrued profits from the cartel. Interestingly, this agreement was unearthed following a series of dawn raids by the Commission in 1991 on the premises

of the seventeen associated company members engaged in the manufacture and distribution of the steel beams. The documentation seized revealed that the cartel had been in operation since 1984 and that those involved had assumed the customary practices of fixing quotas and prices and exchanging what would otherwise have been deemed confidential information.

9. In July 1994, and once again as the result of the Commission initiating its own investigation, nineteen carton board producers were fined ECU 132 million (£104.27 million) for operating what was described by van Miert as Europe's 'most pernicious' price fixing cartel. This clandestine cartel extended across the entire European cartonboard industry and implicitly entailed an agreement on prices and market shares. Within it 'all participants helped to develop a comprehensive system for . . . the monitoring of production, sales volume and capacity utilisation'. In practice those involved raised prices almost simultaneously. Such action prevented their customers taking advantage of what should have been different prices within the European market, and thus thwarted their customers' efforts at securing alternative sources of supply. In short, competition was duly impeded during the operation of this arrangement, and indeed the practice led to a rise in profits of some 86 per cent in the period from 1986 to 1989.
10. In November 1994 the Commission levied a record fine of ECU 248 million (£193 million) on a group of thirty-three national cement producers and associations of the European cement industry for co-ordinating anti-competitive activity since 1983. In Europe's most cartel ridden industry this specific agreement had led to the division of the EU market into distinct national markets and widespread interchange of confidential information amongst all those party to the agreement.
11. This was deemed an infringement of Article 65 of the ECSC. See *Competition Policy Newsletter*, No.2, June, 1998, p. 50.
12. In an analysis of those cases that culminate in the imposition of fines, Montag illustrates how investigations often exceed five years. On average it took almost four years to adopt a decision. In practice, the more companies involved in an infringement, the longer it takes to reach a decision.
13. These have included the *De Minimis* Notice of 1996, the Relevant Market Notice of January 1997 and the 1993 Notice on Co-operation between the EU and the National Authorities.
14. Under the previous system the duration of a cartel agreement was an issue which the Commission examined, but in practice, it made little difference in the calculation of setting of a fine.
15. The DOJ granted immunity from its criminal sanctions regime. The scheme was thoroughly revised in 1993 and has led to a growing number of firms applying for leniency and providing evidence which has enabled the US competition authorities to unearth cartels.

7. The *decussis mirabilis* and the antitrust revolution in Europe, 1999 to the present

If the narrative of EU cartel policy from the 1960s to the 1990s represented one of incremental development, it is one that reaches its pinnacle during a fourth phase of activity which commenced at the turn of the twentieth century and the start of a new millennium. By this point in time the dangers of naked cartellisation within the neo-liberal hegemony were increasingly being appreciated and understood (OECD, 2003). Cartels were held to be costing society billions in dollars, euros and other currencies and seriously thwarting the benefits of market globalisation. It was now generally taken for granted that the existence of hard core cartels (price-fixing and market sharing agreements which aim to restrict competition) damaged consumers by raising prices and reducing output and had negative repercussions on economic efficiency.[1] This universal condemnation and recognition provided the Commission with an apt opportunity to re-examine its own cartel policy and to intensify its war against cartels. It was to culminate in a radical overhaul and restructuring of the entire EU cartel regime. The Commission's anti-trust zeal was in clear evidence in a growing number of decisions against cartel activity), refinements to its leniency initiative, ever higher increasing fines and stricter fining policy (in 2006), an internal restructuring of DG Competition to enable a more concerted and dedicated approach to combat cartels, the publication of its Green (2005) and White Papers (2008) on Private Actions and increased international co-operation. Most of these innovative and imaginative changes proved fairly straightforward for the Commission to introduce, as the refinements did not require the approval of either the Council or the European Parliament. However, the most comprehensive and significant development after 1999, in the form of the new empowering Regulation 1/2003 (which replaced Regulation 17) in 2004, did require and received Council approval.

Together all these changes, sought to modernise the Commission's approach to cartel agreements. In part, however, these changes, if viewed from a positive viewpoint, reflected the Commission's determination fully to tackle cartels, but in part, and viewed from a more negative perspective, bore witness to the long recognised difficulties of hunting cartels. The entire reform package after 1999 represented nothing less than a real revolution in the way cartel policy was now going to be enforced and implemented (Monti, 2004). It was hailed as an essential step in the EU's ongoing evolution into a world-class competition regime (DTI, 2001) and sought to update the existing EU administrative machinery in an effort to ensure more efficient, predictable and legitimate outcomes. This chapter explores this fourth and final phase of EU cartel policy which it categorises as the *decussis mirabilis*. It analyses the nature and the significance of these latest and most radical reforms to the EU cartel regime. Particular attention is paid to the impact of Regulation 1/2003 throughout, but reference is also made to the other notable changes and measures, such as the revision and extension of the Leniency programme, higher fining possibilities, the reorganisation of DG Competition and growing intra-European co-operation, which were pursued by the Commission to make its handling of cartel cases both easier and more effective. This chapter illustrates how these alterations can be understood through the triple lenses of modernisation, decentralisation and even federalisation.

1. THE MODERNISATION OF EU ANTI-CARTEL STRATEGY, 1999–2004

Undoubtedly, the most significant development in this fourth phase of EU cartel activity centres on the overhaul of the mechanics of EU cartel policy which was enshrined in Regulation 1/2003 which came into operation on 1 May 2004. The new regulation has facilitated the Commission's determination to simplify and improve the administrative machinery and modernised at a stroke the rules pertaining to the assessment and handling of restrictive practices (and also firms abusing their dominant position in the market place under Article 82). Although calls for reform date back to the early 1990s, the formal process began in earnest only in 1999 following a Commission White Paper (European Commission, 1999) on the modernisation of the implementing rules of Articles 81 and 82 of the EC Treaty.[2] The significance of this White Paper should not be underestimated. According to Claus-Dieter Ehlermann, a former Director General of DG Competition, 'the White Paper . . . is the most important policy paper the Commission has ever published in more than 40 years of EC Competition policy. It suggests a legal and cultural revolution in proposing the fundamental reorganisation of the existing responsibilities between the Commission national anti-trust authorities and national courts' (Ehlermann, 2000: 537).

The radical nature of this regulation has been echoed by other commentators (McGowan, 2005: 987; and Wigger and Nölke, 2007: 487). The White Paper found support from all member state governments (Wilks, 2005: 435) and rapidly evolved into a proposed draft regulation which was submitted by the Commission to the Council in September 2000 and was then duly approved by the Council, under the Danish presidency on 16 December 2002, and became Regulation 1/2003. It came into effect on 1 May 2004, on the same day as the EU enlarged to take in ten new states (eight from Central and Eastern Europe plus Cyprus and Malta) and extended the EU competition rules across the full membership of the EU25. The later date had been deliberately selected by the European Council to provide this latest wave of member states with sufficient time to make any necessary amendments to their own domestic competition legislation.

Regulation 1/2003 emerged as the final product of extensive discussions and circulation of ideas (see Radaelli and Schmidt, 2004) which had taken place not only between the EU institutions but had also involved the full epistemic competition policy community (Van Waarden and Drahos, 2002) which, alongside competition officials from the European Commission, included officials from the national competition authorities (NCAs) and representatives from private business associations (e.g. the European Round Table of Industrialists (ERT), the Union of Industrial and Employers Confederations of Europe (Business Europe) and the European Office of Consumers Associations (BEUC)).[3] Reform, it must be emphasised was far from being a necessarily automatic, let alone a foregone, conclusion. Discussions and deliberations had revealed a number of detractors early on, and particularly for example in Germany, where repeated concerns were raised by the German Federal Cartel Office (BKartA) over what it deemed to constitute the inherent weaknesses of the suggested new regime. These reservations centred primarily on the degree to which EU decisions were subject to the infusion of politicking in the College of Commissioners. Although the BKartA vocally resisted changes and tried to ensure that Article 81 should serve as a minimum standard, with national competition law being allowed to offer stricter formulations, it was unable to muster a blocking minority in the Council of Ministers, and the German government was left with no other policy option but to seek consensus and the proposals passed.

The key elements of the reform under the new regulation can be neatly summarised under three key headings: the abolition of the notification system; the decentralisation and the sharing of enforcement power with the member states as a means of ensuring the uniformity of application of rules; and lastly, enhanced powers for the Commission. Taking these aspects together, this new regulation marks a sizeable shift in the administration of policy and has ushered in a marked change in approach for all concerned.[4] The reform agenda itself had been driven by two factors: firstly, recognition which the existing practices which had been in place for over forty years were becoming ever more problematic, and, secondly, an expected augmented case load after EU enlargement into Central and Eastern Europe. In short, the reworking sought was designed to facilitate the Commission's cartelbusting enforcement strategies; to create a more level playing field and ensure a greater degree of consistency and certainty for companies and to reduce the bureaucratic processes. Modernisation and decentralisation were the two key hallmarks of this reform package, and both were presented by the Commission as a means to secure better enforcement through redesigning the rules that applied to the handling of Article 81 and through the creation of a European family of competition regulators which brought together the Commission and the national authorities within the European Competition Network (ECN). Did the regulation achieve its authors' ambitions?

2. UNPACKING REGULATION 1/2003

The former (pre-2004) system had placed responsibility for enforcing the competition rules where intra-EU trade was concerned directly onto the Commission. This may have made sense, but the requirement that all agreements which potentially violated Article 81 had to be notified to the Commission, and especially where either a clearance or an exemption was being sought, proved largely unsatisfactory and practically unworkable from an efficiency perspective. This system had effectively pushed DG Competition into a reactive mode from its inception, and had diverted the Competition Directorate's staff and energies away from the more serous hard-core cartels towards the more routine and certainly numerous notifications from companies which simply wished to ensure that their specific agreements did not contravene the provisions of Article 81 or could be exempted from the EU rules if they did.[5] In practice, DG Competition had found itself swamped from the very outset under a sea of notifications. This was problematic not so much in terms of the resources dedicated to such notified agreements, but more in terms of the fact that so few of these agreements, constituted anywhere near a serious breach of the Competition rules (Monti, 2007: 397). Indeed, the Commission prohibited only nine notified agreements in total between 1962 and 1999.

The Commission was only too aware of the surmountable hurdles it faced. The creation of block exemptions, *de minimis* thresholds (which have been regularly revised) and the issuing of comfort letters (as an interim measure which allowed companies to operate safe in the knowledge that they would be exempted from any future negative Commission decision) certainly played a considerable role in easing the caseload, but it did not eradicate the problem entirely and the Commission was never able to digest its workload. Even by the early 1990s the Commission was still facing a backlog of some one thousand cases. Dealing with notifications meant that there was considerably less time to pursue its own proactive investigations into specific economic sectors or individual cases. Indeed, EU enlargement to twenty-seven may not have meant paralysis but it certainly threatened severely to undermine the workings of the EU competition regime. In short, the centralised system established by Regulation 17 hampered 'the application of Community rules by the courts and competition authorities of the member states, and the system . . . prevents the Commission from concentrating its resources on curbing the most serious infringements'.[6]

Regulation 1/2003 makes significant strides in the evolution of DG Competition's cartel wars. In the first instance the system of notifications has been abolished and now follows the American *ex post* model. What this means in practice for the business community is that firms are fully expected to know the rules of the game and familiarise themselves with the mechanics of the new regime as all 'agreements, decisions and concerted practices caught by Article 81(1) of the Treaty which do not satisfy the conditions of Article 81(3) of the Treaty shall be prohibited, no prior decision to that effect being necessary' (Article 1, Regulation 1/2003). In other words 'everything not permitted was forbidden' (Wigger and Nölke, 2007: 496). This alteration and self-assessment model ensures that firms pay close attention to the activities of their competitors and creates a system involving 'a significant privatisation of EC competition law' (Buch-Hansen, 2008: 212). For others (Wilks, 2005) the final version of Regulation 1/2003 in effect created the particular French model of cartel policy which had been advocated in the late 1950s.

In operation Regulation 1/2003 has been designed to enable DG Competition to become much more proactive in protecting competition in the internal market. The European competition regulator should now find itself in a position to focus its resources on combating cartels and other serious breaches of the competition rules, rather than simply processing notifications, but it does raise queries about how far it provides the business community with less security than the former notification system. The varying degrees of potential insecurity in the business sector will certainly secure a lucrative flow of money for the legal community as the former seeks security. It is interesting to reflect that one of the winning groups from the introduction of this new regulation is undoubtedly the legal firms and prospective competition law specialists, who should certainly find much improved career opportunities.

The freeing up of valuable resources from DG Competition's perspective has also been accompanied by the 'decentralisation' of antitrust power and responsibilities. Indeed the decision to decentralise enforcement by enabling the national competition authorities and courts to be able directly to apply Articles 81 and 82 to any agreement which may affect trade between states marks another major development and a decisive shift in the objectives of the new anti-cartel regime. It means that national authorities are now equipped with the means for the first time of applying Article 81 in its entirety themselves. For the cartelbusters, the burden of proving an infringement of Article 81(1) of the Treaty 'rests on the authority alleging the infringement while the firms claiming the benefit of Article 81(3) shall bear the burden of proving that conditions of that paragraph are met' (see Article 2 of Regulation 1/2003). Notably in this regard the European Commission has agreed to surrender its monopoly over Article 81(3) and has allowed the member state authorities to rule on exemptions. This so-called 'deliberate sacrifice' (Goyder, 2003: 551) was a logical step, has been well calculated and brings specific advantages, most notably greater uniformity and consistency. This affirmation of a system of parallel competences and the creation of a flexible mechanism for case allocation between the national and supranational levels is a radical innovation. Put another way, the regulation effectively means that the national competition bodies have been transformed into cartel-like agencies of the European Commission.

Some have interpreted this reform package as an adept masterstroke on the part of the Commission to anchor its pre-eminent position (Wilks, 2005) vis-à-vis the national authorities. Some observers were more critical during the debates and argued that such alterations threatened a complete Balkanisation of competition policy enforcement (Joshua, 2001). Doubts were raised, for example by both the EP and the EESC, about the dangers of inconsistent enforcement across the EU and a loss of legal certainty.[7] These concerns were overridden, as for many any fears that divergent decision making will result from such intended decentralisation which would then undermine both legal certainty and the unity of the system have been overplayed. It is still too early to provide an accurate assessment of the reform and how it will play, but the Commission has already conducted its first survey (which remained open for public comment until the end of September 2008) of how Regulation 1/2003 was working and being greeted in practice. The results were promising.

3. ENHANCED POWERS AND PROACTIVE LEADERSHIP

Sometimes in the history of European competition policy it has seemed that cartels have been sidelined in the press by the more glamorous and politically sensitive areas of the competition brief such as mergers, state aids and the liberalisation of the public utilities. This has been at best unfortunate and at worst a real failing. Let us be clear here, because not only do cartels represent just as exciting an area as the others but they remain the core element of any antitrust authority's activities. Part of the answer why cartels seem to have been downplayed owes much to the nature of cartellisation and the reality that cartelbusting cases have never been as straightforward to process as the handling, for example, of potential mergers, and in part also from many of the legal complexities and arguments surrounding the notion of an agreement and its activities. It is important that we do not let the legal labyrinth deter the greater exploration of cartels. After all, the cartel has become an international phenomenon and problem.

Despite the existence of extensive investigatory powers under regulation 1/2003 the task of detecting cartels has always been and is particularly difficult and the burden of proof has rested squarely with the Commission, which has found itself confronting an onerous task. Experience has shown that there has always been a number of long standing cartel arrangements. In the *Sorbates* case (1P/03/1330) the Commission uncovered evidence that took the formation of this cartel back to 1976. Experience has also shown that certain sectors, such as cement, pharmaceuticals and steel, seem to have more of a propensity towards cartellisation than others (Monti, 2000).

Over the years firms engaged in such practices have become increasingly adept at concealing their moves. For example, experience has shown that there are numerous cases where business records have been stored at the homes of directors or other employees, and to aid the cartelbusters the new regulation grants the European Commission the power (McGowan, 2005: 994; Monti, 2007: 410) for the first time to interview individuals or representatives from an undertaking (Article 19), enables the Commission not only to search business premises where serious violations are suspected (Article 20), but also under Article 21 equips the cartelbusters with the power to search domestic premises (home raids).[8] Complaints from third parties and former cartel members represent a fundamental means of detecting infringements, and from the Commission's perspective it remains essential to establish a clear and efficient procedure for handling complaints. Consequently, the Commission has devised a new

Table 7.1 Cartel cases decided by the European Commission since 1990

Period	Number
1990–1994	11
1995–1999	10
2000–2004	33
2005–2008	24
Total	78

Source: European Commission website, http://ec.europa.eucompetition/index_en.html

official complaint form (Form C) for these parties to complete. Moreover, DG Competition's ability (under Article 17) to conduct its own enquiry into a particular sector of the economy is again reinforced, and in both theory and practice from now on should result in many more cases being opened by the Commission. Although this power is far from new, being provided for in Regulation 17, it does reinforce a genuine commitment and it is expected that this rarely evoked Article (on three occasions in the sugar, beer and telecommunications markets) will be deployed more often. According to the Commission this step is already producing positive results, and enabled it to launch a full enquiry and information gathering exercise into the state of competition in the pharmaceutical sector for those medicines related to human consumption in January 2008 (IP/08/49).

Organisational leadership is absolutely crucial in any anti-cartel strategy and it has been an important feature of EU competition governance over the last two decades. Positively DG Competition has been fortunate in its receipt of its most recent Commissioners who have driven home time and time again the dangers of cartellisation. Mario Monti (1999–2004) emerged as another heavyweight and promoter of neo-liberal policies in 1999 and was always ready in public speeches to advance the need for greater regulation and liberalisation. As a former professor of economics he held a particular interest in and grasp of competition policy and showed a resilient hostility towards cartellisation.[9] EU cartel policy clearly moved further centre stage after 2004 with the appointment of Neelie Kroes (2004–2009) as competition commissioner. An avowed opponent of protectionist tendencies, she focused much of her attention on the cartel problem and a greater need for the identification, targeting and pursuit of cartels. Overall, some commentators have described developments after 1999 as representing a shift 'from the Rhenish to the Anglo-Saxon variety of capitalism' (Wigger and Nölke, 2007: 505). Kroes has pledged to 'be steadfast in applying zero tolerance to those who operate cartels to the disadvantage of customers . . . I have made it crystal clear that the fight against cartels will be one of my top priorities. . . I intend to walk the walk as well as talk the talk'.[10] There is, of course, nothing particularly new in rhetoric behind this anti-cartel drive. The rhetoric is good, but is the Commission delivering?

Throughout the history of EU restrictive practices and cartel policy it is clear that DG Competition's activities have been hampered by too many potential cases coming before it, and this weakness was exacerbated by an insufficient number of staff to deal adequately (in terms of speedy decision making) with all these cases. DG Competition and external commentators had long voiced their concern (and correctly) over insufficient staffing levels, and a backlog arose which restricted DG Competition's pursuit of cartel agreements. Aware of this reality and the prevalence of cartels the Commission has long sought a means to prioritise its fight against such overt anti-competitive practices. This objective has been brought closer with an increase in staff levels. A number of recent rises in overall personnel numbers to some 750 by the end of 2006 (as compared to 411 in 1992) (Cini and McGowan, 2009: 53) is expected to facilitate the competition regulator's efforts to handle more cases (see table 7.2). An augmented pool of staff may work but DG Competition will still be hard pressed, however, as overall numbers are still fairly modest. Indeed, some 357 officials deal with anti-trust, mergers and liberalisation as well as cartels. Yet, from a more positive viewpoint the welcome additional staff numbers have enabled a degree of strategic organisational restructuring and the creation of a new dedicated (and seventy-strong) Cartels Directorate (Directorate G).

Table 7.2 Commission Cartel decisions and annual fines since 2003

Year	No. of Cartels detected	Total Fines
2003	5	404.8 m
2004	6	390.2 m
2005	5	683 m
2006	7	1846 m
2007	8	3338 m
2008	7	2271
2009 (to March)	1[1]	132
Total	39	9065 m

Note: [1] *Marine Hoses* became the first cartel decision of 2009 (IP/09/137) when 6 companies were handed a fine of €131 million.

Source: DG Competition website http://ec.europa.eu/competitionand sourced on 11 March 2009

Table 7.3 Fines imposed for Article 81 violations, 1990–2009

Year	Amount in €
1990–1994	344 282 550
1995–1999	270 963 500
2000–2004	3 207 305 210
2005–2008	8 270 585 100
Total	12 093 136 360

Note: These fines have been corrected where appropriate to accommodate both CFI and ECJ decisions.

Source: DG Competition website, http://ec.europa.eu/competition and sourced on 11 March 2009

It is a welcome development, but in reality more staff are required. The number of decisions in cartel cases is getting better than in the past but still remains somewhat low and is due to resource constraints and arguably a degree of inefficiency within DG Competition, where there is considerable staff rotation and the involvement of too many staff with pending cases and cases before the Courts. The decision making process remains too slow. Even without taking on any new cases it is generally assumed that DG Competition would require several years to clear the existing backlog. Not surprisingly the Commission has continued to seek further deterrents and means to both break up cartels and deter them in the first place. To this end the Commission pushed for the further efforts at modernising the rules to allow its staff actively to hunt for cartels as opposed to spending much of their time processing actual cases.

One of the most visible developments in this fourth period has undoubtedly centred on the Commission's determination to penalise cartel activity with the imposition of ever higher amounts of fines. There have been thirty-nine decisions against cartels (see table 7.2) since the start of 2003, and the scale and scope of the fining arrangements today differ so much from the situation just a decade ago, as table 7.3 shows. Indeed, the seventeen highest fines in the history of EU cartel policy since 1969 (see table 7.4) were all levied after 2000 and eleven of these have occurred after 2005. The *Car Glass* cartel from 2008 (see figure 7.1) and the *Lifts and Escalators* cartel from 2007 embody the two largest fines ever in the history of EU cartelbusting.[11] The lesson being driven forward by the Commission is that cartels are no longer to be tolerated.

These fines clearly reflect a steep upward trajectory, but there have always been questions over whether such corporate fines which were capped actually impacted sufficiently on the companies to hurt them or deter them from further activity. How high is high enough has been an issue which has divided commentators.[12] There is agreement that deterrence requires a heavy financial sanction, but the fines imposed by the Commission may simply fail to outweigh the illegal profits that have been earned. For many commentators (Buiccirossi and Spagnolo, 2006; Motta, 2007) fines have traditionally been set at too low a level and have argued that any real deterrent needs greatly to exceed the original 10 per cent threshold established under Regulation 17. Few fines in the not too distant past came anywhere close!

The Commission recognised such criticisms and finally responded by introducing a new, and the strictest yet, framework notice for the setting of fines in 2006 and one which significantly raises the bar when imposing fines (IP/06/857). It sees a possible tenfold increase in the level of fine that can be imposed and an even higher penalty for repeat offenders.[13] The Commission is making its intention robustly clear, and by stiffening the deterrent is hoping to encourage more whistleblowers. The new fining arrangements mark a major step forward, and it is increasingly difficult to make a case for higher fines without entailing some degree of social costs for the companies concerned. Fining arrangements may represent a useful means to deter existing cartels, but how far do they prevent the formation of new cartels? Under existing arrangements managers and chief executives rarely lose their jobs for cartel activity. Any future move towards the introduction of criminal sanctions (as in the USA and in some EU member states) which includes real and personal risk (prison sentences) to such executives may arguably provide greater results. Indeed, the US experience is illuminating in this regard. Posner (1976: 39) has argued that 'the elimination of the formal cartel from . . . industries is an impressive and remains the major, achievement of the American antitrust law'. The US Department of Justice is convinced that huge fines and lengthy prison sentences are the real keys to the successful pursuit and eradication of cartel arrangements (Hammond, 2005). It is interesting to note how the UK competition authorities have approached this idea (Hammond and Penrose, 2001) and started earnestly to replicate this American model (Cini, 2008), and the same US experience is gaining ground within the staff of DG Competition. The issue of criminal sanctions would certainly prove controversial in terms of wider discussions about EU competences under the current Pillar 1, but such sanctions already apply in many member states (though they are rarely used). Creeping steps towards some form of 'harmonised criminal sanctions' (Daly, 2007: 315) for cartel offences in the EU are probably much closer than many commentators realise, though there is scope to debate the origins and promoters of such developments. Although criminal sanctions remain a distant objective the Commission

Table 7.4 The EU's cartel wars: the seventeen largest fines in EU antitrust history, 1969 to the present[1]

Case name and economic sector	Year fine imposed	Number of cartel members	Amount of fine (in euros)
Car glass	2008	4	1383.8 million
Lift and escalators	2007	5	992.3 million
Vitamins	2001	4	855 million (on appeal reduced to 790.5 million)
Gas insulated switchgear	2007	11	750.7 million
Candle waxes	2008	10	676.0 million
Synthetic rubber	2006	6	519 million
Flat glass	2007	4	486.9 million
Plasterboard	2002	–	458.5 million
Hydrogen peroxide	2006	9	388.1 million
Methacrylates (acrylic glass)	2006	5	344.5 million
Hard haberdashery/zip fasteners	2007	7	328.6 million
Copper fittings producers	2006	11	314.7 million
Carbonless paper	2001	6	313.6 million
Plastic industrial bags	2005	16	290.7 million
Dutch brewers	2007	4	273.7 million
Bitumen Netherlands	2006	14	266.6 million
Chloroprene rubber	2007	6	247.6 million

Note: [1]There were of course a number of smaller cases during this period. It is not the intention to list all here but they included, among others, decisions against FETTCSA (€6.9 million in 2000); Amino Acids (€109 million in 2000); Soda-Ash (€33 million in 2000); SAS/Maersk Air (€52.5 million in 2001); Sodium Gluconate (€57.7 million in 2001); Belgian Brewers (€91 million in 2001); Luxembourg Brewers (€448 000 in 2001); Citric Acid (€135.22 million in 2001); German Banks (€100.8 million in 2001); Austrian Banks (€124.46 million in 2002); Dutch Industrial Gases (€25 million in 2002); Sothebys/Christies (€20.4 million in 2002); Food Flavour Enhancers (€20.56 million in 2002); and Concrete Reinforcing Bars (€85 million in 2002).

Source: European Commission website at http://ec.europa.eu/competition/cartels/overview/faqs_en.html on 12 March 2009

has been eager to adopt a private action scheme which could see those breeching the competition rules facing even higher fines.

For the moment, fines remain the Commission's best weapon and table 7.4 illustrates the severity of the more recent ones. Still, are they severe enough? Fines also impact in another way as evidence illustrates that markets do react rather badly to Commission investigations of cartel activity (as made public in dawn raids), infringement decisions and negative court judgments (Langer and Motta, 2006). In the short term a firm's value actually falls. How far and how damaging such falls may be is open to further question. Positively, however, the fines impact on European consumers in two ways. The first outcome is relatively straightforward and relates to the benefits to consumers from a system of genuine competition (better quality products at lower prices), but the second is equally significant and relates directly to this attempt to mainstream competition policy because these fines are paid directly to the EU and enter the miscellaneous category of the EU budget. The incentives for pursuing and pushing the war against cartels are considerable, but the road is often beset with difficulties as the Commission needs to collect the evidence which is usually well concealed by the members of the cartel.[14] One of the most curious things to note is that many of the cartel offenders are and have been members of the ERT, and this reality raises many issues of trust (especially when co-operation may be more forthcoming over merger applications) and underscores the intrinsic problems of pursuing cartels.

4. WEAPON UPGRADES, STRENGTHENED CO-OPERATION AND COLLABORATION, 2005 TO THE PRESENT

This fourth period of activity also saw an overhauling of the Leniency initiative in 2002 (OJ 2002 C45/3) as a means of making it more straightforward to grant total immunity for the first firm which willingly co-operates and provides DG Competition's officials with substantial information on the operations of the cartel infringement. More total immunity decisions are being made.[15] Leniency had promised to relieve DG Competition's resources and to provide hard evidence to present to the Courts, but did not initially deliver the results as had been imagined. There was one major distinction between the EU and the US leniency schemes. Whereas leniency was automatic under the US regime it was at the Commission's discretion to give and also to determine by how much under the EU system. In its scheme the Commission had devised several categories to reflect the level of reduction in the fine depending on the material and evidence supplied by the firm in question. This form of the leniency initiative, however, proved problematic as it left business unsure about the advantages of pursuing the leniency route and prompted the first overhaul of the Leniency programme in 2002 to provide immediate immunity.

This refinement seems to have made a real and lasting difference. Whereas experience of the first Leniency programme had displayed

Table 7.5 The ten largest fines imposed by the Commission on individual companies for cartel membership

Company	Fine (euros)	Year
Saint Gobain	896 000 000	2008 (Car Glass)
ThyssenKrupp	479 669 850	2007 (Lifts and Escalators)
Hoffmann-La Roche	462 000 000	2001 (Vitamins)
Siemens	396 562 500	2007 (Gas Insulated Gear)
Pilkington	370 000 000	2008 (Car Glass)
Sasol Limited	318 200 000	2008 (Candle Wax)
ENI SpA	272 250 000	2006 (Synthetic Rubber)
Lafarge SA	249 600 000	2002 (Plasterboard)
BASF AG	236 845 000	2001 (Vitamins)
Otis	224 932 950	2007 (Lifts and Escalators)

Source: European Commission website at http://ec.europa.eu/competition/cartels/overview/faqs_en.html on 12 March 2009

considerable reluctance towards this Commission initiative (Reynolds and Anderson, 2006) from the business community the policy is now proving very effective. Indeed, most of the recent cartel investigations conducted by DG Competition commenced following a request for immunity from any fine by whistleblowers under the terms of the Leniency programme. Indeed, whereas the Commission received eighty applications (both for total immunity and a reduction in fines) in the period from 1996 to 2002 it is interesting to note post the 2002 Notice the rise in such requests. In the period from February 2002 until the end of December 2006 104 applications were made. Fifty-six of these were granted partial or complete immunity. It is also significant to note that the introduction of the Leniency programme has also directly led to a significant rise in the number of dawn raids being conducted by the Commission. Nearly two-thirds of all inspections, for example, in the period from 2001 to 2003 were based on leniency requests (Sufrin and Jones, 2008: 879). The system appears to be working well and has 'been an extremely effective device in uncovering cartels and in facilitating the Commission's task to prosecute the companies involved in such cartels' (Motta, 2007: 18). The fact that more and more companies are approaching the Commission for leniency is a sure sign of the programme's impact (see Geradin and Henry, 2005), and success has been enthusiastically welcomed by the Commission. However, two more critical points should be made at this point. Firstly, the Leniency programme has not substantially reduced the length of time needed by DG Competition to handle the case and the competition regulator has carefully to select its cases and prefers to focus on major international cartels. The second issue is important because the Leniency initiative does not provide complete immunity for the whistleblower if a third party (who has been negatively affected by the activities of the cartel) opts to initiate civil proceedings against the entire cartel membership.[16] That said the Commission has continued to tweak the system. The publication of the most recent Leniency Notice in December 2006 (OJ 2006 C 2917; de Broca, 2006) has reinforced the fundamental shift in business' approaches to, and growing acceptance of, the leniency initiative. This revised Notice represents another step to both detect and terminate hardcore cartel activity and reflects the reality that leniency styled programmes are fast becoming the norm in many competition regimes. The 2006 Notice clarifies for companies the information the Commission requires for an undertaking to benefit from immunity, as well as providing greater guidance on how to obtain a reduction in fines.

Accordingly the Commission maintains that the Leniency programme continues to play a crucial role in DG Competition's detection efforts and continues to entice more 'whistleblowers' to come forward. However, it has been suggested that most of the cartels detected through the Leniency programmes would probably have broken up within a couple of years in any case (Lowe, 2007). The fortunes of the companies which have opted to co-operate have been mixed to date. In the very first decision stemming from the 2002 Notice in *Raw Tobacco Italy* the original whistleblower's hope of conditional immunity was dashed when it was discovered that it (Deltafina) had actually pre-alerted its competitors/cartel members to the pending Commission investigation. Nevertheless, Deltafina was deemed to have provided sufficient information and warranted a 50 per cent reduction. *Industrial Bags* began likewise with information from a cartel member (British Polythene Industries) and in the final Commission decision represented an additional increase in the level of fine for one of the companies involved, Bischof and Klein, for allegedly being caught trying to destroy a document during the investigation.

In *Dutch Bitumen* (2006) British Petroleum came forward as a whistleblower and was granted immunity from a Commission fine for clear cartel activity among oil producers. In this case the highest individual fine fell on Shell (€80 million) and provided further evidence of the Commission's determination to punish such habitual cartel offenders (given Shell's earlier involvement in the *PVS* and *Polypropylene* cases) more severely. In *Chloroprene Rubber* (IP-07/1855) Bayer's decision to play whistleblower and inform the Commission of a price fixing and market rigging cartel in the production of rubber ensured that the company received complete immunity from the overall fine, while its former partners (including ENI and Tosoh) were punished for cartel activity that had lasted from 1993 to 2002.

As has been pointed out (Motta, 2008: 211) the Leniency initiative has not reduced the overall length of investigation time. The length of individual case investigation has compelled the Commission to consider the adoption of a settlement procedures scheme which encapsulated a form of plea bargaining as already exists in the United States. The settlement procedure for cartels was introduced in June 2008 (IP/08/1056) and enables the Commission to settle cartel cases through a more simplified procedure. Basically this scheme operates when firms which have been alerted to DG Competition's file and evidence agree to plead guilty to their (the company's) participation in the specific infringement of Article 81. In return the Commission can reduce the fine that it would have imposed by some 10 per cent. The attraction of this course of action is a speedier response and a freeing up of resources and makes it more unlikely that the company will appeal to the Courts. This process should save time and manpower. The process is entirely voluntary, and where no settlement is reached the usual procedure will apply.

In the meantime another and more recent Commission initiative centres on the introduction of a direct actions scheme whereby both companies and consumers could seek private damages from cartel activity. According to Kroes, 'businesses and consumers in Europe lose billions of euros each and every year as a result of companies breaking EU antitrust rules. These people have a right to compensation through an effective system that complements public enforcement, whilst avoiding excessive burdens and abuses'.[17] Direct actions have been rare in EU competition law and in many of the member state jurisdictions, but they hold considerable potential for the competition regulator. The Commission's Green Paper and a Staff Working Paper on Damages Actions for Breach of the EC Antitrust Rules were published in December 2005. The Green Paper's purpose (see Pheasant, 2006) was to launch a debate from stakeholders and to set out a number of possible options to facilitate private damages actions where loss has been suffered as a result of a deliberate infringement of the competition rules.[18] The responses from the public discussion fed directly into the Commission's White Paper on Damages in April 2008 which was once again up for discussion until mid July 2008. If civil actions come into play in cartelbusting it will provide another potential deterrent because, if successful, any private claim for damages would come on top of the fines already imposed by the Commission. The practice marks a new shift in the direction of European anti-trust and one which again derives largely from US experiences and private litigation. The beauty of this approach from the Commission's perspective is the fact that it is completely resource free and is being strongly encouraged. In short, the White Paper embodies an ingenious move and, if approved by the Council, amounts to another radical landmark in the development of EU competition policy.

5. THE DECENTRALISATION OR FEDERALISATION OF EU CARTEL POLICY?

Interestingly the ongoing strategies to eliminate cartels at the EU level occurred practically almost at the same time as national cartel policies had started to converge across the entire EU. Such 'policy isomorphism' (Radaelli, 2000) may not seem so surprising, given the reality that cartel activity is increasingly cross-border and has propelled the necessity of inter-agency dialogue, but its significance should not be underestimated. This convergence marks another critical juncture in the development of the European anti-trust tradition. Some sixty years ago, and as discussed in chapter four, few Western European states contained any meaningful anti-trust provisions on their statute books, the main exceptions being the British and West German anti-cartel regimes. Admittedly, the UK legislation was not as developed until recently (Wilks, 1999) as the emerging EU regime, and offenders usually received a mere regulatory slap on the wrist and only repeat offenders were faced with penalties. However, over the course of the last five decades and very much in line with the shift from embedded liberalism to neo-liberalism (Wigger, 2008) cartel policies were adopted gradually across all states and even arriving as late as the early 1990s in the Italian case. Some mirrored the EEC rules and some did not, but these same cartel laws underwent a process of policy convergence with the EU model during the latter half of the 1990s.

How can such developments be explained? The acceptance of common cartel policy norms can be explored on both the internal and external fronts. In terms of the former it must be realised that consistency of both purpose and rules across all twenty-seven NCAs had to be ensured, and this led to the voluntary adoption of regimes which largely replicated the EU rules across the member states throughout the 1990s and most remarkably in Germany and the United Kingdom. The convergence process with the European model typifies the pull of the integration logic (as neo-functionalism predicted) and very much fed into notions and discussions of Europeanisation (Cini, 2008; McGowan, 2005). For the countries of Central and Eastern Europe the process of convergence took a much more coercive form as EU membership became conditional on the successful negotiation and adoption of a series of thirty plus policy chapters (Schimmelfennig, 2008) by the prospective states. One of these chapters focused on the competition rules and compelled the candidate states to adopt national competition regimes.

This development greatly facilitated the ever stronger dialogue between DG Competition and the NCAs and allowed it to become an even closer relationship and reality through the creation of the European Competition Network (ECN). The ECN promises to foster an ever closer relationship between the Commission and the national competition authorities and should provide for a greater degree of both horizontal and vertical exchanges of information, consultation and interaction between all the members over policy in general and specifically over individual competition cases. It has been designed as a vehicle to lessen the risk that EU competition law might be inconsistently interpreted and applied throughout the entire single market. Regulation 1/2003 specifically states that the NCAs 'must inform the Commission at an early stage of cases that they are investigating under Article 81, requires an exchange of information on such cases and gives DG Competition a complete overview of all cases being investigated throughout the EU'. From the Commission's point of view the provision of such information should supply greater consistency, though it has been suggested that this change is a means for the Commission to instruct the national authorities about what decision to make. This may amount to wishful thinking on the part of DG Competition, but the possibility of such 'pressure' (Pijetlovic, 2004: 361) being indirectly exerted cannot simply be ignored. All information which is forwarded to DG Competition is as a matter of course also transmitted to all members of the network. This is particularly useful as it should avoid parallel proceedings in various states and further enhance the one stop shop principle.

Where difficulties do occur, and are probably to be expected over parallel proceedings, the Commission will intervene directly in the allocation of cases. Even more significantly, the Commission is empowered to investigate any case of its choosing particularly involving intra-state trade, and when it does so the national competition authorities will cease (see Article 11(6)) any investigation already under way. It should also be noted that, as part of its deliberations and discussions, the Commission is still obliged 'to take the utmost account of the opinions delivered by the Advisory Committee on Restrictive Practices and Dominant Positions' (Article 14) which has to be consulted by the Commission prior to any decisions being reached on block exemptions or individual cases.

The establishment of the ECN can be read as an ingenious mechanism to foster and develop a competition culture across the EU and supersedes earlier forms of interaction which Gerber (1999) labelled both the

BOX 7.1 THE CAR GLASS CARTEL

The Commission's decision to levy fines of over €1383 million on the members of the Car Glass cartel (IP/08/1685) marks yet another milestone in the history of EU cartelbusting for two reasons. This fine, which was based on the 2006 guidelines (IP/06/857), represents the highest ever levy for an infringement of Article 81 and secondly, represents the highest ever fine against an individual company (Saint Gobain) in its role as a repeat offender (see table 7.5). The cartel had been in operation from 1998 to 2003 and had actively sought to restrict competition by fixing prices and allocating markets. Car glass itself is used in a variety of ways by the car industry in the manufacture of windscreens, wing mirrors, windows and sun-roofs. The cartel bore the familiar characteristics. Meetings had been arranged to take place in airports and hotels in different European cities where confidential information was exchanged by the parties concerned. Neelie Kroes was scathing in her comments about the objectives of this cartel, and argued that these companies had cheated the car industry and car buyers for five years in a market which was estimated to be worth two billion euros in the last year of the cartel. Given the size of the market the Commission regarded this cartel as a 'very serious infringement' of the antitrust rules and was extremely critical of the activities of the cartel members which comprised Asahi, Pilkington, Saint-Gobain and Soliver. Together the four offenders controlled more than 90 per cent of the EU market (including the EEA) for branded replacement glass for cars. The case was also interesting in its own right as an 'own initiative' case to which DG Competition had been alerted by an unknown third party and suggests that the recent reforms are bearing fruit. Asahi was granted a 50 per cent reduction in its fine as it supplied information under the Leniency Notice.

'foundational model' and the 'solar model'. In operation it is hoped that the ECN will potentially strengthen information symmetry and reduce conflict. It will certainly strengthen the 'federal' relationship. Indeed, the Commission remains very much the 'ring master' of EU cartel policy, and this fact is in evidence in the allocation of cases. These are to be determined following discussions within the network, and in most instances should not prove too problematic as it will be clear which authority is best placed to handle the case. The key here is the strengthening of this 'federal' relationship which involves an exchange of information, including confidential information, but for the purpose of applying Article 81.

According to the Commission, however, the ECN is already proving effective as a forum for consultation and information exchange. So far, disputes have not occurred. Indeed, one of the first positive outcomes of such dialogue centres on the readiness of national competition authorities to alert the Commission and other ECN members about potential cartel infringements, and thereafter to embark on joint co-operation in the very early stages of the investigations. Others (Riley, 2003; Wilks, 2007) remain to be fully convinced and hold that the ultimate success of the ECN will depend on the powers of enforcement and the reality that some of the national authorities (e.g. the British, French and German) are unquestionably more significant players within the ECN in terms of budget and case-load than many of the others.

Others have wondered whether the EU modernisation plan was 'deeply flawed' (Joshua, 2001). Federalising competition policy with a system of federal courts was a radical idea, but doubts were raised about the challenge that the fragmentation of enforcement poses for legal predictability and consistency in a multi-level governance system like the EU, and especially in Central and Eastern Europe. It is one thing to enact competition legislation and another to implement it. In order to prevent any inconsistency in approach the Commission has moved to finance training programmes to the value of €600 000 to train and retrain national judges about the latest developments in competition law. Considerable co-operation within the EU seems to be becoming a reality, but time will tell how secure and pronounced this actually is.

Interpretations and enforcement remain important issues. Since the late 1990s fewer Commission decisions have been overturned by the Courts as the Commission started to receive much more substantive evidence and proof through the Leniency programme. However, although the Courts have not rejected any of the more recent Commission decisions they have usually opted to lower slightly many of the actual Commission fines (Motta, 2008). Recourse to the Courts makes sense for firms which hope at least for a reduction in the size of the overall fines. In order for cartel policy to be effective there needs to be a general consensus on the part of both the Commission and the Courts over facts and stances. Constant friction and disagreements would seriously undermine policy effectiveness. Both have come to realise this. In 2005, for example, the European Courts reviewed eight cartel decisions (some four in 2004) and, significantly, backed the Commission's stance in each case (Table 7.6). The Commission has also taken to welcoming Court judgments as in the CFI's ruling on *Plasterboard* when the Commission's initial fines were reduced from €478

Table 7.6 Judgments from the courts in 2005

Sector	Court	Decision date	Decision
Speciality graphite	CFI	June 2005	Supported Commission's view and reasoning
Preinsulated pipes	ECJ	June 2005	Confirmed Commission's 1998 decision; dismissed appeal and upheld CFI's 2002 decision
Alloy surcharge	ECJ	July 2005	Rejected appeals against CFI (Dec'01 judgment) which had upheld earlier Commission decision
SAS Maersk	CFI	July 2005	Upheld the Commission's 2001 decision
Luxembourg brewers	CFI	July 2005	Confirmed Commission decision
Belgian brewers	CFI	October and December 2005	Confirmed Commission's 2001 decision
Vitamins	CFI	October 2005	Annulled Commission's 2001 decision as far as two companies concerned
Zinc Phosphate	CFI	November 2005	Fully endorsed the Commission's decision and dismissed all applications for annulment

Source: Compiled from the European Commission, Competition Policy Newsletter, June 2006, pp. 58–60.

million to €458 million (MEMO/08/489 Date: 08/07/2008). Advances are being made in the Commission's war against cartels, but let's be clear; even with the recent increases in staffing levels it is clear that DG Competition is still under-resourced, and this is particularly true for the fight against cartels. This explains why the Commission continually seeks new mechanisms and means to aid its activities.

6. CONCLUSIONS

EU cartel policy in the period after 1999 provides a fascinating study of supranational enforcement activity, and one where once the Commission had accrued its powers, developed its arguments and bolstered its position

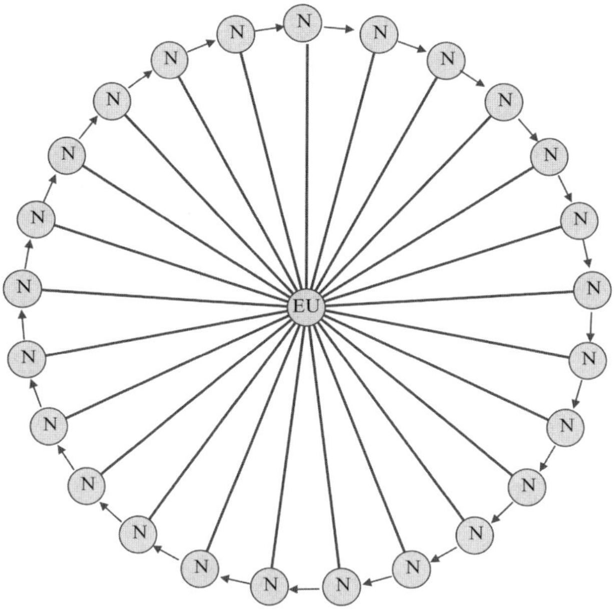

Note: N = 27 National Competition Authorities
EU = European Commission

Figure 7.1 Visualising EU Cartel policy in operation after 2004

as a puissant and determined regulator, it was handed weapons to secure its objectives but also devised and upgraded these tools (through, for example, a higher fining policy) to tackle cartels. The Commission has consistently displayed both imagination and drive in its efforts to combat cartels through initiatives such as the decentralisation of its remit, the leniency notices, the imposition of higher fines and moves towards direct actions. Having been empowered by the member states the Commission has been able to graft on new notices and guidelines itself to make cartel policy more efficient. Building in mechanisms (such as the ECN) as a means of securing greater co-operation and consistency with the national competition authorities is one such route which hopes to enhance detection and foster a common competition culture. The changes post-1999 truly represent a revolution in the history of European anti-trust. Time will tell how effective it will be but it appears for some to be working well already (ABA, 2005).

Developments in European cartel governance in both the form of policy convergence and the new. More significantly, the notions of a market led economy had heralded nothing less than a real revolution for the former Soviet satellite states of Central and Eastern Europe. Competition policy had not featured at all as an aspect of the command economy approach which had been pursued by these states since the late 1940s. Yet all successfully adopted competition policies and established competition authorities prior to joining the EU. We should readily dismiss neither the different philosophies, approaches and national provisions which existed and shaped cartel policy even in the states with competition laws in Western Europe nor the lack of contact between the EU rules and the national systems (Riley, 2003). Can these different experiences prevent the arrival of a single European cartel policy?

The under-resourced Commission has shown degrees of flair and imagination. As DG Competition's resolve intensifies so it appears does the determination of cartels not to be caught. Indeed, cartels are becoming ever more sophisticated and better equipped to evade the cartel hunters. It is clear that DG Competition has used its authority and powers to create norm interpreting administrative rules which take the form of guidelines, communications, notices and letters (see Hofmann, 2006). It was handed weapons to secure its objectives, but also devised and upgraded its own means to tackle cartels. It has developed and deployed simultaneously both carrot and stick approaches to deter cartellisation. The new fining arrangements should prove an invaluable upgrade and will lead neither to bankruptcies nor higher prices for consumers as is so often claimed (see Motta, 2008). Indeed, the Commission should publicise more widely to a general audience how its anti-cartel strategies benefits consumers directly (the benefits of greater competition) and indirectly (fines are paid into the EU budget). Ultimately the fact that cartels still exist strongly suggests that fines at current levels do not act as sufficient deterrents, but can they go much higher and further? Moves towards the criminalisation of cartel activity – and some member states including the UK now allow for such sanctions – may yet provide the better deterrent, but the issue of criminal sanctions raises questions about the nature and powers of the EU. Criminal sanctions for cartel offences seem, however, inevitable in the longer term.

From a positive perspective DG Competition has correctly opted to prioritise its cartelbusting activities and its record over the last decade has been pretty impressive. This *decussis mirabilis* has built directly on the work of the previous four decades and has seen horizontal price fixing and market sharing agreements being attacked robustly. Yet, judging just how successful European cartel policy actually is remains an arduous task, for we get to learn only about the cartels which have been unearthed. Just how many unknown agreements proliferate through the entire global economy? Are the cartel authorities really making an impact on attitudes?

Officials are prepared to state that they are probably discovering only the tip of the iceberg and that the challenge confronting all cartel-busting regulators is immense. According to Phillip Lowe (2007), the current Director General of DG Competition, the Commission will uncover only about 10 per cent of cartel activity (Lowe, 2007). This confession not only demonstrates just how wedded many firms are to cartel arrangements but further reinforces the difficulty of detecting cartel activity and the shortage of manpower within the Commission. Ultimately, cartels as an element of the business world in all probability will never be vanquished. The regulator's task is an immense one, and each must create the best possible conditions that deter cartellisation. It is fair to say that the Commission is making progress. Detection is getting easier, but finding the right deterrent remains somewhat elusive for now within the EU context. In its efforts to tackle cartels the Commission has increasingly pursued international co-operation.

NOTES

1. Hard-core infringements (which divide markets, fix prices and/or apply conditions of sale) are deemed under Article 81 to constitute infringements even where in theory they might be able to, but in practice cannot, make a case for efficiency benefits. Interestingly, agreements where there are no specific hard-core clauses can still fall foul of the EU rules if they have the effect of restricting actual competition.
2. The reform was formally set in motion under Karel van Miert's tenure though the process fell to his successor Mario Monti to complete.
3. Large business groups have played a decisive role at times in pushing closer economic integration, particularly since the mid 1980s. The ERT, for example, is one of the best known and most powerful groups. It comprises the chief executives of Europe's leading private business companies and was an enthusiastic advocate of the single market programme and rapidly engaged in a neoliberal 'competitiveness discourse' (Buch-Hansen, 2008: 199) and, more recently, in the pursuit of the Lisbon Agenda. For discussion of the ERT see van Appeldoorn, 2002. There is an argument to be made about how the Commission's engagement with outside groups provides it with greater legitimacy.
4. This wider policy community plays a vital role in any future design of competition policy. The Commission places considerable emphasis on hearing the views of business and legal practitioners as to how policy could be improved. Be it regular competition conferences (as run, for example, by AMCHAM EU) or comments on Green Papers this input is valued and arguably necessary. The views on the latter are often extensive and are disseminated on DG Competition's web pages.
5. The Commission has always been keen to stress the degree to which it has been overburdened by the notification system, though some (see Riley, 2003) question whether the Commission actually overplayed this issue. The backlog of cases under Articles 81 and 82 had declined throughout the 1990s from some 1,500 to 473 in 2004 (see Monti, 2007: 400).
6. See recital 3 and recital 1, Council Regulation (EC) No 1/2003 on the Implementation of the Rules laid down in Articles 81 and 82 of the Treaty, OJ 2003 L1/1.
7. See the EP's report on the Commission's 1999 White Paper, Final A5-0069/1999 of 30 November 1999 and also the Opinion of the Economic and Social Committee on the

Commission Proposal for a Council Regulation on the Implementation of the Rules on Competition as down in Arts 81 and 82 of the Treaty, OJ 2003 C155/73.

8. See recital 26, Council Regulation (EC) No 1/2003 on the Implementation of the Rules laid down in Articles 81 and 82 of the Treaty, OJ 2003 L1/1.
9. Monti had wanted to stay and serve a second term as competition commissioner but the rules on the composition of the College of Commissioners were changed in 2004 to accommodate the enlargement to an EU25. At this point the five largest states (France, Germany, Italy, Spain and the United Kingdom) which had traditionally appointed two of their nationals to the College were now allowed (under the Treaty of Nice) to appoint only one to the incoming Barroso College. Rocco Buttiglione was the favoured choice of the Italian government as the new Italian Commissioner and almost immediately plunged the Commission into a renewed crisis!
10. This was stated by EC Competition Commissioner, Neelie Kroes, 'Introductory remarks at a press conference on the chlorine chloride cartel and EDP/ENI/GDP merger decision', Brussels, 9 December 2004.
11. In February 2007 the Commission imposed its then highest fine to date of €990 million on bid rigging cartels which had deliberately been created to deal with the installation and maintenance of lifts and escalators in hospitals, railway stations and shopping centres throughout Belgium, Germany, Luxembourg and the Netherlands. The *Lifts and Escalators* cartel comprised seventeen subsidiaries of the Otis, KONE, Schindler and ThyssenKrupp companies and had been in operation between 1995 and 2004. This particular cartel had angered DG Competition not only on account of both the wide geographical market that its instigators had covered (given the limited number of lift manufacturers) and the maintenance contracts which would keep the firms active for years to come, but also because this cartel arrangement had even fitted out the refurbishments to the Berlaymont building and the European Courts in Luxembourg. DG Competition's investigation of this suspected cartel began with a number of' 'dawn raids' on the premises of the companies in question in January 2004. These inspections confirmed suspicions of cartel activity. In response the companies immediately filed for immunity or at least a reduction in fines for providing information on the cartel.

    This particular Article 81 violation epitomises the archetypal and classic form of a cartel, as its members had rigged the bids for procurement markets, fixed prices, allocated projects to each other and not only shared markets but exchanged both commercial and confidential information (on bidding practices and prices). The seriousness of the infringement was never going to be in question. The Competition Commissioner, Neelie Kroes, stated that 'it is outrageous that the construction and maintenance costs of buildings, including hospitals, have been artificially bloated by these cartels. The national management of these companies knew what they were doing was wrong, but they tried to conceal their action and went ahead anyway'. This was a serious accusation for the managers of each of the companies if true, and DG Competition collected evidence that many of the meetings relating to the cartel's operations were taken in bars and restaurants and that the managers even used pre-paid mobile phone cards to avoid detection and tracking.

    The cartel represented one of the worst infringements of Article 81 in the EU's anti-trust history and the amount of the overall fine reflected the size of the market, the duration of the agreement and the weight of the firms involved. It is significant to note that they even tried to share their involvement within the Commission's leniency programme. The KONE subsidiaries were granted full immunity from the fines with respect to the cartel's operations relating specifically to Belgium and Luxembourg while Otis received the same outcome for providing the first information on the cartel's activities in the Netherlands. ThysssenKrupp was far less fortunate and given its role as a repeat offender had its fines increased by some 50 per cent and faced a final bill of €480 million. It should be noted that the cartel's impact extends far beyond the dissolution of the agreement in question, as many of the purchasers of these lifts and escalators are already tied to these companies for regular maintenance and repairs for the foreseeable future.

12. See OECD, Report on Hard Core Cartels, 2002.
13. The actual level of fine is calculated to reflect both the length and seriousness of a particular infringement and also to punish those habitual offenders. New draft guidelines were published in June 2006 (to update the 1998 Notice) and approved in the autumn of 2006 and present a revised and tougher framework for the setting of fines. Under the new rules companies will be fined a so-called 'entry fee' automatically, and this will amount to somewhere in the region of 15–25 per cent of their specific annual turnover from the infringement in question, while repeat offenders can expect even tougher examples of how fines are set.
14. Monti (2000) has openly shared his frustration over the difficulties at unearthing cartels as they destroy copies of documents and often meet outside the jurisdictional territory of the states in question.
15. There is a growing list here which includes some of the most famous Commission cartel decisions since 2000 such as *Vitamins*, *Acrylic Glass*, *Industrial Bags*, *Sorbates*, *Rubber Chemicals*, *Gas Insulated Switchgear*, *Road Bitumen* and *Lifts and Escalators*.
16. This issue became a particular concern under the US system where civil cases gererally increased the overall fine some threefold until the US antitrust system was amended with the adoption of the Antitrust Criminal Penalty Enhancement and Reform Act of 2004. It is a means to ensure that 'informers' continue to come forward.
17. See the Commission's Competition website at http://ec.europa.eu/comm/Competition/antitrust/actionsdamages/index.html which was accessed on 11 August 2008.
18. The public consultation on this Green Paper was open until 21 April 2006. The Commission received substantial comments from business and law firms across Europe and beyond and has put all submissions on its website at http://ec.europa.eu/comm/Competition/antitrust/others/actions_for_damages/gp_contributions.html.

8. The internationalisation of cartel policy and the challenges ahead

Cartel policy and wider competition policy have played an integral role in the European integration project. Over the course of the last five decades the Commission has been able to carve out for itself a space from which to expand its competition remit, but also one which gradually came to encroach on and influence the shape, style and substance of domestic anti-trust regimes throughout the entire European continent. This process of policy convergence has been remarkable. The intensification of the war on cartels over the last decade bears witness to the determination of the European Commission to tackle such anti-competitive activity. It has made significant strides, re-invested its institutional energies and resources and conceived new means of combating cartellisation. Still, the regime is increasingly facing a new and arguably its greatest challenge to date as questions abound about how, where and if cartel enforcement should be regulated at the international level. Pressure for some form of agreement to deal with cartels has been growing since the early 1990s and determination, perseverance, innovative initiatives and higher fines have become the hallmarks of serious anti-cartel regimes. Although major successes can be reported it is fact that not only has cartel activity not been suppressed, but those wishing to engage in such action are going to greater lengths to conceal any such evidence of illegal activity through, for example, the use of encryption software to protect e-mails and anonymous mailboxes. In *Industrial Bags* evidence was unearthed by the Commission of a company document which stated that any information and materials indicating figures for 'allocating markets and prices must be destroyed' (see Whish, 2009: 498). Detecting cartels was proving to be a formidable challenge, and even more so as cartel arrangements do not stop at European borders and are not just European constructs. Many are international, and given the global nature of many cartels there has followed a growing recognition that much greater co-operation between competition authorities in Europe and beyond is required if cartels are going to be effectively pursued and deterred.

This international dimension of cartel policy presents a new set of challenges and opportunities for the Commission and the other anti-trust regulators about how much and what types of co-operation are envisaged and raises questions about the compatibility of the various regimes. Cartel detection and enforcement have become a priority internationally. The ideas of international cartel regulation have been an almost omnipresent feature of trade discussions since the late 1940s, although real progress is only being made now. The Commission has displayed an eagerness to engage in the ongoing debate which began in earnest in the early 1990s about some form of global competition rules (Baker, Campbell, Reynolds and Rowley, 1997; Jacquemin, 1993; Sullivan and Filion, 2004). Interestingly the Commission's own anti-cartel strategy has been echoed in other industrialised states, and its focus and energies against cartels were being mirrored in other non-European jurisdictions and especially in North America and Oceania. Just as DG Competition reorganised itself to be in a better position to counter cartels, so other agencies increased their own resources in this area.[1] The pursuit of an international competition policy is a relatively new departure (Aydin, 2009; Cini and McGowan, 1998; Damro, 2003), but one where a good deal of co-operation (Woolcock, 2003) already exists and is rapidly developing, and where there is an augmenting literature on developments in states from across the globe. It is not without its problems and difficulties, notably that the EU rules are dealt with under a civil law regime, in contrast to the criminal law system in use in the United States and Canada. This chapter cannot cover all the aspects but focuses on the European Commission's pro-active involvement in the international anti-cartel arena and explores the degree to which cartel policy has been and can be successfully internationalised.

This chapter comprises four sections. The first sets the scene and provides a short overview of the steps taken to internationalise competition policy. It explores the extent to which the Commission has been able to export its own EU competition rules across Europe, in relation to candidate states, potential candidate states and the few remaining other states in Europe. The second provides a short narrative of efforts at international co-operation on competition matters after 1945 and looks briefly at both the OECD and the General Agreement on Tariffs and Trade (GATT)/ World Trade Organisation. Discussion is extended specifically in the third section to illustrate how the war against cartels has become the focus of competition regulators worldwide, and how efforts at fostering co-operation have gathered pace since the late 1990s through the OECD, the WTO and the International Competition Network (ICN). The final section addresses the new challenges posed to this very regime by the onset of global recession and the return of unemployment.

1. EXPORTING THE COMPETITION PRINCIPLE THROUGHOUT EUROPE

Understanding the context in which EU competition policy operates is essential, for it opens up discussions on a wider debate about the desirability and attainability of some form of international competition code or policy. In a world where not only goods and services, but also people, capital and ideas have adopted trans-national characteristics, the absence of international rules on private business practices has increasingly become a source of concern for those governments, business undertakings and international organisations that are working to promote open and competitive markets. Anti-competitive practices are an intrinsic aspect of transnational commerce. They surface as major issues for example, when firms opt to fix prices and arrange markets of operation to the detriment of the consumer, when firms opt to abuse their dominant position and engage in abusive behaviour (such as predatory pricing to eliminate rivals) and when firms opt to merge and thereby possibly threaten to undermine competitors. All have ensured the salience and political dimension of competition policy.

As we have seen, such issues surface at national, regional and supranational (i.e. EU) levels, and accordingly states have designed institutional mechanisms to regulate against anti-competitive conduct, but when such issues arise in the globalised market place who is best placed to fulfil the task of regulator? These issues become particularly problematic, given the distinct approaches to the operationalisation and implementation of competition policy in different states and the reality that progress on common rules has proved to be difficult and sensitive, given the degrees of incompatibility that prevail between the approaches of the different regimes. Progress to date has been modest, but things are now changing very rapidly as the international dangers posed by cartellisation are recognised. The pressure to uncover and punish such collusive activities has forced competition agencies to explore the possibilities for co-operation. To this end there has been growing evidence (in terms of sharing information and joint inspections) and increasing co-operation between competition authorities and the Commission over cartels. Such cross-border collaboration is to be welcomed, but just how much co-operation has there actually been, how has it been structured and just how effective has it been in the war against cartels? The European Commission has successfully exported its model across Europe.

The evolution and expansion of the European Union (EU) have had repercussions on its member states and especially on how they have responded to this dimension of governance and its challenges. EU power has also been felt by potential EU applicant states through the enlargement process also even by third states which do not have any intention of joining the EU at all. EU competition policy provides an excellent example of the actual pull of EU governance on non-member states and actually represents one, if an often overlooked, form of the EU's external relations (Lavenex, 2004). The Commission's efforts at exporting its own brand of competition rules beyond its borders have met with mixed success. The actual efforts can be examined by exploring both the pan European and global contexts of policy development. The Commission has been particularly keen to encourage the adoption of its own brand of competition rules, and particularly in the European context where the requirements of the internal market have provided a sound rationale for this type of policy convergence. The Commission's efforts have been visible in agreement on the European Economic Area (EEA) and also emerged as an integral aspect of the EU enlargement process into Central and Eastern Europe. Both are considered briefly.

2. EXTENSION 1: THE EUROPEAN ECONOMIC AREA

The agreement establishing the EEA, which came into force in 1994, effectively extended the size of the Single European Market to encompass the EU member states and most EFTA members.[2] The agreement clearly demonstrated how the EU was able to extend its competition rules and norms beyond its own borders.[3] In signing the EEA Agreement, the EFTA states agreed to apply and abide by internal market legislation even though they had had no formal influence over making it. It is not surprising that, under these circumstances, accession should become an extremely attractive proposition. This agreement contains specific competition provisions which practically mirror the European Union's competition regime. Indeed, in substantive terms, the wording of the EEA competition provisions (Articles 53 and 54 of the EEA Agreement) is identical to that of Articles 81 and 82 and the procedural framework reflects the provisions of Regulation 17.[4] The Agreement (in Articles 56 and 57) also established an institutional framework which included the EFTA Surveillance Authority (ESA) as the EEA's version of the Commission, and the EFTA Court, to mirror the European Court of Justice.

With almost identical substantive, institutional and procedural characteristics, the Agreement establishes a homogeneous system of competition throughout the EEA. The only real novelty, then, involves the allocation of cases between the two sets of institutions. Even this is achieved in a fairly straightforward fashion, with responsibility resting with the ESA in cases directly involving and concerning the EEA states or where firms from the EEA states have a foothold of at least 30 per cent in the EU market. In all other cases, DG Competition assumes the lead. In essence, the EEA competition provisions operate on the basis of two principles: the 'two-pillar' system, that is, ESA and the EU; and the 'one-stop shop' principle (with only one body being able to act on a case at any one time) (Stragier, 1993: 30). The export of the EU's competition rules to the EEA marks the first step in the creation of a pan-European competition regime. The novelty of the EEA project should not be understated, but a very different approach was adopted, although with similar outcomes in terms of competition policy, for the countries of Central and Eastern Europe.

3. EXTENSION 2: CENTRAL AND EASTERN EUROPE

The logic guiding the extension of the competition rules to the enlarged single market within the EEA was present at the outset of discussions surrounding the EU's further expansion to the countries of Central and Eastern Europe (CEECs). Indeed, the priority in this case was even greater, as most of these states (apart from Cyprus and Malta) possessed zero experience of the competition principle and were in the process of being transformed from centrally planned economies into full functioning market economies. The initial encouragement given to the CEECs on the domestic competition policy front formed only one strand of the EU's broader strategy towards Eastern Europe, which had commenced with the rather conventional trade and co-operation agreements of the late 1980s, and fed, for example, into the PHARE (Poland–Hungary Aid for Economic Reconstruction) programme of technical and financial assistance and the more detailed association (Europe) agreements in the early 1990s. The twin-track emphasis after 1992 on both market and democratic reform saw the EU offering advice and support to the CEECs. In performing this role, '[it] was instinctive to advocate that the CEECs imitate west European policy models and rules' (Sedelmeier and Wallace, 1996: 356). It soon became clear that this advocacy of West European rules was going to be tied to the prospect of EU membership, and that the adoption of rules compatible with the internal market was in effect a condition of EU membership. Encouragement had given way to direct pressure and expectation (Schimmelfennig and Sedelmeier, 2004)!

The Europe Agreements became the means by which the EU imposed specific requirements (in terms of policy design and implementation) on the CEECs. These Agreements gave the CEECs associate status and held out the prospect of eventual membership. The chapter dealing with competition policy was included in part V of Title V on 'Payments, Capital, Competition and Other Economic Provisions, Approximation of Laws', where the rules on competition were identified as a priority area (Van den Bossche, 1997: 52). By mid-1997, ten agreements (with Poland, Hungary, the Czech Republic, Slovakia, Romania, Bulgaria, Estonia, Latvia, Lithuania and Slovenia) had been signed. The competition provisions represented a new approach and indeed innovation for the CEECs because the former centrally planned economies were not based on competition. The competition rules were fairly similar in style and substance in all the Europe Agreements. The first paragraph of the competition provisions identified practices and types of behaviour (such as restrictive agreements between firms, abuses of a dominant position and public aid which distorts or threatens to distort competition) which were incompatible with the single market. The second paragraph stipulated that any assessment of such anti-competitive behaviour was to be based on the criteria in Articles 81, 82 and 88. The third paragraph compelled the signatories of the Europe Agreements to adapt their national legislation in line with the competition Articles and within three years of the respective agreements coming into force. The importance of competition policy in the EU's pre-accession strategy was confirmed both at the Essen European Council in December 1994 and in the Commission's influential (though non-binding) White Paper of June 1995 (COM(95)163 final). The White Paper defined and prioritised both the legislation and the legal and administrative frameworks needed for CEECs to adapt to the internal market.[5]

The campaign for policy convergence had begun and was a conscious one on DG Competition's part (see table 8.1). It is interesting to reflect on the extent to which the Commission's advocacy of competition alignment and harmonisation could be described as economic imperialism on the part of DG Competition. The Commission certainly was keen to encourage the emergence of national systems of competition regulation throughout Europe, and with access to the single market held up as the prize candidate, states saw the attractiveness of developing compatible systems of competition. By the mid 1990s DG Competition was also pursuing closer links with the former Soviet states, most notably with Belarus, Kazakhstan, Kyrgystan and Moldova. It also led into discussions with the states of the southern Mediterranean, and compelled Turkey to harmonise its domestic legislation in line with European competition law after the setting up of the 1996 Customs Union as an 'alternative' to membership.

The extension of EU-style competition systems to the countries of Central and Eastern Europe was evident in the two most recent enlargement waves in 2004 and 2007 respectively, and the same impetus is driving the current negotiations which involve the next seven potential future member states in the Balkans (Albania, Bosnia-Herzegovina, Croatia, Macedonia, Montenegro, Serbia and Turkey). EU membership is the incentive that is often the persuasive factor (Lavenex and Schimmelfenning, 2008). Moreover, the EU's developing European Neighbourhood Policy (ENP), which applies to all those states primarily in the territories of the former Soviet Union (with the exception of Russia), is constructed around a series of non-binding action plans which contain some competition provisions (Aydin, 2009). The competition principle has also been built into the Cotonou Agreement which regulates trade and development aid with the former European colonies in the African, Caribbean and Pacific (ACP) states.[6] By 2009 states on the European continent had sought to operate their economies within a common or a mutually compatible framework of competition rules (see table 8.1). Could the same logic driving policy convergence throughout Europe be exported to third and non-European states?

Table 8.1 The expansion of the competition principle in Europe, 1990 to the present[1]

Wave 1	Wave 2	Wave 3
Cyprus, 1990	Estonia, 1993	Bosnia-Herzegovina, 2001
Hungary, 1990	Iceland, 1993	Croatia, 2003
Poland, 1990	Norway, 1993	Macedonia, 2005
Czechoslovakia, 1991[2]	Slovenia, 1993	Montenegro, 2005
Latvia, 1991	Ukraine, 1993	
Russia, 1991	Malta, 1994	
Belarus, 1992	Turkey, 1994	
Bulgaria, 1992	Albania, 1995	
Finland, 1992	Switzerland, 1995	
Lithuania, 1992	Georgia, 1996	
Moldova, 1992	Romania, 1996	
	Serbia, 1996	

Notes:
[1] It should be remembered that a successful competition policy rests very much on its implementation. Having one on the statute books is a start, but is not sufficient in itself. Negotiations between the EU and Croatia on competition had not yet begun by the start of 2009.
[2] Although this territory split into the Czech Republic and Slovakia in 1994 the competition rules from the unified state are extended into its two successor states.

4. THE COMMISSION'S STRATEGIC ENGAGEMENT IN STRENGTHENING INTERNATIONAL CO-OPERATION ON COMPETITION POLICY

The objective of establishing some form of international competition code may indeed seem logical, but attempts at securing any such agreement have been both difficult and problematic. Moves in this direction have often been hindered and by a clash of cultures and ways of handling the economy in general and different interpretations of the exact value of, and approaches to, anti-trust. Nevertheless, the internationalisation process began earnestly in the mid 1940s. The 1947 Havana Charter (McGowan, 1998) represented the first major post-war multilateral initiative (Brown, 1950), and one which not only embraced substantive antitrust rules (which reflected the US model) to ease international trade but also espoused the creation of a new institution, the International Trade Organisation (ITO) in 1946. The original schematics for the ITO had included provisions which not only dealt with anti-competitive behaviour on an international front but also aimed to compel ITO members to adopt national competition laws to enable the successful implementation of an international cartel policy. This drive towards an anti-cartel strategy was informed by events in the 1930s (see chapter 3), the salience of the theme in printed form (Hexner, 1946; Stocking and Watkins, 1946) and firm convictions that cartels were the tools of authoritarian regimes. In retrospect, it was an extremely bold aspiration to be made in the 1940s when few states possessed domestic competition legislation, and it ran into political difficulties almost immediately, but it reflected the political and economic concerns of the time. Rather ironically the greatest pressure (often the US government) and the greatest resistance emanated from the United States. It was primarily American opposition and the House of Congress' worries not about the antitrust rules but concerns about losing any regulatory sovereignty (Woolcock, 2003) which led to the US government's refusal to ratify the ITO, which in turn ensured that the ambitious plan was effectively stillborn.

The General Agreement on Tariffs and Trade (GATT) emerged in 1947 as an alternative multilateral vehicle (although a shadow of the ITO proposal) to promote international trade, but it was primarily concerned with enacting tariff cuts. In contrast, the idea of pursuing an international competition policy code was effectively sidelined despite the existence of some ardent supporters.[7] The opportunity to discuss competition policy issues arose within the rubric of another new international forum, namely the United Nations Conference on Trade and Development (UNCTAD).

Again, however, discussions of cartel issues were sporadic and the significance of the few resolutions on anti-competitive activities that were agreed can be questioned as they were non-binding on the members. That said, UNCTAD did play a fundamental role and managed to keep the theme alive within a much wider political spectrum, and even adopted several measures such as the Code on Restrictive Business Practices in 1980 (Benson, 1980). More recently it has also drawn up and periodically revises its own model competition law for those countries seeking to enact policy for the first time, and has been particularly active at providing technical assistance for developing countries in this area.

Overall, however, rather minimal progress of any kind was made on moving towards any substantive multilateral competition rules from the late 1940s until the late 1980s. This picture began really to change, however, only with the advance of neo-liberalism and the growing recognition of the reality of globalised markets and global business players in the late 1980s. The Commission had taken an interest in the international dimension to competition policy which reflected the sudden wave in merger activity in the late 1980s as barriers to trade were brought down (Damro, 2006b) and questions arose over who exactly was empowered to regulate the processes of transnational concentration.

In considering its approach to the international dimension of cartel policy the Commission was faced with a series of possible strategic options to pursue. These encompassed multilateral, bilateral and unilateral perspectives. The Commission strongly favoured the multilateral approach, was actively involved in a series of multilateral initiatives such as UNCTAD's activities, was a member of the latter's Intergovernmental Group of Experts on Competition Law and Policy and pursued the idea of global rules through venues such as the WTO. In the absence of any concrete steps towards a global multilateral competition regime, the real threat of a return to purely unilateral methods of international competition enforcement presented itself as one viable, if unwelcome, route. Not only does this course of action prove an inadequate way of dealing with transnational practices, but it can also provoke retaliation from aggrieved competitor states.

The controversial issue here surrounds the extension of domestic competition law beyond the borders of a particular state when a national or regional law seems to impinge on another state's sovereignty or territorial integrity. Both the US and EU competition regimes allow for what is known as the extraterritorial application of competition law. While an American tendency to resort to extraterritorial solutions when faced with international trade difficulties has frequently provoked harsh criticism from the Europeans, the extraterritorial application of the EU rules has also at times proven controversial. For here we see one aspect of competition policy which impinges directly on the 'high politics' of trade policy. In applying the concept of extraterritoriality, the Commission's competition policy is said to affect all companies operating within, and importing goods into, the single market, including companies the headquarters of which are not within the EU. In the absence of multilateral solutions, and in efforts to avoid unilateral action, bilateral agreements, such as that between the US and the EU or that between Canada and the EU, offer a convenient alternative.[8] The globalisation of trade and the new geo-political realities of the post-Cold War world had propelled both states to re-examine their 'special' relationship, and the decision of both to agree a bilateral agreement on competition policy reflected growing need for co-operation (Van Miert, 1996). The bilateral agreement aimed to smooth the path to greater co-ordination. Judged positively it created a framework for meaningful and useful co-operation and enabled both signatories to become more familiar with each other's rules and enforcement techniques, and led to a series of bi-annual meetings between DG Competition and the US Fair Trade Commission. A joint investigation into Microsoft in 1995 proved one of the first examples of this new-found co-operation in practice at work which has 'contributed greatly to the effective resolution of a number of cases' (Van Cauwelaert, 1997: 52). However, difficulties remained, and such arrangements do not compensate for the absence of an international competition code. Despite the heralding of the 1991 US–EU Co-operation Agreement as a landmark, the limits of bilateralism become all too clear when we consider the 1997 dispute over the proposed merger between Boeing and McDonnell Douglas (McGowan and Cini, 1999) and the later tensions over the GE/Honeywell merger in 2001 (Fox, 2007; Morgan and Maguire, 2004).[9]

With the likelihood of any international agreement on competition policy seeming remote in the 1990s, given the potential for conflict between discrete policy models, the competition agenda turned instead to explore the scope for policy co-operation and mutual accommodation. The Commission, together with national competition authorities such as the American Federal Trade Commission (FTC) and the German Federal Cartel Office and international organisations such as the United Nations Conference on Trade and Development (UNCTAD), the OECD, the G8 and the WTO, has, at one time or another, been involved in encouraging harmonisation and co-ordination measures (Cini and McGowan, 1998). An increasing awareness of the importance of the international dimension has led to the emergence of a network of agreements between states, and the inclusion of competition policy arrangements in international treaties such as, for example, the 1993 North Atlantic Free Trade Agreement

(NAFTA). Indeed, two international organisations, namely the OECD and the General Agreement on Tariffs and Trade (GATT), became important arenas in which these issues of internationalisation were discussed. Both are now considered briefly in turn.

5. THE ORGANISATION FOR ECONOMIC CO-OPERATION AND DEVELOPMENT (OECD) AND COMPETITION POLICY

The OECD has become one of the most significant arenas for discussions of the purpose and desirability of an international cartel policy. This body was established in 1961 as a research body for the world's most industrialised nations and still serves as a forum in which member states can study and formulate policies based on best practice.[10] Its purpose is to encourage co-operation amongst its thirty members, especially in areas where domestic policy has transnational implications.[11]

The OECD was initially involved in some non-binding (soft law) recommendations on competition policy from its inception, but its early attempts to raise cartel related matters in the 1960s and 1970s met with substantial opposition from its members.[12] At the time, competition policy was judged to be an almost exclusively domestic concern, and it was not until the 1980s that a political interest in the international dimension of competition policy emerged to allow the first substantive moves on this issue. It was in this changed environment, however, that the OECD's role became better defined, through the work of its own Competition Policy and Law Committee (CPL).[13] The CPL, the members of which come from the national competition authorities from the OECD member states and DG Competition, spends much of its time publishing reports and providing data on competition and competition matters. It holds conferences on competition policy, provides regular reviews of the state of competition and cartel policy in member states and sees itself as 'the world's premier source of policy analysis and advice to governments on how best to harness market forces in the interests of greater global economic efficiency and prosperity' (OECD, 2009). The OECD approach towards cartels has been built on consensus, and it has deliberately avoided seeking to present itself as searching for a common global competition policy (Doern, 1996: 316). The OECD has sought to encourage co-operation between states and even attempted to steer it. Its reports and expertise have gradually earned the OECD a solid reputation. Its 1986 Memorandum on Co-operation between Competition Authorities, for example, was influential in launching a coherent case for the need to harmonise competition rules and to make the case for greater international co-operation in anti-trust matters. Although its advocacy of harmonisation and internationalisation did not initially bear much fruit, it was in retrospect a first and important step forward in persuading members to implement and enforce their own competition policies, using common analytical approaches.

By the mid-1990s issues such as cartel policy convergence, the interaction between international trade policies and competition policy (which led to the setting up of a Joint Group on Trade and Competition), the connections between economic regulation and competition (which was especially important as member countries deregulate and reformed their regulatory regimes), and the enforcement of international competition by competition officials all took centre stage. DG Competition once again was fully engaged in these and in other areas of the OECD's work. DG Competition has participated in a working party on public support measures, in an examination of the 'competition advocate' role played by competition authorities, and in general discussions on 'essential infrastructure projects', small and medium-sized enterprises, the liberal professions and firms holding a dominant position (Commission, 1996). As such, the OECD has become an important focal point of contact for DG Competition, and the latter has increasingly involved itself in the pursuit of international accord on competition rules and entered a new phase of heightened anti-cartel activity after 1995 (see below).

6. THE WORLD TRADE ORGANISATION (WTO)

The GATT initially might have seemed a more appropriate international forum for addressing competition issues. However, while some of its activities – those involving anti-dumping and the grant of government subsidies for example – were on the margins of competition policy, GATT was reluctant to involve itself in debates about policy harmonisation, given the fervent opposition of some of its members. Indeed, until the late 1980s, its only involvement in the policy was through an annual Intergovernmental Group of Experts on Restrictive Business Practices which was effectively a forum for discussion. Not until the mid-1980s was it possible to identify any change of emphasis which led to the establishment of an International Anti-trust Code Working Group in 1992 (Trebilcock, 1996). Composed mainly of German anti-trust experts (though comprising other Europeans, Americans and Japanese academics), the Working Group produced a draft International Anti-trust Code, which was submitted to GATT in the summer of 1993 (Drexl, 2003). The Code advocated minimum standards for competition rules to cover horizontal and vertical agreements, mergers and monopolies, and recommended the setting up of an independent International Anti-trust Agency and a Disputes Settlement Panel under the auspices of the WTO. Although the draft was widely criticised on both sides of the Atlantic, it did succeed in drawing attention to the international dimension of competition and cartel policy.

Since 1995, GATT's successor, the WTO, has continued to involve itself in competition matters.[14] As an organisation entrusted with the promotion of trade flows, the advancement of economic liberalisation through negotiation and the establishment of impartial dispute-settlement mechanisms, competition-related issues certainly seem to lie at its heart. However, in the first two years of its existence, the WTO's only dealings with competition matters were on specific trade. This began to change in 1996 at the Singapore ministerial meeting where ministers agreed to establish several new working groups, including one which would deal with trade and competition policies. The idea for such a working group originated in a report, known as the Van Miert Report (COM(95)359 final). The Report discussed the idea of establishing an international anti-trust code which it deemed unrealistic, and proposed in the interim that all WTO countries should be encouraged to develop competition policies and that bilateral ant-trust agreements should be encouraged. This working group began its work at the start of 1997 with the task of providing the WTO with analytical and exploratory materials. The Commission was convinced that the WTO provided the best means to work towards a multilateral framework on competition principles, and one which would be built gradually around the industrialised states but would in time also bring in the developing nations (Weinrauch, 2004: 158). The US was always rather sceptical about moving towards any multilateral deal, but it agreed to participate in the working group (Marsden, 2003: 60). This group proved reasonably active and met regularly, some three times per year from 1997 to 2004, to discuss policy matters and in effect seek to forge a 'competition culture'.

However, actual progress can be described as minimal at best as major differences between the competition systems prevailed. One of the areas where it had been hoped that substantial progress could have been made in the Doha Round discussions, given a wide consensus, was the need to tackle those hard-core cartels which determined price and output and added little in the way of improved productivity.[15] The WTO was – and correctly – convinced that cartels are far from being a coincidental convergence of interests on the part of their members, but on the contrary, deliberate and professionally run creations which impact negatively on price. It was estimated by the WTO that cartels on average led to price rises of some 10 per cent, with even more significant increases in the developing world (Levenstein, 2001). More worryingly the WTO appreciated that many cartels go undetected. Despite the general agreement on the dangers posed by cartels there was little headway made with anything like the WTO having the power to impose a cartel ban. The different national perceptions about what types of agreements were actually damaging and problematic simply prevented any agreement on cartel policy. US opposition towards any multilateral arrangement which threatened to undermine the principles of American anti-trust was always at the forefront and, given the differences, it was far from surprising when the WTO General Council decided to drop competition policy from the negotiations in the Doha Round. Consequently, its committee was dissolved in 2004 and is now 'inactive' (WTO, 2009). Overall discussions on the entire trade round were to collapse later in Cancun. The failure of the WTO initiative was certainly unfortunate and dented the move towards greater multilateral co-operation, but it represented only one possible attempt at achieving agreement on rules pertaining to an international competition regime. In the absence of such a body were there other possibilities of facilitating greater co-operation against international cartels?

7. CONSTRUCTING AN INTERNATIONAL COALITION TO COMBAT CARTELS

Agreement may have been difficult to attain, but there was growing recognition among competition regulators that the role and anti-competitive strategies of some business concerns, and especially the growing reality of international cartel activity, necessitated co-operation on the competition policy front at a global level. Most competition agencies have long realised the pressures, but how exactly was this goal going to be managed divided states. Co-operation between agencies rapidly emerged as the path ahead, as opposed for the moment to direct policy convergence. Co-operation has its advantages as it has the possibility to alert any relevant competition agencies about cartels which may be active and operating in their own jurisdiction, it holds the promise of sharing information, but, more importantly, co-ordinating antitrust activities, and may avoid the risk of destruction of evidence if one agency moves before any others where a cartel is active. Co-operation also enables agencies to learn, collect and collate useful information from other bodies and facilitates contact and staff discussions. Information exchanges and co-operation can occur at the pre-investigatory level, the investigatory level itself and the post-investigatory level. Essentially, the information that can be imparted at all three levels includes the exchange of information from one public agency to another; the sharing of collected information obtained from private sources (e.g. other rival companies) which is not available within the public domain but the sole possession of the authority in question; possible existing information/past history notes on the companies concerned about past misdemeanours, and new ways to facilitate cross-agency exchanges. Such co-operation is already occurring at a number of levels and is seen in the UNCTAD, in the shape of the OECD and in a growing series of regional/trade integration agreements, and in a growing number (some twenty+) of bilateral agreements (Woolcock, 2003).

The first tentative efforts at facilitating co-operation against cartels were undertaken under the auspices of the OECD. Its 1995 report on 'Recommendations between Agencies' signals a modest starting point, but one which was heading in the right direction by seeking greater interaction, exchanges of non-sensitive information and the co-ordination of investigations between the competition authorities. This objective was never going to be as straightforward in cartel cases as in merger and dominance cases, and so experience proved. The OECD's determination found a more developed expression in the OECD Council's 'Recommendation on effective Action against Hard-Core Cartels' from 1998, which basically urged its members to be aware of the dangers posed by hard-core cartels and to identify ways to deter them by intensifying enforcement procedures. This plea added further pressure because traditionally what co-operation had existed – and it was at best minimal in the cartel policy field – had very much depended on the nature of agreements between the NCAs themselves, and more often than not these same agencies displayed a reluctance to both share and exchange confidential information.

The OECD was effectively taking a leadership role and steering its states towards some form of best practices approach. It has continued to advocate co-operation and to underline the significance and danger posed by cartels. To this end it produced its 'Report on Leniency Programmes to fight Hard-Core Cartels' in 2001 which focused very much on how the best regimes operated, how far the role of whistleblowers could facilitate cartel detection and whether additional incentives could also be handed out to whistleblowers as in the UK system. A further 2002 'Report on the Nature and Impact of Hard Core Cartels and Actions against Cartels under National Competition Laws' reinforced its anti-cartel message and its conviction that fines had yet to reach an optimal level truly to create an effective deterrence. Its 'Third Report on the Implementation of the 1998 Recommendation' from 2005 reiterated the anti-cartel message, but also incorporated another angle when it suggested that the wider public should be made more aware of ways in which international cartels impacted on their lives.

The realities of international cartels and the increasing salience of the

OECD's reports had almost certainly created a changed atmosphere, and one which facilitated the creation of the ICN (International Competition Network). The ICN was established in 2001 as a vehicle and forum for the competition authorities themselves to discuss experiences and their respective approaches on a wide range of competition issues such as policy style, policy development and policy enforcement. Ultimately this network sought to foster a competition culture and move towards greater policy understanding rather than policy convergence. To this end the ICN quickly created a small number of select working groups within it, for example, one on mergers, one on dominant positions and one on cartels. It has further developed its interest in the cartel area by holding an annual ICN cartel workshop, and it has already produced a couple of reports on anti-cartel policy. As a founding member the Commission has been eager to play an instrumental role in the development of the ICN and it took on the responsibility in 2005, on behalf of its fellow ICN members, to examine the role and degree of co-operation between the competition agencies in cartel investigations and to ascertain how much had changed.

The Commission conducted its survey in the form of a questionnaire (Commission, 2007), and its 2007 assessment provided a fairly sober picture of developments. Progress was taking place but it remained slow and sporadic. Positively, some agencies did admit to using informal exchange mechanisms and found them useful, but they were utilised less in cartel cases than in mergers or monopoly cases. It seems that formal information exchanges were often limited to simple notification at the start of investigations in other jurisdictions. Indeed, information tended to be disseminated more readily at the pre-investigation stage (with the provision of background information, details about the sector/industry, co-ordination of searches and raids, and travel by officials to conduct interviews) but still occurred during actual investigations (e.g. informing other agencies about the state of play, a general assessment of the case and shared interviews). More interaction, agency learning and mutual respect should intensify cooperation in the future. To this end the OECD is pursuing the issue and has even begun the task of pulling together a cartel enforcement manual, and even 'created a template for ICN members to set out their rules governing cartel enforcement' (Commission, 2009).

A second means to enhance co-operation stems from existing provisions under national law which allow competition agencies to exchange information. Competition authorities such as the BKartA, the Canadian Competition Bureau, the US Department of Justice and the Romanian Competition Council are entitled to share information, but in practice issues arise over exactly what materials should be shared, as sensitivities remain. For example, the latest alterations to the German GWB which came into force in 2005 incorporate not only the provisions implementing Article 12(1) of Regulation 1/2003 which openly advocates the sharing of information between agencies within the ECN, but also authorises the German authority to enter into co-operation with authorities outside the EU.[16] In a similar vein the UK Enterprise Act of 2003 enables the OFT to supply information which it has gained from its own investigations to another authority to aid the prosecution of criminal activity, and this includes cartels.

A third factor facilitating stronger links and co-operation between competition agencies occurs when specific bilateral agreements on competition policy have been made between jurisdictions. The first bilateral competition agreement was signed between the USA and West Germany in 1976 and has become a standard type of agreement to regulate co-operation.[17] The European Union's three dedicated bilateral agreements with the United States, Canada and Japan serve as prototypes, and commit the agencies party to each agreement to exchange information and to co-ordinate their enforcement activities. The EU has other co-operation agreements (built on the OECD's 1995 recommendations) with China and Korea. These agreements are largely similar in terms of both style and purpose and are structured around notifying other competition authorities where it is relevant, sharing information where appropriate and conducting parallel or joint investigations. Most such agreements do include a caveat, however, which prevents co-operation where it may endanger business confidentiality.

Within Europe the ECN is proving to be an invaluable facilitator. As a singular and unique regulatory agency it deliberately provides for greater co-operation between the ECN member agencies. This, of course, has become more straightforward and even easier as all the NCAs are applying the same competition rules. Under Article 12 of Regulation 1/2003 all ECN members are urged to exchange information, including confidential information, and this co-operation can take place at all three levels of investigation. It is just left to the agencies themselves to determine how and where they interact as part of the ECN. All members have to inform the others when an investigation is launched if EC law is applied. Importantly in the realm of cartel policy information on raids can be supplied after the event, although the actual NCAs will be contacted beforehand if inspection is to be carried out in order to co-ordinate responses, and if need be organise simultaneous searches. As part of this network the Commission is obliged to inform the relevant NCAs in advance of any inspection and the NCAs are expected to give assistance to the Commission if requested. Moreover, the Commission can actually request that an appropriate NCA carry out the investigation on its behalf. There has been progress but caution is still required, because the co-operation is not without its own problems. Case complexity still abounds and the procedures from start to finish are lengthy, especially where the judicial authorities are brought into the equation. Co-operation has intensified and fascinating questions arise over whether we are moving towards some degree of policy convergence. Such notions may seem premature, but the evolution of European cartel policy (through the introduction and refinement of the leniency programme and the pursuit of private actions) finds its origins in the US experience, has led some (McGowan and Morgan, forthcoming) to argue that changes to the EU regime really represent nothing more than Americanisation for slow learners. Is it not inevitable that the EU regime introduced criminal sanctions as part of its cartel enforcement regime?

8. CONCLUSIONS: CARTEL POLICY IN A CHANGING ECONOMIC ENVIRONMENT

There is little doubt that competition policy finally came of age in the course of the last twenty years (Leon Brittan, as quoted in Devuyst, 2000: 134). Various aspects of the EU regime, be it mergers, monopolies or state aids, provide ample evidence of its salience, but it is cartel policy which has best demonstrated the innovative and imaginative role of the European Commission in tackling the most fundamental aspect of anti-competitive activity, and it is cartel policy that has been at the forefront of international cartel enforcement. Developments in European competition policy can be approached theoretically through the three interconnected logics which have recently been applied to the evolution and study of EU foreign policy (Smith, 2009). Whereas the first logic of the integration process focuses on the pressures for policy change (to create a fully functioning single market) and adaptation, the second logic of external opportunity structures explores the ways and degrees to which networks (e.g. ECN, legal firms) and actors (the Commission) can push for developments and incremental change. The third and final logic of identity is very much concerned with how member state governments perceive and react to policy initiatives, and it is this final one where we may indeed see greater member state involvement and more direct intervention in the competition arena than in the past. It is interesting to speculate just how stable the entire competition regime actually is today. Until the latter half of 2008 EU competition policy and the competition principle had been king and had resisted for the most part political pressures, and usually successfully dismissed any notions of industrial policy when it came to making decisions, but can the system deflect the seismic economic and political shocks of a new economic recession?

The sudden and unexpected collapse of Lehman Brothers in the US in September 2008 marked a decisive moment in the fortunes and immediate stability of the global economy. It represented the beginnings of the onset of the worst economic crisis to confront the western industrialised world since the 1929 Wall Street Crash. Output has since slumped as many order books are increasingly rather empty, and many firms have since collapsed under the weight of the economic strain, which in turn has propelled the number of unemployed back to early 1990s levels. The impact of such economic and social turmoil is being felt in many quarters and the competition policy arena is unlikely to remain totally immune from events. The central question facing the western world once again centres on how government responds to and approaches the ongoing economic and increasingly social crisis. If belief in the free market comes to be discredited how will it impact on the design and operation of competition policy?

Questions are going to be raised about whether the competition principle will come under increasing attack from member state governments (Wilks, 2009) which are responding to the needs of wider society in the face of ongoing recession. It seems almost certain that enforcement in particular aspects of the competition brief is going to be affected, and particularly the area of state aids and mergers. Indeed, the Commission at the start of 2009 sanctioned some state subsidies exceeding some €3,000 million to help rescue the banking system. It may even be that the old conflict between industrial policy and competition policy may re-emerge to an extent as the objectives of both once again clash. In times of recession should the competition regulators be as determined to enforce the competition rules? Do they really want to insist on the maintenance of competition if it makes a tough situation even tougher? Do they want a number of companies going out of business (Stephan, 2009)? Can and should social policy concerns, for example, supersede competition policy? Time will tell exactly how far and whether the belief in competitive markets will triumph. It is tempting to use words such as retrenchment and decline but these would be to overdramatise the events.

It can be anticipated that merger control may be relaxed, and almost certainly that the approach to state aid will soften considerably. However, the two traditional cornerstones of antitrust, namely cartels and abusive monopolies, will remain untouched.[18] Whatever the future holds for European competition policy – and softening is expected in certain areas – the war against cartels is unlikely to change, and what change may come will probably occur with the re-emergence of sanctioned crisis cartels (for example, in the much troubled car industry). Cartels remain a reality, and even more so in times of economic recession, and we should expect to see many more episodes of such cheating and collusive activity, and as such the wars will continue and must be intensified further. It is to be expected that 'unquestionably leniency programmes are the greatest investigative tool ever designed to fight cartels' (Hammond, as quoted in Spratling and Arp, 2004) will make detection easier and more frequent, and it is also assumed that increased co-operation and co-ordination among competition authorities will enable more cartels to be discovered. The final message for companies (and increasingly for individuals where cartel activity constitutes a criminal offence) is clearer than ever. They should avoid entering into price fixing and market sharing agreements if they are to avoid the serious consequences that will arise and the growing determination of cartel regulators worldwide to eradicate cartellisation.

NOTES

1. Case studies from Australia and New Zealand provide excellent examples of how cartels have come to feature more heavily on the radar screens of the Australian Competition and Consumer Commission and New Zealand's Competition Commission, and how both have recorded the imposition of ever higher fines and the introduction of leniency programmes. (See Simpson Grierson, 2009.)
2. Switzerland was a member of EFTA, but did not participate in the EEA because a referendum on EEA membership was rejected narrowly in December 1992. The original EFTA agreement had provided for interaction between the member state governments on competition matters (Martin, 1961). However, the EFTA Council did not possess any powers to conduct investigations and, in effect, such aspirations were meaningless.
3. For many of the European Free Trade Association (EFTA) states, however, the agreement was little more than a stepping stone to accession. It offered access to the internal market as a half-way house between non-membership and membership of the EU. Three of the original participants, Sweden, Austria and Finland, joined the EU in January 1995, leaving only Iceland, Liechtenstein and Norway as the three remaining EFTA parties to the agreement. The EEA Agreement sought to create the largest single market in the world. Fundamental to this aim was the introduction of the so-called 'four freedoms' (goods, services, labour and capital), although the Agreement also included co-operation in the fields of research and the environment, and financial aid through the European Investment Bank (EIB). Certain European Union policies, including Economic and Monetary Union and Common Foreign and Security Policy, were not covered by the Agreement.
4. It should be noted that merger policy was treated somewhat differently, however, as it was intended that the EU's Merger Control Regulation should be modified to cover the entire EEA region. The state aid provisions contained within Articles 61–63 of the Agreement reflected those within the EC Treaty (Articles 88–90).
5. Drafted by the DG responsible for the single market and supported by DG Competition, it foresaw two ways in which the Commission could assist the CEECs in building an effective competition policy: first, by drawing up an inventory of state subsidies granted by the CEECs and, second, by running competition policy training programmes.
6. The Cotonou Agreement (OS 2000 L 317/3) was signed in June 2000 and came into force in April 2003, is valid for twenty years and is based around three pillars – political

co-operation, trade links and development assistance. Article 45 of the Agreement obliges the ACP states to adopt and implement sound competition policies.

7. These supporters came mainly from Western Europe including Germany. The issue of cartels was raised in the mid 1950s (Lloyd and Sampson, 1995) and a 1961 report made the case of the suitability of GATT as a vehicle for tackling cartels. (See also Edwards, 1967 for a greater discussion.) Little interest existed among most GATT members as concerns prevailed about the dangers of losing political control over the process and also widely held views that cartels were not deemed to represent any significant problem.
8. The EU/US bilateral agreement came into force in 1995 and was followed swiftly by a similar agreement with Canada.
9. The first real test of the US–EU Co-operation Agreement came with the proposed merger of two US aircraft manufacturers, Boeing and McDonnell Douglas, in 1997. This merger was expected to create a firm with a $48 billion (£29 billion) turnover and 20,000 employees. The alliance was approved conditionally by the US's FTC early in July 1997. However, DG Competition had strong reservations about its impact on competition with Airbus and especially in terms of market share and the exclusive twenty year contracts with Delta, Continental and American Airlines to supply all their aircraft. The Americans were convinced that the Commission's criticism of the merger had more to do with general industrial policy fears and an impulse to protect Airbus than with any provisions within the Merger Regulation. A trade war between the EU and the US loomed as negotiations between Boeing and the Commission continued throughout the summer, with both sides hoping that the other would back down. Ultimately Boeing proposed one final set of concessions which clinched a deal and Commission acceptance. The *Boeing/McDonnell Douglas* case demonstrated the limits of the US–EU Co-operation Agreement and the perpetuation of the extraterritorial application of competition policy. There was certainly a heavy political dimension to the case.
10. The OECD was the successor to the Organisation for European Economic Co-operation (OEEC). The latter was established as an intergovernmental organisation in 1947 as a means of liberalising trade and encouraging the growth of agricultural and industrial production in Western Europe. It originally comprised sixteen member states – Austria, Belgium, Denmark, France, Greece, Iceland, Ireland, Italy, Luxembourg, the Netherlands, Norway, Portugal, Sweden, Switzerland, Turkey and the United Kingdom. West Germany joined in 1955 and Spain in 1959. The OEEC ceased to function in December 1961.
11. The OECD's membership was extended to eighteen in 1960 when both Canada and the United States were accepted as members, as was Japan in 1964. Its membership grew rapidly after 1990 with the addition of many of the CEECs. Discussions for further membership began with Chile, Estonia, Israel, Russia and Slovenia in May 2007.
12. The first ever recommendation from the OECD's Competition Policy and Law Committee was made in 1967. Revisions to this document in the 1970s made little headway, though interestingly the recommendations (in 1973 and 1979) referred to issues such as notification, sharing of information and co-operation.
13. The OECD also produces its own *OECD Journal of Competition Law and Policy*.
14. The WTO had some 153 members in 2008.
15. When the Doha Round of the ongoing trade negotiations was launched in 2001 competition policy was included as one of the themes.
16. Article 50a section 1 of the GWB stipulates that 'in accordance with Article 12(1) . . . the Competition authority has the power to disclose any mater of fact or law to the European Commission and the competition authorities of other member states and to supply the relevant document and data. This data may include confidential information, in particular trade and business secrets. In return the competition authority has the power to request and receive such information from other competition authorities and can use it in evidence.'
17. Such bilateral agreements can be labelled as first generation (see ICN, 2009) attempts

to foster co-operation, and have developed further into second generation style accords which allow for the direct exchange of confidential information between competition authorities. To date there is only one example of the latter and it centres on an agreement between the US and Australian authorities. This so-called Antitrust Mutual Enforcement Assistance Agreement (AMEAA) was signed in 1999.

18. The highest ever fine of €1.06 billion (£948 million) under Article 82 (abusive monopolies) was imposed on Intel (computer chipmaker) in May 2009 for having paid a manufacturer to use its chips over those of its rival companies. See http://news.bbc.co.uk/1/hi/business/8047546.stm.

Appendix: The numbering and renumbering of the rules on competition under the treaties

Treaty of Rome (EEC), 1957	Treaty of Amsterdam (ToA), 1997	Treaty of Lisbon, (TFEU)*, 2007
Article 85	Article 81	Article 101
Article 86	Article 82	Article 102
Article 87	Article 83	Article 103
Article 88	Article 84	Article 104
Article 89	Article 85	Article 105
Article 90	Article 86	Article 106
Article 91	Article 87	Article 107
Article 92	Article 88	Article 108
Article 93	Article 89	Article 109

Note: * TFEU is the abbreviation for the Treaty on the Foundations of the European Union but more commonly known as the Treaty of Lisbon. When it comes into force it will renumber the rules on competition for a second time. This particular treaty was signed in December 2007 and came into effect in December 2009 after successful ratification from each of the twenty-seven Member States.

Bibliography

Adler, M. (1969), 'Specialization in the European Coal and Steel Community', *Journal of Common Market Studies*, **8**, 175–89.

Albert, M. (1993), *Capitalism against Capitalism*, London: Whurr Publishers.

ALDE (2006), Competition Policy Paper, October, at: http://www.alde.eu/fileadmin/files/Download/CompetitionPolicy_EN1_web.pdf.

Allen, D. (1977), 'Policing or Policy Making? Competition Policy in the European Communities' in Wallace, H., Wallace, W. and Webb, C. (eds), *Policy-Making in the European Communities*, London: John Wiley and Sons.

Amato, G. (1997), *Antitrust and the Bounds of Power*, Oxford, Hart Publishing.

American Bar Association Section on Antitrust Law Brown Bag Program (ABA) (2005), 'The European Competition Network: What it is and Where it is going', 19 April, 2002, at http://www.abanet.org/antitrust/source/07-05/Jul05-ECNBrBag7=28f.pdf.

Areeda, P. and Turner, D. (1975), 'Predatory Prices and Related Practices under Section 2 of the Sherman Act', *Harvard Law Review*, **88**(4), 697–733.

Asch, P. and Seneca, J.J. (1976), 'Is Collusion Profitable?', *Review of Economics and Statistics*, **68**, 1–12.

Aydin, U. (2009), 'Promoting Competition: European Union and the Global Competition Order', paper presented at the EUSA Biennial Conference, Los Angeles, 23–25 April.

Baker, D.L., Campbell, A.N., Reynolds, M.J. and Rowley, J.W. (1997), 'The Harmonization of International Competition Law Enforcement' in Waverman, L., Comanor, W.S. and Goto, A. (eds), *Competition Policy in the Global Economy: Modalities for Co-operation*, New York: Routledge.

Ball, G.W. (1973), *The Past has another Pattern*, London: W.W. Norton and Company.

Barbezat, D. (1989), 'Cooperation and Rivalry in the International Steel Cartel, 1926–33', *Journal of Economic History*, **49**(2), 435–47.

Barbezat, D. (1990), 'International Cooperation and Domestic Cartel Control. The International Steel Cartel', *Journal of Economic History*, **50**(2), 436–38.

Barnikel, H.H. (1988), *Marktwirschaft – Kartelle, Konzentration, Kontrolle*, Heidelberg: D & M.

Barry, N. (1989), 'Political and Economic Thought of the German Neo-liberals' in Peacock, A. and Willgerodt, H. (eds), *The German Social Market,* Basingstoke: Macmillan.

Beaud, M. (2000), *Histoire du Capitalisme de 1500 à 2000*, Paris: Points Economie.

Bebr, G. (1953), 'The European Coal and Steel Community: A Political and Legal Innovation', *Yale Law Journal*, **63**(1), 1–43.

Benson, S.E. (1980), 'UN Conference on Restrictive Business Practices', *The American Journal of International Law*, **74**(2), 451–3.

Berghahn, V. (1986), *The Americanization of West German Industry*, Leamington Spa: Berg.

Bishop, M. (1993), 'European or National? The Community's New Merger Regulation' in Bishop, M. and Kay, J. (eds), *European Mergers and Merger Policy*, Oxford: Oxford University Press.

Bishop, S. and Walker, M. (2002), *The Economics of EC Competition Law: Concepts, Application and Measurement*, London: Sweet and Maxwell, 2nd edition.

Bomberg, E., Peterson, J. and Stubb, A. (eds) (2007), *How does the European Union Work?*, Oxford: Oxford University Press, 2nd edition.

Boserup, W. and Schlichtkrull, U. (1962), 'Alternative Approaches to the Control of Competition' in Miller, J.P. (ed.), *Competition Cartels and Their Regulation,* Amsterdam: North-Holland Publishing Company.

Bowie, R. (1989), 'Réflexions de Jean Monnet' in *Témoinages à la memoire de Jean Monnet*, Lausanne, Fondation Jean Monnet pour l'Europe.

Braithwaite, J. and Drahos, P. (2000), *Global Business Regulation*, Cambridge: Cambridge University Press.

Brown, W.A. (1950), *The United States and the Restoration of World Trade*, Washington, DC: The Brookings Institution.

Buch-Hansen, H. (2008), 'Rethinking the History of European Level Merger Control: A Critical Economy Perspective', PhD Thesis, Copenhagen: Copenhagen Business School, No. 26.

Buiccirossi, C.P. and Spagnolo, G. (2006), 'Optimal Fines in the Era of Whistleblowers', *CEPR Discussion Paper*, N.5465, January.

Büthe, T. (2007), 'The Politics of Competition Policy in the European Union: The First 50 Years' in Meunier, S. and McNamara, K.R. (eds), *The State of the European Union*, Vol. 8, Oxford: Oxford University Press.

Büthe, T. and Swank, G. (2005), 'The Politics of Antitrust and Merger Review in the European Union: Institutional Change and Decisions from Messina to 2004', *Working Paper*, Mimeo, Duke and Stanford Universities.

Campbell, A.N. and Trebilcock, M.J. (1997), 'Interjurisdictional Conflict in Merger Review' in Waverman, L., Comanor, W.S. and Goto, A. (eds), *Competition Policy in the Global Economy: Modalities for Cooperation*, New York: Routledge.

Carter, C. and Smith, A. (2008), 'Revitalizing Public Policy Approaches to the EU', *Journal of European Public Policy*, **15**(2), 263–81.

Cecchini, P. et al. (1988), *The European Challenge 1992: The Benefits of the Single Market*, Report of the Cost of Non-Europe Steering Committee, Aldershot: Wildwood House.

Chamberlain, E.H. (1947), *The Theory of Monopolistic Competition*, Cambridge, MA: Harvard University Press.

Childs, D. (1986), *The GDR: Moscow's German Ally*, Hemel Hempstead: George Allen and Unwin.

Church, C. and Phinnemore, D. (2002), *The Penguin Guide to the European Treaties*, London: Penguin.

Cini, M. (2006), 'The Europeanization of British Competition Policy' in Bache, I. and Jordan, A. (eds), *The Europeanization of British Politics*, Basingstoke: Palgrave.

Cini, M. (ed.) (2007), *European Union Politics*, Oxford: Oxford University Press.

Cini, M. and McGowan, L. (1998), *Competition Policy in the European Union*, Basingstoke: Macmillan.

Cini, M. and McGowan, L. (2009), *Competition Policy in the European Union*, Basingstoke: Palgrave, 2nd edition.

Clark, J.M. (1940), 'Toward a Concept of Workable Competition', *American Economic Review*, **30**(2), 241–56.

Clarke, R. and Morgan, E. (2006), *New Developments in UK and EU Competition Policy*, Cheltenham: Edward Elgar.

Coen, D. and Thatcher, M. (2009), 'National Regulators Attitudes to Formal European Networks of Regulators', paper presented at the EUSA Biennial Conference, Los Angeles, 23–25 April.

Commission of the European Communities (1973–), *Annual Reports on Competition Policy*, Luxembourg: Office for Official Publications of the European Union).

Commission of the European Communities (1977), 'Sixth Report on Competition Policy', *Annual Competition Policy Report*, Luxembourg: CEC.

Commission of the European Communities (1980), 'Ninth Report on Competition Policy', *Annual Competition Policy Report*, Luxembourg: CEC.

Commission of the European Communities (1984), 'Thirteenth Report on Competition Policy', *Annual Competition Policy Report*, Luxembourg: CEC.

Commission of the European Communities (1985), *Completing the Internal Market*, White Paper from the Commission to the Council, COM(85)310 Final, Luxembourg: CEC.

Commission of the European Communities (1999), *White Article on Modernisation of the Rules Implementing Articles 85 and 86 of the EC Treaty*, Commission programme no. 99/027, 28 April 1999.

Commission of the European Communities (2005), Green Paper on 'Damages Actions for Breach of the EC Antitrust Rules' at http://europa.eu.int/comm/competition/antitrust.others/actions_for_damages/gp.en#.

Commission of the European Communities (2008), *White Paper on Damages Actions for Breach of the EC Antitrust Rules,* COM(2008)165.

Connor, J.M. (2001), 'Our Customers are our Enemies: The Lysine Cartel of 1992–1995', *Review of Industrial Organisation*, **18**(1), 5–21.

Consumers' Association (2002), 'Criminalisation of Cartels: What is all the Fuss about?', *Briefing Paper*, 19 February.

Council of Europe (1951), *Memorandum on the Recommendation of the Consultative Assembly for the Preparation of a European Convention for the Control of International Cartels and Draft Convention prepared by the Secretariat General*, SG/R (51) 15, 28 November.

Daly, K. (2007), 'Cartels and Deterrence – Creeping Criminalisation and the Class Action Boom', *Bloomberg Business Law Journal*, **1**(35), 315–26.

Damro, C. (2006a), 'The New Trade Politics and Competition Policy: Shopping for Convergence and Co-operation', *Journal of European Public Policy*, **13**(6), 867–86.

Damro, C. (2006b), *Cooperating on Competition in Transatlantic Economic Relations*, Basingstoke: Palgrave.

Damro, C. and Guay, T. (2009), 'Comparing International EU Competition Cases: What can Business and Politics Learn', paper presented at the EUSA Biennial Conference, Los Angeles, 23–25 April.

De Broca, H. (2006), 'The Commission Revises its Guidelines for Setting Fines in Antitrust Cases', *Competition Policy Newsletter*, (Autumn), 1–6.

De Jong, H.W. (1973), 'The Economics of Concerted Practices (Collusion)' in *European Competition Policy: Essays of the Leiden Working Group on Cartel Problems*, The Europa Institute of the University of Leiden, Leiden: A.W. Sijthoff.

Devuyst, Y. (2000), 'Transatlantic Cooperation Relations' in Pollack,

M. and Schaffer, G.C. (eds), *Transatlantic Governance in the Global Economy*, Oxford: Rowman and Littlefield.

Diebold, W. (1959), *The Schuman Plan: A Study in Economic Co-operation, 1950–59*, New York: F.E. Praeger.

Diegmann, A. (1993), 'American Deconcentration Policy in the Ruhr Coal Industry' in Diefendorf. J.M. et al. (eds), *American Policy and the Reconstruction of West Germany, 1945–55*, Cambridge: Cambridge University Press.

Dinan, D. (1999) *Ever Closer Union*, Basingstoke: Macmillan.

Dinan, D. (2006), *Origins and Evolution of the European Union*, Oxford: Oxford University Press.

Djelic, M.-L. (1998), *Exporting the American Model: The Postwar Transformation of European Business*, Oxford: Oxford University Press.

Doern, G.B. and Wilks, S. (eds) (1996), *Comparative Competition Policy: National Institutions in a Global Market*, Oxford: Clarendon Press.

Doleys, T. (2007), 'Managing the Paradox of Discretion: Commission Authority and the Evolution of EU State Aid Policy', paper presented at UACES Research Conference, Portsmouth, UK, 3–5 September.

Drexl, J. (2003), 'Do we Need Courage for International Trust Law? Choosing between Supranational and International Principles of Enforcement' in Drexl, J. (ed.), *The Future of Transnational Anti-trust: From Comparative to Common Competition Law*, The Hague: Kluwer Law International.

DTI (2001), *Productivity and Enterprise – A World Class Competition Regime*, London: The Stationery Office, Cm5233, July 2001.

Eckbo, P.L. (1976), *The Future of World Oil*, Cambridge: Ballinger Publishing.

Edwards, C.D. (1967), *Control of Cartels and Monopolies: An International Comparison*, New York: Oceana.

Ehlermann, C.-D. (2000), 'The Modernization of EC Anti-Trust Policy: A Legal and Cultural Revolution', *Common Market Law Review*, **37**, 537–90.

Ehrmann, H.W. (1954), 'The French Trade Associations and the Ratification of the Schuman Plan', *World Politics*, **6**(4), 453–81.

Eichner, A.S. (1969), *The Emergence of Oligopoly: Sugar Refining as a Case Study*, Baltimore: Johns Hopkins University Press.

Ellison, G. (1994), 'Theories of Cartel Stability and the Joint Executive Committee', *Rand Journal of Economics*, **25**(1), 37–57.

Epstein, E.J. (1982), *The Rise and Fall of Diamonds*, London: Schuster and Schuster.

Erhard, L. (1957), *Wohlstand für Alle*, Düsseldorf: Econ.

ERT (2000), *ERT Proposals for the Reform of EU Competition Policy*, Brussels: ERT.

Estrin, S. and Holmes, P. (1998), *Competition and Economic Integration in Europe*, Cheltenham: Edward Elgar.

Eucken, W. (1990), *Grundsätze der Wirtschaftspolitik*, Tübingen: UTB (reprint).

Eucken, W. and Hensel, K.P. (1952), *Grundsätze der Wirtschaftspolitik*, Tübingen: Mohr and Siebeck.

Evenett, S.J.M., Levenstein, M.C. and Suslow, V.Y. (2001), 'International Cartel Enforcement: Lessons from the 1990s', *The World Economy: Special Global Trade Policy Issue*, **24**(9), 1221–45.

Eyre, S. (1999), *The Politics of Merger Control in the EU and UK*, PhD thesis, Politics Department, University of Exeter, UK.

Eyre, S. and Lodge, M. (2000), 'National Tunes and a European Melody? Competition Law Reform in the UK and Germany', *Journal of European Public Policy*, **7**(1), 63–79.

Farrelly, P. (2001), 'Cartel that Conceals its Cutting Edge', *Observer*, 4 March.

Faull, J. and Nikpay, P. (2007), *The EC Law of Competition*, Oxford: Oxford University Press, 2nd edition.

Fear, J. (2006), 'Cartels and Competition: Neither Markets nor Hierarchies', *Harvard Business School Working Paper* 07 (11).

Featherstone, K. and Radaelli, C. (eds) (2003), *The Politics of Europeanization*, Oxford: Oxford University Press.

Feldenkirchen, W. (1985), 'Das Zwangskartellgesetz von 1933: Seine wirtschaftliche Bedeutung und seine praktischen Folgen' in Pohl, H. (ed.), *Kartelle und Kartellgesetzgebung in Praxis und Rechtsprechung von 19. Jahrhundert bis zur Gegenwart*, Stuttgart: Steiner.

Feldenkirchen, W. (1988), 'Concentration in German Industry, 1870–1939' in Pohl, H. (ed.), *The Concentration Process in the Entrepreneurial Economy since the Late Nineteenth Century*, Wiesbaden: Steiner Verlag.

Feldenkirchen, W. (1991), 'Banking and Economic Growth: Banks and Industry in Germany in the Nineteenth Century and their Changing Relationship During Industrialisation', in Lee, W.R. (ed.), *German Industry and German Industrialisation*, London: Routledge.

Feldenkirchen, W. (1992), 'Competition Policy in Germany', *Business and Economic History*, **21**, 257–69.

Fishwick, F. (1993), *Making Sense of Competition Policy*, London: Kogan Page.

Fitzpatrick, E. (1995), 'Articles 85 and 86: Control of Restrictive Practices and Abuses of Dominant Positions', in Davidson, L., Fitzpatrick, E.

and Johnson, D. (eds), *The European Competitive Environment,* Oxford: Butterworth-Heinemann.

Fox, E.M. (2007), 'GE/Honeywell: The US Merger that Europe stopped: A Story of the Politics of Convergence', *SSRN Working Paper Series*, at http://ssrn.com/abstract=1002647.

Freyer, T. (1992), *Regulating Big Business: Anti-trust in Great Britain and America, 1800–1990*, Cambridge: Cambridge University Press.

Friedman, J.W. (1972), 'A Non-Cooperative Equilibrium for Supergames', *Review of Economic Studies,* **80**(5), 906–50.

Friedman, M. (1972), 'Comments on the Critics', *Journal of Political Economy* and reprinted in Gordon, R.J. (ed.) (1974), *Milton Friedman's Monetary Framework: A Debate with His Critics*, Chicago, IL: University of Chicago Press.

Gauer, C. and Jaspers, M. (2006), 'The European Competition Network. Achievements and Challenges – a Case in Point: Leniency', *Competition Policy Newsletter*, No. 1 (Spring), 8–11.

Gavin, B. (2001), *The European Union and Globalisation*, Cheltenham: Edward Elgar.

Gebhardt, G. (1957), *Ruhrgebau: Geschichte, Aufbau und Verflechtung seiner Gesellschaften und Organisationen*, Essen: Glückauf.

Gehler, M. and von der Gröben, H. (2002), 'Europäische Integration aus historischer Erfarung: ein Zeitzeugengespräch mit Michael Gehler/Hans von der Gröben', *Zentrum für Europäische Integrationsforschung (ZEI) Discussion paper*, Bonn: Rheinisch Friedrich-Wilhelms-Universität.

Genesove, D. and Mullin, W.P. (1998), 'Testing Static Oligopoly Models: Conduct and Cost in the Sugar Industry, 1890–1914', *Rand Journal of Economics*, **29**(2), 355–77.

Genesove, D. and Mullin, W.P. (2001), 'Rules, Communication and Collusion: Narrative Evidence from the Sugar Institute Case', *American Economic Review*, **91**(3), 379–98.

Geradin, D. and Henry, D. (2005), 'The EC Fining Policy for Violations of Competition Law: An Empirical Review of the Commission Decisional Practice and the Community Courts' Judgments', GCLC Working Paper No. 2/05, University of Tilburg, at SSRN: http://ssrn.com/abstract=671794 or DOI: 10.2139/ssrn.10.2139/ssrn.671794.

Gerber, D. (1994), 'The Transformation of European Community Competition Law', *Harvard International Law Journal*, **35** (1), 97–147.

Gerber, D. (1998), *Law and Competition in Twentieth Century Europe: Protecting Prometheus*, Oxford: Clarendon Press.

Gerber, D.J. (1999), 'The US–European Conflict over the Globalization of Antitrust Law: A Legal Perspective', *New England Law Review*, **34**(1), 123–31.

Gerschenkron, A. (ed.) (1962), 'Economic Backwardness in Economic Perspective' in Gerschenkron, A. (ed.), *Economic Backwardness in Economic Perspective: A Book of Essays*, Cambridge, MA: Bellnap Press.

Gillingham, J. (1985), *Industry and Politics in the Third Reich: Ruhr Coal, Hitler and Europe*, London: Methuen.

Gillingham, J. (1991), *Coal, Steel and the Rebirth of Europe, 1945–1955*, Cambridge: Cambridge University Press.

Gillingham, J. (2003), *European Integration, 1950–2003: Superstate or New Market Economy?*, Cambridge: Cambridge University Press.

Gillingham, J. (2006), 'The German Problem and European Integration' in Dinan, D. (ed.) *Origins and Evolution of the European Union*, Oxford: OUP.

Goyder, D.G. (1993), *EC Competition Law*, Oxford: Clarendon Press, 2nd edition.

Goyder, D.G. (2003), *EC Competition Law*, Oxford: Clarendon Press, 4th edition.

Grant, C. (1994), *Delors: Inside the House that Jacques Built*, London: Nicholas Brealey Publishing Ltd.

Green, E.J. and Porter, R.H. (2007), 'Non-cooperative Collusion under Imperfect Price Information' in Levenstein, M. and Salant, S.W. (eds), *Cartels*, Cheltenham: Edward Elgar.

Green, N. and Robertson, A. (1999), *The Europeanisation of UK Competition Law*, Oxford: Hart.

Griffin, J.W. (2007), 'An Inside Look at the Cartel at Work: Common Characteristics of International Cartels', speech given on 6 April 2000 and reprinted in Levenstein, M. and Salant, S.W. (eds), *Cartels*, Cheltenham: Edward Elgar.

Grosser, A. (1985), *Der Staat in der Wirtshaft der Bundesrepublik*, Opladen: UTB.

Gyselen, L. (1993), 'The Commission's Fining Policy in Competition Cases' in Slot, P.J. and McDonnell, A. (eds), *Procedure and Enforcement in EC and US Competition Law*, London: Sweet and Maxwell.

Haas, E.B. (1958), *The Uniting of Europe: Political, Social and Economic Forces 1950–1957*, Stanford, CA: Stanford University Press, 2nd edition.

Haas, E.B. (1970), 'The Study of Regional Integration', *International Organisation*, **24**(4), 91–108.

Haas, E.B. (2004), 'Introduction: Institutionalisation or Constructivism?' in *The Uniting of Europe: Political, Social and Economic Forces 1950–1957*, Notre Dame, IN: University of Notre Dame Press, 3rd edition.

Hall, P. (1986), *Governing the Economy: The Politics of State Intervention in Britain and France*, Cambridge: Polity Press.

Hallstein, W. (1962), *United Europe: Challenge and Opportunity*, Cambridge, MA: Harvard University Press.

Hambloch, S. (2007), 'Competition Policy in the EEC in the 1960s', paper presented at the Workshop on European Competition Policy, 1930–2005, Paris; Sorbonne University, 14–15 September.

Hammond, A. and Penrose, R. (2001), *Proposed Criminalisation of Cartels in the UK*, Report for the UK Office of Fair Trading (November) [2002] UKCLR 97.

Hammond, S. (2005), 'An Overview of Recent Developments in the Antitrust Division's Criminal Enforcement Programme', speech delivered to the American Bar Association, Kona, Hawaii, 10 January.

Harding, C. and Joshua, J. (2003), *Regulating Cartels in Europe*, Oxford: OUP.

Harmsen, R. and Wilson, T.M. (eds) (2000), *Europeanization, Institution, Identities and Citizenship*, Amsterdam and Atlanta, GA: Rodopi.

Henderson, W.O. (1967), *The Industrial Revolution on the Continent, 1800–1914*, London: Frank Cass and Co.

Herlitzka, N. (1963), 'Bemerkungen zur historischen Entwicklung von Kartellen' in Kastl, L. and Metzner, M. (eds), *Kartelle in der Wirklichkeit Festschrift für Max Metzner zu seinem fünfundsiebzigsten Geburtstag*, Cologne: Heymann.

Hexner, E. (1946), *International Cartels*, London: Pitman.

Hix, S. (2005), *The Political System of the European Union*, Basingstoke: Palgrave.

Hoffmann, S. (1966), 'Obstinate or Obsolete? The Fate of the Nation-state and the Case of Western Europe', *Daedalus* **95**(3), 862–915.

Hofmann, H.C.H. (2006), 'Negotiated and Non-Negotiated Administrative Rule Making: The Example of EC Competition Policy', *Common Market Law Review*, **43**(1), 153–78.

Hofstadter, R. (1964), 'What happened to the Antitrust Movement? Notes on the Evolution of an American Creed' in Cheit, E.F. (ed.), *The Business Establishment*, London: Wiley.

Hovenkamp, H. (1994), *Federal Antitrust Law: The Law of Competition and its Practice,* St Paul, MN: West publishing Co, 2nd edition.

International Antitrust Code Working Group (1993), *Draft International Antitrust Code*, Munich, July.

Jacquemin, A. (1993), 'The International Dimension of European Competition Policy', *Journal of Common Market Studies*, **31**(1), 91–102.

Jenny, F. (1990), 'French Competition Policy in Perspective' in Comanor, W.S. et al., *Competition Policy in Europe and North America: Economic Issues and Institutions*, London: Harwood Academic Publishers.

Jephcott, M. and Lübbig, T. (2003), *Law of Cartels*, London: Jordans.
Jones, A. and Sufrin, B. (2004), *EC Competition Law*, Oxford: OUP, 2nd edition.
Jones, A. and Sufrin, B. (2008), *EC Competition Law*, Oxford: OUP, 3rd edition.
Joshua, J. (1986), 'Information in EEC Competition Law Procedures', *European Law Review*, **11**(4), 409–29.
Joshua, J. (2001), 'Flawed Thinking about Price Fixers: Fighting Cartels in Europe Calls for a Review of the Law rather than the Commission's Ramshackle Solution', *Financial Times*, 3 August.
Joshua, J. (2002), 'A Sherman Act Bridgehead in Europe, or a Ghost Ship in Mid-Atlantic?: A Close Look at the United Kingdom Proposals to Criminalise Hardcore Cartel Conduct', *European Competition Law Review*, **23**(5), 231–45.
Judge, D. and Earnshaw, D. (2008), *The European Parliament*, Basingstoke: Palgrave, 2nd edition.
Kassim, H. and Wright, K. (2009, 'Network Governance and the European Union: The Case of the European Competition Network', paper presented at the EUSA Biennial Conference, Los Angeles, 23–25 April.
Kastl, L. And Metzner, M. (1963), *Kartelle in der Wirklichkeit Festschrift für Max metzner zu seinem fünfundsiebzigsten Geburtstag*, Cologne: Hetmann,
Kerse, C.S. (1998), *EC Antitrust Procedure*, London: Sweet and Maxwell, 4th edition.
Kiersch, G. (1963), 'Die Internationalen Stahlkartelle zwischen den beiden eltkriegen' in Kastl, L. (ed.), *Kartelle in der Wirklichkeit*, Cologne: Carl Heymanns Verlag.
Kleeberg, J.M. (2004), 'German Cartels: Myths and Realities', available at cedar.barnard.columbia.edu/~econhist/papers/Kleeberg_German_Cartels.pdf.
Kon, S.D. (1980), 'The Delicate Balance between Municipal Law and Community Law in the Application of Articles 85 and 86 of the Treaty of Rome' in Hirwitz, L. (ed.), *Contemporary Perspectives on European Integration, Attitudes, Non-Governmental Behaviour and Collective Decision Making*, London: Aldwych Press.
Kon, S. (1982), 'Article 85, para. 3: A Case for Application by National Courts', *Common Market Law Review,* **19**(4), 541–61.
Korah, V. (2007), *An Introductory Guide to EC Competition Law and Practice*, Oxford: Hart Publishing, 9th edition.
Kroes, N. (2004), 'Introductory Remarks at a Press Conference on the Chlorine Chloride Cartel and EDP/ENI/GDP Merger Decision', Brussels, 9 December.

Kroes, N. (2006a), 'Delivering on the Crackdown: Recent Developments in the European Commission's Campaign against Cartels', speech delivered at the 10th Annual Competition Conference at the European Institute, Florence, 13 October.

Kroes, N. (2006b), 'More Private Antitrust Enforcement through Better Access to Damages: An Invitation for an Open Debate' at the conference on Private Enforcement in EC Competition Law: the Green Article on Damages Action, Brussels, 9 March.

Kroes, N. (2008), 'Consumers at the Heart of EU Competition Policy', speech delivered at the BEUC, dinner, Strasbourg, 22 April.

Kronstein, H. and Leighton, G. (1946), 'Cartel Control: A Record of Failure', *Yale Law Journal*, **55**(2), 297.

Langer, J. and Motta, G. (2006), 'The Effect of EU Anti-trust Investigations and Fines on a Firm's Valuation', *CEPR Discussion Paper 6176*, London, March.

Lavenex, S. (2004), 'EU External Governance in Wider Europe', *Journal of European Public Policy*, **11**(4), 680–700.

Lavenex, S. and Schimmelfenning, F. (2008), 'Relations with the Wider Europe', *Journal of Common Market Studies*, **46**(1), 145–64.

Lehmkuhl, D. (2008), 'On Government, Governance and Judicial Review: The Case of Competition Policy', *Journal of Public Policy*, **28**(1), 139–59.

Leucht, B. (2008), 'Transatlantic Policy Networks and the Creation of a European Antitrust Law, 1950–1', in Kaiser, W., Leucht, B. and Rasmussen, M. (eds), *Origins of the European Polity: Transnational and Supranational Integration, 1950–72*, London: Routledge.

Leucht, B. and Seidel, K. (2007), 'Ruptures and Continuities in European Competition Policy, 1950–62', paper presented at conference on European Competition Policy 1930–2007 at the University of Paris IV-Sorbonne, September.

Levenstein, M. (1996), 'Do Price Wars Facilitate Collusion?: A Study of the Bromine Cartel Before World War One', *Explorations in Economic History*, **33**(1), 1107–37.

Levenstein, M. and Salant, S. (2007), *Cartels*, Cheltenham: Edward Elgar.

Levenstein, M.C. and Suslow, V.Y. (2001), 'Private International Cartels and their Effects on Developing Countries', paper prepared for the World Bank's *World Development Report, 2001*, December.

Levenstein, M.C. and Suslow, V.Y (2006), 'What Determines Cartel Success?' *Journal of Economic Literature*, **44**(1), 43–95.

Levy, H. (1968), *Monopoly, Cartels and Trusts in British Industry*, London: Frank Cass and Co, 2nd edition and a translation of the 1927 original.

Levy, N. (2005), 'Mario Monti's Legacy in EC Merger Control', *Competition Policy International*, **1**(1), 130–32.

Liefmann, R. (1930), *Kartelle, Konzerne und Trusts: Die Unternehmungen und ihre Zusammenschlüsse*, Stuttgart: Ernst Heinrich Moritz, and translated as Liefmann, R. (1932), *Cartels, Concerns and Trusts*, New York: E.P. Dutton and Co.

Lindberg, L.N. (1963), *The Political Dynamics of European Economic Integration*, Stanford, CA: Stanford University Press.

Lister, L. (1960), *Europe's Coal and Steel Community: An Experiment in Economic Union*, New York: Twentieth Century Fund.

Lodge, M. (2000), 'Isomorphism of National Policies? The "Europeanisation" of German Competition and Public Procurement Law', *West European Politics,* **23**(1), 89–107.

Lodge, M. (2002), 'Varieties of Europeanization and the National Regulatory State', *Public Policy & Administration*, **17**(2), 43–67.

Lowe, P. (2007) 'Introduction to Cartels Working Group Plenary Session', ICN Annual Conference, Moscow, 31 May.

McChesney, F.S. and Shughart, W.F. (eds) (1995), *The Causes and Consequences of Antitrust: The Public Choice Perspective*, Chicago, IL: University of Chicago Press.

McGowan, L. (1993), 'The Evolution of German Competition Policy: The Bundeskartellamt, its Role and Competences', *RUSEL Working Paper, No.14*, Politics Department, University of Exeter, UK.

McGowan, L. (1994), 'Half-baked rather than Whole-hearted? Competition Policy in Germany', *Debatte*, **2**(1), 129–49.

McGowan, L. (1997), 'Safeguarding the Economic Constitution: The Commission and Competition Policy' in Nugent, N. (ed.), *At the Heart of the European Union: Studies of the European Commission*, Basingstoke: Macmillan.

McGowan, L. (1998), 'Protecting Competition in a Global Market: The Pursuit of an International Competition Policy', *European Business Review*, **98**(6), 328–39.

McGowan, L. (2000), 'At the Commission's Discretion: Fining Infringements Under the EU's Restrictive Practices Policy', *Public Administration*, **78**(3), 639–56.

McGowan, L. (2005), 'Europeanization Unleashed and Rebounding: The Modernisation of EC Cartel Policy', *Journal of European Public Policy*, **12**(6), 986–1004.

McGowan, L. (2007a), 'Theorising European Integration: Revisiting Neo-functionalism and Testing its Suitability for Explaining the Development of EC Competition Policy?', *European Integration On-Line Papers*, **55**(3).

McGowan, L. (2007b), 'Competition and Industrial Policies' in Menon, A. and Hay, C. (eds), *European Politics*, Oxford: Oxford University Press.

McGowan, L. and Cini, M. (1999), 'Discretion and Politicization in EU Competition Policy: The Case of Merger Policy', *Governance*, **12**(2), 175–200.

McGowan, L. and Wilks, S. (1995), 'The First Supranational Policy of the EU: Competition Policy', *European Journal of Political Research,* **28**(2), 141–69.

McLachlan, D.L. and Swann, D. (1967), *Competition Policy in the European Community: The Rules in Theory and Practice*, Oxford: Oxford University Press.

Maes, I. (2004), 'Macroeconomic and Monetary Thought at the European Commission in the 1960s', *EUI Working Paper* RSCAS No. 2004/01, European University Institute.

Maher, I. (2002), 'Competition Law in the International Domain: Networks as a New Form of Governance', *Journal of Law and Society*, **29**(1), 112–36.

Maher, I. (2006), 'The Rule of Law and Agency: The Case of Competition Policy', *Chatham House Working Paper (*International Economics Programme), IEP WP 06/01.

Marsden, P. (2003), *A Competition Policy for the WTO*, London: Cameron May.

Marsh, D. (1992), *The Bundesbank*, London: Mandarin.

Martin, A. (1961), 'Restrictive Trade Practices in the European Free Trade Association', *International and Comparative Law Quarterly Supplement No. 1: Legal Problems of the EEC and EFTA* (BIICL), 89–107.

Martin, S. (2004), *Coal and Steel: First Steps in European Market Integration* at http://www.kranert.purdue.edu/faculty/smartin/via/E15060D.pdfandescsfig.pdf.

Martin, S. (2006), *The Goals of Antitrust and Competition Policy*, at ftp://ftp.zew.de/pub/zew-docs/veranstaltungen/rnic/papers.StephenMartin.pdf.

Mason, C.F. and Polasky, S. (2005), 'What motivates Membership in Non-Renewable Resource Cartels: The Case of OPEC?', at http://www.sciencedirect.com/science/article/B6VFJ-4GTVYJ3-1/2/95d635ecbf6f3e33ef1ec647f7b3a7a2.

Michelmann, H. (1978), *Organisational Effectiveness in a Multinational Bureaucracy*, Farnborough: Saxon House.

Milward A.S. (1992), *The European Rescue of the Nation State*, London: Routledge.

Milward A.S. (2000), *The European Rescue of the Nation State*, London: Routledge, 2nd edition.

Mirow K.R. and Maurer, H. (1982), *Webs of Power: International Cartels and the World Economy*, New York: Houghton Mifflin.

Monnet, J. (1978), *Memoirs*, New York: Doubleday.

Montag, F. (1996), 'The Case for Radical Reform of the Infringement Procedure under Regulation 17', *European Competition Law Review*, **17**(8), 428–37.

Monti, G. (2007), *EC Competition Law*, Cambridge: Cambridge University Press.

Monti, M. (2004), 'The EU gets New Powers for the 21st Century', *Competition Policy Newsletter*, No. 4 (special edition).

Morgan, E.J. (2001), 'A Decade of EC Merger Control', *International Journal of the Economics of Business*, **8**(3), 451–73.

Morgan, E. (2009), 'Cartels in the EU: Are Fines Enough', paper presented at the EUSA Biennial Conference, Los Angeles, 23–25 April.

Morgan, E. and Maguire, S. (2004), 'Transatlantic Divergence: GE-Honeywell and the EU's Merger Policy', *Journal of European Public Policy*, **11**(1), 39–56.

Möschel, W. (1972) *70 Jahre Deutsche Kartellpolitik*, Tübingen: Walter Eucken Institut.

Motta, M. (2004), *Competition Policy: Theory and Practice*, Cambridge: Cambridge University Press.

Motta, M. (2007), 'Cartels in the European Union: Economics, Law and Practice', paper presented at the conference on Fifty Years of the Treaty: Assessment and Perspectives of Competition Policy in Europe, Barcelona, 19–20 November.

Motta, M. (2008), 'On Cartel Deterrence and Fines in the European Union', *European Competition Law Review*, **29**(4), 209–19.

Nazerali, J. (1998), 'Plus ça change, plus c'est la même chose', *Business Law Review*, **19**(4), 84–5.

Neale, A. and Goyder, D.G. (1980), *The Antitrust Laws of the United States of America*, Cambridge: Cambridge University Press, 3rd edition.

Neumann, M. (1998), 'The Evolution of Cartel Policy in Germany' in Martin, S. (ed.), *Competition Policies in Europe*, Amsterdam: North Holland.

Neven, D., Papandropoulos, P. and Seabright, P. (1998), *Trawling for Minnows: European Competition Policy and Agreements Between Firms*, Brussels: Centre for European Policy Research.

Nipperdey, T. (1994), *Deutsche Geschichte, 1800–1866*, Munich: Beck.

Nörr, K. W. (1994), *Die Leiden des Privatrechts, Kartelle in Deutschland vor der Holzstoffkartellentscheidung zum Gesetz gegen Wettbewerbsbeschränkungen*, Tübingen:

Nugent, N. (2010), *The Government and Politics of the European Union*, Basingstoke: Palgrave, 6th edition.

Nussbaum, H. (1986), 'International Cartels and Multinational Enterprises' in Teichova, A., Levy-Leboyer, M. and Nussbaum, H. (eds), *Multinational Enterprises in Historical Perspective*, New York: Cambridge University Press.

OECD (1986), *Memorandum on Co-operation Between Competition Authorities*, Paris: OECD.

OECD (1995), 'Recommendation of the Council Concerning Co-operation Between Member Countries on Anti-competitive Practices Affecting International Trade', 27 July, C(95)130/FINAL.

OECD (1998), 'Recommendation of the Council Concerning Effective Action Against Hard Core Cartels' at http://www/oecd.org/dataoecd/39/4/2350130.pdf.

OECD (2001), 'Report on Leniency Programmes to Fight Hard Core Cartels', *OECD Observer*, September, at www.oecd.org/daf/clp/CLP_reports/Leniency-e.pdf.

OECD (2002), *Report on the Nature and Impact of Hard Core Cartels and Actions Against National Competition Laws*, April, DAFFE/COMP (2002)7.

OECD (2005), 'Hard Core Cartels: Third Report on the Implementation of the 1998 Recommendation' at http://www.oecd.org/dataoecd/58/1/35863307.pdf.

Pace, L.F. (2007), *European Antitrust Law: Prohibitions, Merger Control and Procedures*, Cheltenham: Edward Elgar.

Palatzke, A.K. (2008), 'State Entities as Addressees of Antitrust Law', paper presented at the Third Joint Seminar between the University of Konstanz and Fudan University Shangai, 16 October.

Pate, E.H. (2004), 'International Anti-Cartel Enforcement', paper presented at the 2004 ICN Cartels Workshop, Sydney, Australia, at http://www.usdoj.gov/atr/public/speeches/206428.htm.

Peacock, A. and Willgerodt, H. (1989), *The German Social Market*, Basingstoke: Macmillan.

Peeperkorn, L. (2001), 'New Notice on Agreements of Minor Importance (de minimis Notice)', *Competition Policy Newsletter*, No. 2 (June), 4–60.

Peritz, R.J.R. (1996), *Competition Policy in America, 1882–1992: History, Rhetoric, Law*, Oxford: Oxford University Press.

Peters, B.G. (1996), 'United States Competition Policy Institutions: Structural Constraints and Opportunities' in Doern, G.B. and Wilks, S. (eds), *Comparative Competition Policy: National Institutions in a Global Market,* Oxford: Clarendon.

Peters, L.L. (1989), 'Managing Competition in German Coal, 1893–1913', *Journal of Economic History*, **49**(2), 419–33.

Pheasant, J. (2006), 'Damages Action for Breach of the EC Antitrust Rules: The European Commission's Green Paper', *European Competition Law Review*, **27**(7), 365–81.

Pierenkemper, T. and Tilly, R.H. (2004), *The German Economy During the Nineteenth Century*, New York: Berghahn.

Pijetlovic, K. (2004), 'Reform of EC Antitrust Enforcement: Criticism of the New System is Highly Exaggerated', *European Competition Law Review*, **25**(6), 356–69.

Pogge von Strandman, H. (1969), 'Domestic Origins of Germany's Colonial Expansion', *Past and Present*, **42**, 140–59.

Pollack, M. (2000), 'The End of Creeping Competence? EU Policy-making since Maastricht', *Journal of Common Market Studies*, **38**(3), 519–38.

Pope, D. (1993), 'Some Reflections on Italian Flat Glass', *European Competition Law Review*, **14**(4), 172–6.

Posner, R.A. (1970), 'A Statistical Study of Antitrust Enforcement', *Journal of Law and Economics*, **13**(2), 365–419.

Posner, R.A. (1976), *Antitrust Law: An Economic Perspective*, Chicago, IL: University of Chicago.

Posner, R.A. (2001), *Antitrust Law: An Economic Perspective*, Chicago, IL: University of Chicago, 2nd edition.

Radaelli, C. (2000), 'Whither Europeanization? Concept Stretching and Substantive Change, *European Integration Online Papers*, vol. 4 (2000), No. 8, at http://eiop.or.at/eiop/texte/2000-008a.htm.

Ramirez, S. (2007), 'The Competition Policy of the EEC in the Automobile Sector: The Case of the Block Exemption for Automobile Distribution, 1962–1985', paper presented at the Workshop on European Competition Policy, 1930–2000, Sorbonne University, Paris, 14–15 September.

Resch, A. (2002), *Industriekartelle in Österreich vor dem Ersten Weltkrieg*, Berlin: Duncker and Humblot.

Resch, A. (2005), 'Phases of Competition Policy in Europe', *Working Paper AY0504*, Vienna University of Economics and Business Administration.

Reynolds, M.J. and Anderson, D.G. (2006), 'Immunity and Leniency in EU Cartel Cases: Current Issues', *European Competition Law Review*, **27**(2), 82–90.

Riley, A. (2003), 'EC Antitrust Modernisation: The Commission Does Very Nicely-Thank You Part Two: Between the Idea and the Reality: Decentralisation Under Regulation 1', *European Competition Law Review*, **24**(4), 657–72.

Risse, T., Cowles, M.G. and Caporaso, J. (2001), 'Introduction' in

Cowles, M.G., Caporaso, J. and Risse, T. (eds), *Transforming Europe: Europeanization and Domestic Change*, Ithaca, NY: Cornell University Press.

Ritter L.W., Brown, W.D. and Rawlinson, F. (1991), *EEC Competition Law: A Practitioner's Guide*, Dordrecht: Kluwer Academic Publishers.

Rosamund, B. (2000), *Theories of European Integration*, Basingstoke: Macmillan.

Rosamund, B. (2005), 'The Uniting of Europe and the Foundation of EU Studies: Revisiting the Neo-functionalism of Ernst B. Haas', *Journal of European Public Policy*, **12**(2), 237–54.

Rutherford, M. (1974), 'West Germany: People before Profits' in Rowley, A. (ed.), *The Barons of European Industry*, London: Taylor and Francis.

Sakkers, H.G.B. and Ysewyn, J. (2008*), European Cartel Digest*, Dordrecht: Wolters Kluwer.

Sanekata, K. and Wilks, S. (2006), 'The Fair Trade Commission and the Enforcement of Competition Policy in Japan' in Doern, G.B. and Wilks, S. (eds), *Comparative Competition Policy: National Institutions in a Global Market,* Oxford: Clarendon.

Scharpf, F. (2002), 'The European Social Model: Coping with the Challenges of Diversity', *Journal of Common Market Studies*, **40**(4), 645–70.

Scherer, F.M. and Ross, D. (1990), *Industrial Market Structure and Economic Performance*, New York: Houghton Mifflin, 3rd edition.

Schimmelfening, F. and Sedelmeier, U. (2004), 'Governance by Conditionality: EU Rule Transfer to the Candidate Countries of Central and Eastern Europe', *Journal of European Public Policy*, **11**(4), 661–79.

Schröter, H.G. (1994), 'The International Potash Syndicate' in Barjot, D. (ed.), *International Cartels Revisited 1880–1980*, Caen: Editions-diffusion du Lys.

Schröter, H. (1996), 'Cartellisation and Decartellisation in Europe, 1870–1995: Rise and Decline of an Economic Institution', *Journal of European Economic History*, **29**(1), 129–53.

Schulze, R. and Hoeren, T. (eds) (2000), *Dokumente zum Europäischen Recht (Band 3 – Kartellrecht (bis 1957)*, Berlin: Springer Verlag.

Sedelmeier, U. and Wallace, H. (1996), 'Policies towards Central and Eastern Europe' in Wallace, H. and Wallace, W. (eds), *Policy-Making in the European Union*, Oxford: OUP, 3rd edition.

Seidel, K. (2007), 'Establishing an Economic Constitution for Europe: DGIV and the Origins of a Supranational Competition Policy', paper presented at the UACES annual conference, University of Portsmouth.

Simpson/Grierson (2009), 'Cartel Cases – the New Wave of Competition Law Litigation' at www/simpsongrirson.com/publications/fyis/fyi-competition-law/cartel-cases-t.

Slade, M. (1990), 'Cheating on Collusive Agreements', *International Journal of Industrial Organisation*, **8**(4), 519–33.

Slot, P.-J. and Johnston, A. (2006), *An Introduction to Competition Law*, Oxford: Hart Publishing.

Smith, A. (1976), *An Inquiry into the Nature and Causes of the Wealth of Nations* (1776), Harmondsworth: Penguin.

Sosnick, S.H. (1958) 'A Critique of Concepts of Workable Competition', *Quarterly Journal of Economics*, **72**(3), 380–423.

Spar, D.L. (1994), *The Competitive Edge: The Internal Politics of International Cartels*, Ithaca, NY: Cornell University Press.

Spratling, G.R. and Arp, D.J. (2005), 'The Status of International Cartel Enforcement Activity in the US and Around the World 2005', paper presented at the IBRAC and International Bar Association's Antitrust and Trade Law Section conference, Rio de Janeiro, May, 1–62.

Stephan, A. (2009), 'Will the Recession make Cartels More Likely and Cartel Enforcement More Difficult', *Centre for Competition Policy Newsletter*, University of East Anglia, No.16.

Stevens, D. (1994), 'The Comfort Letter: Old Problems, New Developments', *European Competition Law Review*, **15**(5), 81–8.

Stigler, G. (1964), 'A Theory of Oligopoly', *Journal of Political Economy*, **72**(2), 44–61.

Stocking, G.W and Watkins, M.W. (1946), *Cartels in Action*, New York: Twentieth Century Fund.

Stragier, J. (1993), 'The Competition Rules of the EEC Agreement and their Implementation', *European Competition Law Review*, **14**(1), 30–38.

Strieder, J., Gras, N.S.B. and Hartsough, M.L. (2001), *Jakob Fugger: The Rich*, London: Beard.

Sturm, R. (1996), 'The German Cartel Office in a Hostile Environment' in Doern, G.B. and Wilks, S. (eds), *Comparative Competition Policy: National Institutions in a Global Market,* Oxford: Clarendon.

Sullivan, E.T. (1991), *The Political Economy of the Sherman Act: The First One Hundred Years,* Oxford: Oxford University Press.

Sullivan, M. and Filion, J. (2004), 'The Basics of International Cartel Enforcement in Canada', paper presented for the Osgoode Hall Continuing Legal Education Program at the Osgoode Hall Law School, York University, 14 January, at http://www.competitionbureau.gc.ca/eic/site/cb-bc.nsf/eng/01064.html.

Suslow, V. (1991), *Cartel Contract Duration: Empirical Evidence from International Cartels*, Mimeo.

Thomas, K. and Wishlade, F. (2009), 'Locational Tournaments in the European Union and the United States', paper presented at the EUSA Biennial Conference, Los Angeles, 23–25 April.

Van Appeldoorn, B. (2000), 'Transnational Class Agency and European Governance: The Case of the European Round Table of Industrialists', *New Political Economy*, **5**(2), 157–81.

Van Bael, I. (1995), 'Fining à la Carte: The Lottery of EU Competition Law', *European Competition Law Review*, **16**(4), 237–43.

Van den Bergh, R.J. and Camesasca, P.D. (2006), *European Competition Law and Economics: A Comparative Perspective*, London: Sweet and Maxwell, 2nd edition.

Van den Bossche, A.M. (1997), 'The International Dimension of EC Competition Law: The Case of the Europe Agreements', *European Competition Law Review*, **18**(1), 24–37.

Van der Pijl, K. (1984), *The Making of an Atlantic Ruling Class*, London: Verso.

Van Gerven, W. (1974), 'Twelve Years of EEC Competition Law (1962–73) Revisited', *Common Market Law Review*, **11**(2), 36–81.

Van Miert, K. (1996), 'Transatlantic Relations and Competition Policy', *Competition Policy Newsletter*, **3**(2), 1–5.

Van Waarden, F. and Drahos, M. (2002), 'Courts and (Epistemic) Communities in the Convergence of Competition Policies', *Journal of European Public Policy*, **9**(6), 913–34.

Vesterdorf, B. (1994), 'Complaints Concerning Infringement of Competition Law within the Context of EC Law', *Common Market Law Review*, **31**(1), 77–104.

Vito, F. (1939), *I Sindacati Industriali – Cartelli e Gruppi*, Milan: Giuffrè.

Voigt, F. (1962), 'German Experience with Cartels and their Control during Pre-War and Post-War Periods' in Miller, J.P. (ed.), *Competition, Cartels and Their Regulation,* Amsterdam: North Holland Publishers.

Von der Groeben, H. (1961), 'European Parliamentary Debates, 19 October', *Economic Journal,* **73**(289), 54–79.

Von der Groeben, H. (1987), 'The European Community. The Formative Years', Brussels: *The European Perspectives Series*, Luxembourg: Office for Official Publications of the European Community.

Wagner, K. (1956), *Die Diskussion über ein Gesetz gegen Wettbewerbsbeschränkungen in Westdeutschland nach 1945,* Zurich: Polygraphischer.

Wallace, W., Wallace, H. and Pollack, M. (2005), *Policy Making in the European Union*, Oxford: Oxford University Press, 5th edition.

Walsh, D. (2008), 'The White Paper on Damages Actions in EC Competition Law – One Step Forward, Two Steps Back', paper delivered at UACES Research Conference, Edinburgh, 1–3 September.

Warzoulet, L. (2006), 'At the Core of European Power: The Origins of

Competition Policy (1957–64)', *History*, Working Paper, Paris: Sorbonne University, at www.heirs-wu.ord/documents/heirscolloquium2005pdf.
Waverman, L., Goto, A. and Comanor, W.S. (1997), *Competition Policy in the Global Economy: Modalities for Co-operation*, London: Routledge.
Weinrauch, R. (2004), *Competition Law in the WTO*, Vienna: Neuer.
Wells, W. (2002), *Antitrust and the Formation of the Post War World*, New York: Colombia University Press.
Whish, R. (2003), *Competition Law*, London: Butterworths, 5th edition.
Whish, R. (2009), *Competition Law*, London: Butterworths, 6th edition.
Wigger, A. (2008), 'Competition for Competitiveness: The Politics of the Transformation of the EU Competition Policy Regime', Ph.D thesis, Vrije Universiteit Amsterdam.
Wigger, A. and Nölke A (2007), 'The Case of Antitrust Enforcement', *Journal of Common Market Studies*, **45**(2), 487–513.
Wilks, S. (1999), *In the Public Interest*, Manchester: Manchester University Press.
Wilks, S. (2005), 'Agency Escape: Decentralisation or Dominance of the European Commission in Competition Policy', *Governance*, **18**(3), 431–52.
Wilks, S. (2007), 'Agencies, Networks, Discourses and the Trajectory of European Competition Enforcement', *European Competition Journal*, **3**(2), 437–64.
Wilks, S. (2009), 'Regulatory Capitalism, Economic Constitutions and European Competition Policy (in the Wake of the Credit Crunch)', paper presented at the EUSA Biennial Conference, Los Angeles, 23–25 April.
Wilks, S. and Bartel, I. (2002), 'The Unanticipated Consequences of Creating Independent Competition Agencies', *West European Politics*, **25(**1), 148–72.
Wilks, S. and McGowan, L. (1996), 'Competition Policy in the European Union: Creating a Federal Agency' in Doern, G.B. and Wilks, S. (eds), *Comparative Competition Policy: National Institutions in a Global Market,* Oxford: Clarendon.
Willis, F.R. (1968), *France, Germany and the New Europe, 1945–67*, Stanford, CA: Stanford University Press.
Wils, W.P.J. (1998), 'The Commission's New Method for Calculating Fines in Antitrust Cases', *European Law Review*, **23**(3), 252–63.
Wils, W.P. (2008), *Efficiency and Justice in European Antitrust Enforcement*, Oxford: Hart Publishing.
Woolcock, S. (2003), 'International Competition Policy and the World Trade Organisation', paper for the LSE Global Dimensions/Federal Trust Forum on the 'Singapore Issues' in the WTO, 25–27 March, London School of Economics.

Index